John Shaw Banks

Our Indian Empire

Its Rise and Growth

John Shaw Banks

Our Indian Empire
Its Rise and Growth

ISBN/EAN: 9783337059910

Printed in Europe, USA, Canada, Australia, Japan

Cover: Foto ©ninafisch / pixelio.de

More available books at **www.hansebooks.com**

OUR INDIAN EMPIRE:

ITS RISE AND GROWTH.

BY THE
REV. J. S. BANKS,
AUTHOR OF 'MARTIN LUTHER, THE PROPHET OF GERMANY,' ETC.

JEYPORE.

London:
WESLEYAN CONFERENCE OFFICE,
2, CASTLE STREET, CITY ROAD;
SOLD AT 66, PATERNOSTER ROW.
1880.

CONTENTS.

CHAP.		PAGE
I.	INTRODUCTORY	1
II.	TO THE BATTLE OF PLASSEY, 1757, AND THE END OF CLIVE'S FIRST ADMINISTRATION, 1760—THE STRUGGLE WITH THE FRENCH	8
III.	TO THE ADMINISTRATION OF WARREN HASTINGS, 1760–1772—SECOND ADMINISTRATION OF CLIVE—FIRST WAR WITH MYSORE	27
IV.	ADMINISTRATION OF WARREN HASTINGS, 1772–1785—FIRST MAHRATTA WAR—SECOND MYSORE WAR	43
V.	LORD CORNWALLIS AND SIR JOHN SHORE—THIRD MYSORE WAR—INTERNAL REFORMS. 1786–1798	63
VI.	LORD WELLESLEY—FOURTH MYSORE WAR—SECOND MAHRATTA WAR—AFFAIRS OF OUDE, ETC. 1798–1805	76
VII.	SIR GEORGE BARLOW AND LORD MINTO. 1806–1813	103
VIII.	LORD HASTINGS—NEPAUL WAR—PINDARI WAR—EXTINCTION OF THE MAHRATTA POWER, ETC. 1813–1823	114
IX.	LORDS AMHERST AND WILLIAM BENTINCK—FIRST BURMESE WAR—SIEGE OF BHURTPORE—INTERNAL REFORMS, ETC. 1823–1835	135
X.	LORD AUCKLAND—AFGHAN WAR. 1835–1842	154
XI.	LORD ELLENBOROUGH — AFGHAN WAR — CONQUEST OF SCINDE—AFFAIRS OF GWALIOR. 1842–1844	171
XII.	LORDS HARDINGE AND DALHOUSIE—FIRST AND SECOND SIKH WARS. 1844–1848	186
XIII.	LORD DALHOUSIE (CONTINUED) AND LORD CANNING—ANNEXATIONS—SECOND BURMESE WAR—INTERNAL IMPROVEMENTS—SEPOY MUTINY. 1848–1862	214
XIV.	HISTORY OF PROTESTANT MISSIONS IN INDIA	257

LIST OF ILLUSTRATIONS.

Lord Clive	*Frontispiece*
Jeypore	*Title*
Tower of Koutub, Delhi	viii
Mausoleum at Agra	7
Temple at Ellore	9
Hyder Ali	26
Warren Hastings	42
Seringapatam	62
Marquis Wellesley	77
Temple at Elephanta	100
Palace of Vellore	102
Hindu Temple, Chandernagore	113
Rangoon	115
Troop of Mahrattas	134
View in Calcutta	153
Cabul	155
Benares	168
Khyber Pass	170
Sir Charles Napier	178
British Troops Entering Mooltan	187
Sir Herbert Edwardes	202
Lucknow	213
Sir James Outram	215
Lord Lawrence	229
Sir Henry Havelock	239
Lord Clyde	247
Mosque in Cawnpore	254
View of Calcutta	256
Lahore	279

TOWER OF KOUTUB, DELHI.

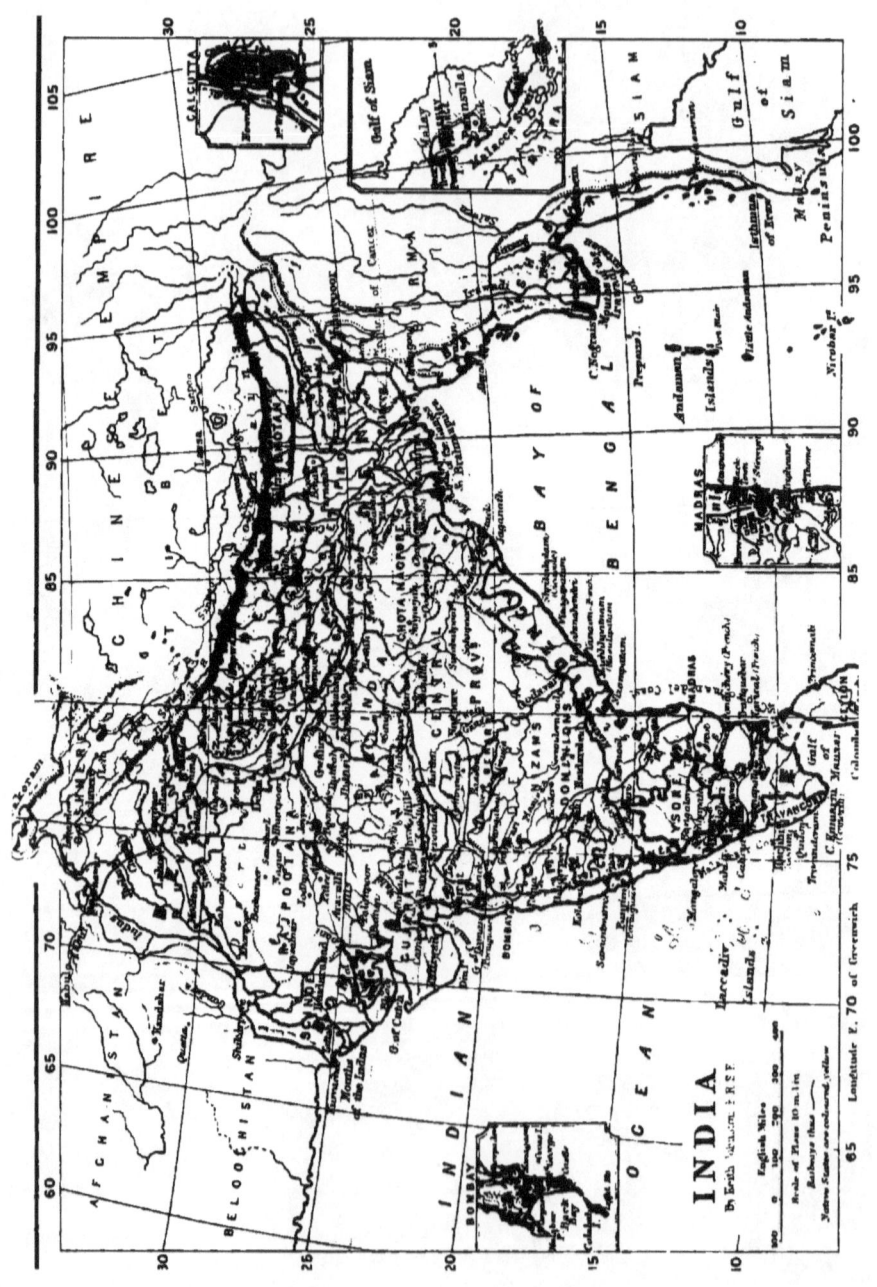

OUR INDIAN EMPIRE.

CHAPTER I.
INTRODUCTORY.

WE premise a few of the more striking physical characteristics of the Indian continent. In extreme length it measures one thousand nine hundred miles, in extreme breadth one thousand five hundred. The area of British India, apart from tributary and independent states, is twelve times that of Great Britain and Ireland, seven times that of France.

Northern India, *i.e.*, India north of the Vindhya Mountains and Nerbudda River, is sometimes distinguished as Hindostan, Southern India as the Deckan (from *dakshana*—south). The population of the continent is two hundred and forty millions, of whom five-sixths are Hindus, one-sixth Mohammedans. In shape India forms a triangle, the base of which is buried under the snows of the Himālayas, the apex within a few degrees of the equator, and the two sides washed by the Bay of Bengal and the Indian Ocean. The whole interior of the Deckan is a lofty table-land, the home of large kingdoms, and enjoying of course a cooler climate than the narrow plains which stretch thence to the sea. The mountain-sides of this plateau are called ghauts (*steps*).

India is thus clearly marked off by nature from surrounding countries, and admirably adapted to be the abode of a self-contained people, such as the Hindus have always been. The Brahmins, indeed, who have moulded the civilization of India, cannot claim to be its original inhabitants. These are found in the few, scattered mountain-tribes, such as the Bheels, Kols, and Gonds, who have nothing in common with modern Hindus.

A later deposit, but still anterior to the coming of the Brahmins, is probably represented by the five vernacular languages of South India known as the Dravidian tongues. Thus, strictly speaking, the Brahmin language, caste and faith are as foreign to India as Mohammedan and British institutions. But the coming of the Brahmins dates so far back, and they have so thoroughly stamped their character on everything Indian, that they are to all intents and purposes the Hindu people. They may be considered the Normans of the East. When and in what circumstances they came to India, it would be useless to attempt to conjecture. Indeed, the entire history of India before the arrival of the Mohammedans is a blank. Of India, during the time when the Hindus were masters in their own house, there are no historical records. The Hindus have no prose history. They have names which can be compared with Homer, Euripides, and Virgil, but none that can be compared with Herodotus, Thucydides, Livy, and Tacitus. Ask a Hindu for the history of his country, and he puts into your hands epic and mythological poems like the Rāmāyana, Maha-Bhārata, and Purānas, infinitely more extravagant and less credible than the *Æneid* and *Paradise Lost*. Great kingdoms grew up, a highly artificial language and civilization reached their climax, systems of philosophy and religion ran their course, wars were carried on, generation after generation of living men and women joyed and sorrowed; and of all this the only record is in books in which it is impossible to distinguish between fact and fiction. The temples in which the people worshipped, the laws they made, the poems they sang, the works in which they embodied their thoughts on God and man and nature, on art and science, remain to us, but all other trace of their lives has passed away for ever. When India first comes into the daylight of history, it is as a conquered country. For example, in the sixth century B.C. Buddhism arose as a protest against idolatry and caste, and, according to tradition, became the established religion of India; but subsequently it declined or was exterminated from the entire continent. Of the details of this wonderful revolution we know nothing. Asōka, Vikramāditya, and Sālivāhana are probably historical names, but they are only names. Under Asōka Buddhism was triumphant; the era of Vikramāditya begins 57 B.C., and is current in Hindostan; the era of Sālivāhana begins 78 A.D., and is current in the Deckan.

It is with the Mohammedan conquests that India first emerges from the obscurity of myth and legend. The first serious Mohammedan attacks on India were made in the eleventh century by Māhmud, Sultan of Ghuzni in Afghanistan. In twenty-five years he led no fewer than twelve expeditions from the poor Afghan heights to the wealthy plains of India. But his object was plunder, not conquest; and in that object he succeeded to a degree which would surpass belief, did we not remember that his were the first plundering hands laid on the accumulated treasures of generations. From single temples he carried off wrought and unwrought gold and silver, pearls, diamonds, and jewels by the hundred-weight. The numbers swept into slavery were such that they could not find purchasers at four shillings each. It was Māhmud who carried off the sandal-wood gates of the temple of Somnāth (A.D. 1024), which long ages after Lord Ellenborough restored. Ghuzni grew into a magnificent city from the spoils of India. Several interesting stories are told of Māhmud. One is of a delicate reproof to his ambition by one of his ministers. This minister professed to be able to interpret the language of birds. To test his professions, Māhmud asked him what an owl, perched on the ruins of a village, was saying. 'He is wishing long life,' was the reply, 'to the Sultan Māhmud, because while he lives there will be no lack of ruined villages to become the habitations of owls.' As good a reproof was administered by a poor widow, to whose demand for justice on her son's murderer Māhmud alleged the impossibility of preserving order in so wide an empire: 'Then why do you take countries which you cannot govern, and for the protection of which you must answer in the day of judgment?' It is worth noticing that the Mohammedans conquered India from the side of Afghanistan. Long before they thought of establishing themselves in the country, they made innumerable raids and held Indian provinces in a state of dependence on Ghuzni.

The real conqueror of India and founder of the Mohammedan empire there is Shahab-u-din, or Mohammed Ghori (1157—1206), who successively subjugated the Hindu states of Ajmir, Canouj, Oude, Behar, and Bengal. Under his successor Kutb-u-din (like many of the Mogul emperors, originally a Turkish slave), all connection with Ghuzni was severed and Mohammedan rule in India started on an independent course.

The chief characteristic of that rule was incessant warfare. From the coming of the Mohammedans India may be said to have been a stranger to peace. An instance of undisputed succession to the throne was the exception. Each monarch had either to obtain or keep his throne at the cost of a war, if he did not take the more effectual way of putting to death all possible rivals. Even Akbar, by far the greatest of the whole line of sovereigns, and Aurungzib, whom Mohammedan writers put first, who each reigned nearly fifty years, were engaged in incessant wars of conquest or defence. In their wars of aggression no question of right was regarded, no scruples about means were felt, the sole consideration taken into account was their ability to accomplish their ends. It would be an endless and unwelcome task to give in detail even specimens of the perfidy and cruelty which stain the Mogul annals. Massacres in cold blood, impaling, flaying alive, were common. We should have to tell how the emperor Ala-u-din murdered in cold blood fifteen thousand Moguls, whom he had discharged from his service, for a conspiracy of some of their number; how Humayun put out his brother's eyes; how Aurungzib gained the throne by deposing his father and slaying his two elder and younger brothers; how Jehanghir impaled seven hundred rebels in a line from the gates of Lahore. In point of fact, India was conquered twice over by the Mohammedans. The invasion of Tamerlane (1398 A.D.), coming upon weak reigns and internal dissensions, crumbled the empire to dust, and the great Baber had to build it again from the foundation. Thus, India over its whole extent underwent the horrors of two separate conquests. The entire Deckan was never thoroughly subdued or long acquiescent; the Hindu defence there was desperate, and renewed at every opportunity. There arose the Mahratta power, which exhausted the Mogul resources by incessant attacks. Aurungzib spent the last fifteen years of his life in a vain attempt to reduce the Deckan, an enterprise which had the same effect on the Mogul empire as the invasion of Spain had on Napoleon's. During the five and a half centuries of the Mohammedan rule, forty-five emperors occupied the throne, an average of twelve years each.

To crown the sufferings of India, the same period witnessed three invasions from without,—that of Tamerlane in 1398, Nadir Shah in 1739, and Ahmed Shah in 1756. On each occasion Delhi was given over to pillage and slaughter, and the scenes of horror and outrage enacted were indescribable. Nadir Shah carried off treasure to the amount of £34,000,000, the plunder including Shah Jehan's famous peacock-throne and slaves innumerable. Before the last invasion the sceptre had fallen into weak hands, and the shock completed the ruin of the empire.

It is not inconsistent with this account to refer to the wealth and state of the Mogul emperors; as, for example, of Shah Jehan, whose peacock-throne, all set in gems and rubies, was variously estimated as worth from one to six millions, and whose mausoleum, the Tāj Mahāl at Agra, to the memory of his wife, is one of the wonders of the world. After all his great works, such as the canal at Delhi called by his name, he left £24,000,000 in his treasury. It may be questioned whether, in an Eastern despotism, royal wealth and splendour are any index of the condition of the people. Too often lavish waste in the palace means oppression and misery among the masses. Sir Thomas Roe, an ambassador from James I. to Jehanghir, was not more astounded at the splendour of the court than at the sordid and downtrodden state of the people, on whom, of course, at last the cost of ceaseless war and extravagant show fell. It is not impossible that, in a country as vast as India, considerable prosperity was here and there enjoyed. Probably no amount of misgovernment and oppression could exhaust the resources of such a country and population. The Mogul history is full of romantic episodes. Few stories are more wonderful than those of the emperors Baber and Humayun, and of Nur Jehan

('Light of the World'), Jehanghir's famous queen. Their histories present every vicissitude of human fortune. The emperors were served from time to time by statesmen and soldiers of the greatest ability and highest character, the best of whom were rewarded with treachery, ingratitude and jealousy. We dwell, however, with most satisfaction on the great public works by which the masses were benefited, such as canals, reservoirs, caravanseras, roads, bridges. Shere Shah (1540—1545) cut a road two thousand miles in length from the Indus to the Bay of Bengal. Unfortunately, these works are not sufficiently numerous to determine the character of the whole period. We fear that every one who studies the history in the impartial and even favourable pages of Mountstuart Elphinstone, our best authority for this period, must come to the conclusion that, to be in keeping with the contents, the history of the Mohammedan rule in India would need to be written in blood. We know that in fairness the standard of comparison should be mediæval, not modern, Europe. But even measured by that standard, the difference in the number, character and scale of crimes under the Mogul rule is startling beyond expression.

We wish to emphasize the fact that the English took India, not from Hindu, but from Mohammedan hands. In few cases was it a Hindu dynasty that was displaced. It was one foreigner succeeding another. The rulers dispossessed were Mohammedan governors who had either recently become independent kings or still professed nominal dependence on the phantom-emperor at Delhi. The sceptre of supreme sovereignty had fallen from Mogul hands, and waited for the first comer strong enough to pick it up. The native Mahratta had tried to do so, and failed. Mr. Marshman says: 'With the exception of the Rajpoot chiefs and the puppet emperor at Delhi, not one of the kingdoms which were subsequently absorbed in the British empire had been in existence even a quarter of a century when the English first took up arms in Hindostan.' How India had fared under the Mogul we have seen. There could scarcely be a more striking contrast than exists between the principles and methods of Mohammedan and British government. Take only

INTRODUCTORY. 7

the question of religious toleration, a thing forbidden by Mohammedan law. The only one of the emperors tolerant on principle was Akbar, and he is always reproached by Mohammedan writers with unfaithfulness to his creed. The Mohammedan religion, in its very essence, is fiercely, cruelly intolerant, as the Hindus have too often found. Aurungzib imposed a poll-tax—*jezzia*—on all Hindus as a badge of religious inferiority. Proselytism by force, the destruction of temples and images, outbreaks of wild fanaticism were common occurrences all through the Mohammedan period. With British rule a brighter prospect opens before an oppressed and distracted country.

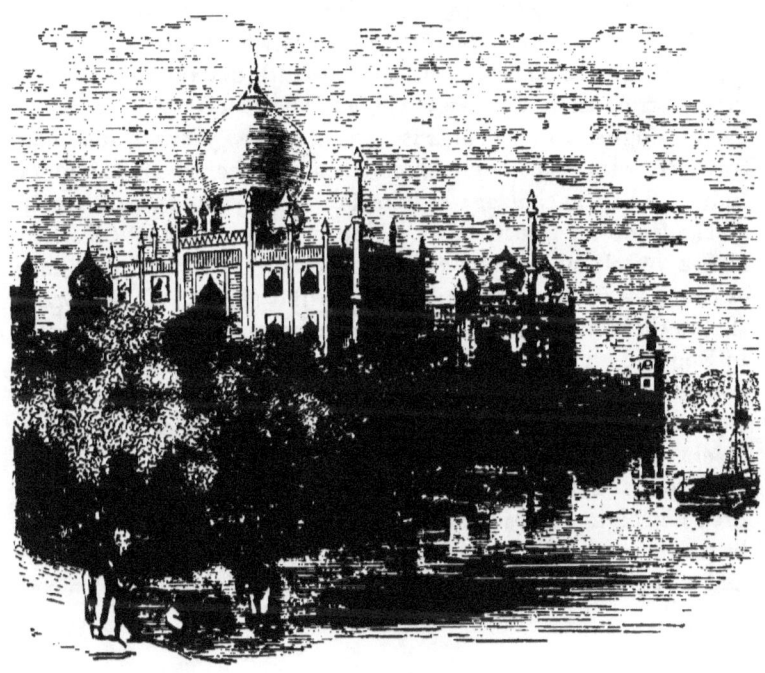

MAUSOLEUM AT AGRA.

CHAPTER II.

TO THE BATTLE OF PLASSEY, 1757, AND THE END OF CLIVE'S FIRST ADMINISTRATION, 1760—THE STRUGGLE WITH THE FRENCH.

IT is an old story by this time, that the British empire in India grew out of a trading company. So imperceptible and undesigned was the growth, that it would not be easy to say where trading ended and government began. For a long time the two characters were inextricably blended. Each separate step seemed to follow by inevitable necessity. To point out any alternative course would be difficult. And yet the total result is what we see.

The first English company for trading with the East Indies was formed in 1599, during the reign of Elizabeth in England and Akbar in India. The circumstances which led to the company being formed were, the great wealth derived by the Portuguese from their Eastern trade, and the reports brought home by an Englishman called Fitch, who a few years before had travelled with some companions through the whole extent of India. The first charter was issued in 1600, granting a monopoly of the trade for fifteen years. The first trading fleet consisted of five vessels, and sailed from Torbay in 1601, the forerunner of countless fleets, mercantile and warlike, since. We may note that in the charter of 1661 the company were authorized to deport to England all unlicensed Englishmen and to administer justice, two undoubted functions of government. Throughout its history the East India Company never lost its jealousy of the 'interlopers' who infringed its monopoly.

The first English factory was established at Surat, one hundred and eighty miles to the north of Bombay, and was confirmed by a firman of the Emperor Jehanghir in 1613. For a century and a half after this the English establishments in India con-

TEMPLE AT ELLORE.

FIRST SETTLEMENTS.

tinued mainly commercial, everything being subordinated to trade and profit, and only so much of the functions of government being assumed as was necessary to the wellbeing of the community. The factory included warehouses, offices, and the residences of the company's servants. The latter dined in common, as in an ancient monastery or modern regiment.* The salaries seem surprisingly small. A century after this time the president at Calcutta received £300 per year; eight members of council, £40 each; junior merchants, £30; factors, £15; writers, £5: but they received board and lodging in addition, and enjoyed the privilege of private trade, which often meant a great fortune. But Surat was soon superseded by Bombay, which was ceded to the company by the Crown in 1668, the Crown having received it from Portugal a few years before as part of the Queen's dowry. But the Bombay Presidency, though founded early, was the latest in territorial development, owing to the fact that the anarchy on the dissolution of the Mogul government was not so great in the west as in the east, the native Mahratta power preserving in the west some semblance of strength and order.

For a long time no footing could be gained in Bengal, the Emperor Shah Jehan having taken offence at the conduct of the Portuguese, and being resolved to keep all Europeans outside. The nearest point to Bengal at which the company could get permission to settle was the port of Piply, near Balasore in Orissa. This permission was granted by an imperial firman in 1634. But two years later an English surgeon, called Boughton, who had cured a daughter of Shah Jehan, requested as a reward permission for the English to trade in Bengal duty free, and to establish factories at Balasore itself and at Hooghly, a town about twenty-six miles above the present Calcutta. Of course in the circumstances the request could not be refused. The

---

* Not many know that it is to the convivial factors at Surat that we owe the modern drink called punch. It was composed of five ingredients: brandy, sugar, limes, spice, and water. The name was borrowed from the Hindustani and Sanscrit numeral *pancha*, five. What punch is made of now, the writer knows not.

trade grew so rapidly that Bengal was formed into a separate Presidency. The first governor was Mr. Hedges, with a modest guard of one corporal and twenty European soldiers. The company had no end of trouble with the local governors and authorities, who were practically independent of the emperor at Delhi, and in spite of imperial firmans levied duties and expected presents on every sort of occasion. One year the nabob exacts sixty thousand rupees, two years after thirty thousand, the next twenty-two thousand; and so on. Once three English sailors got into a quarrel in the streets of Hooghly, and the difficulty was only solved by the town being bombarded by the English ships. The exactions interfered so seriously with the profits of the company, that Job Charnock, an early governor, retired from Hooghly to the present site of Calcutta, and at last from Bengal altogether. In face of subsequent events there is something amusing in these firmans, in this arrogance on one side, and almost abject dependence on the other. Little did the Mogul dream of what his reluctant firmans would lead to; and so far were the English from thinking of empire in India that they actually sent out two strong fleets to form a settlement at Chittagong in Aracan, farther to the east, both of which failed. In 1690 the English returned to Bengal, on the invitation of the Nabob, or viceroy, of Bengal, who missed the profits of their enterprise. The permission to return was granted, so ran the proclamation, in consequence of the English having 'made a most humble and submissive petition that the crimes they had committed should be forgiven.' On the site of three native villages, called Calcutta, Chuttanutty, and Govindpore, Calcutta was founded. The present given to the viceroy for the site was sixteen thousand rupees (£1,600). The Court of Directors characteristically thought the price 'very high.' Such was the origin of the 'City of Palaces.'

The founder of Calcutta was a shrewd trader, but by no means a model in other respects. The general punishment for offences among the natives was whipping. The cries of the victims were evidently music to the governor's ears, for the punishment was inflicted while he sat at dinner. He married a native wife, whom he had rescued from the funeral pile, and by her was converted to Hinduism. After her death, he annually sacrificed a cock on her tomb. It is said, that native murderers, instead of being hanged, were whipped to death.

From Mr. Wheeler's *Early Records of British India*, we get many details of English life in Bengal in those days. The English factory, which was simply 'an emporium of trade, with its warehouses, workshops, offices, and outlying houses, covered about a hundred acres on the banks of the Hooghly. The native town consisted of three or four large villages, more or less remote from the English factory and from each other. Some houses may have been built of brick and chunam; some were made of clay, and whitewashed; the bulk were hovels of mud and straw. These have grown into a metropolis of brick and stone. The outlying village of Chowringhee, with the surrounding marshes and rice-fields, has become the aristocratic quarter of the European population. The swamp and jungle which separated Chowringhee from the river has been formed into the large grassy plain known as the "Maidan."' The commercial character of the English at Calcutta stamped itself on all their proceedings. The governor was the agent of the Court of Directors. The term survives in the 'political agents' of modern days. The English 'bought, sold, overlooked, kept accounts, wrote letters, regulated establishments and expenditure. Large ships from Europe brought woollen goods, cutlery, iron, copper, quicksilver. The same ships carried away cotton piece-goods, fine muslins, silks, indigo, spice, saltpetre, Indian rarities. Buying and selling at outcry or auction was one of the excitements of Calcutta life.' There were subordinate factories at Dacca, famous for muslin, Cossimbazar, Patna. It must be remembered that then India sent cotton goods to England, not the reverse. It was only at the close of the century that Manchester began to compete with Bengal; 'calico' is an Indian term. Between 1780 and 1790 the Court of Directors was alarmed by the rivalry of Manchester. On the other hand, English calico-printers petitioned Parliament ' to prevent the emigration of artists to India; to prohibit the exportation of plates, blocks, and materials for printing;

and also to lay such additional duty upon goods printed in India as would be sufficient to put the white piece-goods printed in England on an equal footing with Indian goods.'

As to the private life of the English we are told that 'the mornings were devoted to business. Then followed the midday dinner and the afternoon siesta. In the cool of the evening they took the air in palanquins, or sailed on the river in budgerows. They angled for mango-fish, or shot snipe and teal. The evening wound up with supper. There were quarrels, scandals and controversies; possibly there were some religious exercises. There was always the show of religion and decorum which characterized the early life of the eighteenth century; the chaplain read prayers every morning, and preached on Sundays. There were intervals of excitement apart from the daily business. Ships brought news from Europe, from the outer presidencies, from the far-off settlements in China, Sumatra, Pegu, and other remote quarters. Many of these features belong to Anglo-Indian life still.' Within the English settlement the company was supreme. In course of time the governor's judicial functions were transferred to a mayor and nine aldermen, who sat in quarter sessions for the trial of civil and criminal cases among Europeans. A capital sentence had to be confirmed by a royal warrant from England. Among the native population on English ground a servant of the company acted as zemindar, collecting the revenue and administering justice in all respects like the native zemindars. Many of the taxes on trade and different articles were farmed out to individuals. In 1755 the English zemindar collected from all sources taxes to the amount of little more than £10,000. In 1876 the municipal taxation of Calcutta amounted to £260,000. If taxation is one evidence of advancing civilization, there can be no doubt respecting the improvement of India.

The French were established in Bengal at Chandernagore, the Dutch at Chinsurah, the Danes at Serampore.

From 1741 to 1751 Bengal was subject to annual raids by the Mahratta hordes, who carried destruction and death everywhere. They ruined a country as effectually as locusts, and in addition tortured and slew without pity. The Mahrattas were

MAHRATTA RAIDS.

perhaps the most accomplished plunderers the world has ever seen. They would suddenly swoop upon a town or district, seize everything valuable, and were away on their swift steeds before any force could be gathered to cope with them. Their ravages extended from Delhi to Tanjore. Any government was guaranteed against plunder on condition of annually paying the *chout*, or one-fourth of its revenues. In 1751 Bengal engaged to do this. When Bengal came, a few years later, under English influence, the *chout* ceased. But in truth the Mahrattas only exceeded the ordinary native rulers in the scale of their extortions and cruelties. Ali-verdi Khan became Nabob of Bengal in 1740. He had risen from a humble position by talent and bribery. There was a petty rāja near Monghyr, against whom Ali-verdi had a pique. One day as an English convoy was going to Patna with goods and treasure, the leaders hailed a passing boat to obtain some fish; the six baskets in the boat were found to be filled with the heads of the rāja and his thirty followers, who had been treacherously slain by the khan's order. The baskets were on their way to the nabob. About this time a subordinate officer of the nabob in Bengal invented the following punishment. He had a pond dug and filled with all imaginable filth, to which he gave in derision the name of *veikunta*, the Hindu name for 'paradise.' When a zemindar's payments were not forthcoming, he was dragged by means of ropes under the arms, through this pond; the officer would also force his victims to put on loose trousers, into which live cats were then introduced. The Mahratta Ditch round Calcutta is a relic of the Mahratta invasions. It was intended as a barrier against the clouds of Mahratta horse, and, if completed, would have described a semi-circle of seven miles; but only three miles were completed, as the panic passed away. A sobriquet of the citizens still is, 'Inhabitants of the Ditch'; just as once the English in Ireland were, 'the People of the Pale.'

The first soil actually possessed by the English in India was the present site of Madras. They needed something more for their valuable trade on the Coromandel Coast than a factory, but the Moguls would neither grant land nor permit forts. But in

1639 the English obtained what they wanted from the Hindu rāja of Chandragiri, whose seat was about seventy miles inland. The land ceded was about six miles long by one broad. According to the grant, which was engraved on a gold plate, the rent to be paid for this was £600. It does not seem to us easy to understand why the English chose a site with nothing but an open roadstead, in which a high surf rolls ceaselessly and ships are compelled to put to sea on the appearance of a storm. The recommendation was that the strip of territory included a small island, four hundred yards by one hundred, formed by a river and the sea. This island was the seat of the settlement, and gave protection against plundering horsemen. Only Europeans were allowed to live on the island, which was called White Town and Fort St. George. The native town was and is still called Black Town.

It was in Madras that the English were first involved in war. They had to fight a long battle for existence. It was carried on with the French, who deliberately formed the plan of driving them out of India. This was done for the most part under the cover of native alliances, the English and French espousing opposite sides in the disputes of native princes for the throne. There was an abundant crop of such disputes in this part of India, where the pressure of the Mogul empire was least felt and the anarchy on the fall of the empire greatest. In the beginning of the conflict the advantage was decidedly with the French. Their ardour carried everything before them. But their power sank even more rapidly than it had risen. It was not for want of able governors and soldiers that the French missed the Indian empire on which their hearts were set, and which had once been within their grasp. Labourdonnais, Dupleix, Bussy, and Lally were equal to any names on the other side. Several causes explain the result; as, want of unity among the leaders, the lack of persistence and tenacity in the French character, blunders on the part of the home government, shameful treatment of unfortunate governors and commanders on their return home. It would be beside our purpose to enter into the French plans and operations except in so far as they touch on English affairs.

FRENCH WARS.

The war between France and England which began in 1744 led to hostilities in the East. In September, 1746, Labourdonnais captured Madras, after a bombardment of five days. The walls were in a poor state of defence, and manned by only two hundred European soldiers, while the French brought to the attack eleven hundred, beside four hundred Malagasees and four hundred sepoys, whom the French were the first to train and use. As his instructions from home prevented him from holding or destroying the town, Labourdonnais ransomed it for forty-four lacs of rupees. The French settlement, Pondicherry, one hundred miles to the south of Madras, was governed by Dupleix, a man of extraordinary ability, ambition and intrigue, and as jealous and vain as he was able. He denounced the capitulation, and sent Labourdonnais with larger forces to destroy the town; but the enterprise failed. Labourdonnais returned to France, was kept prisoner in the Bastille three years, and died broken-hearted soon after his liberation.

A slight conflict which took place at this time was attended by momentous results. The Nabob of the Carnatic,* Anwar-u-din, in whose territories Madras lay, expected that the French, according to promise, would deliver Madras up to him. When he saw that he was deceived, he sent his son with ten thousand men to chastise them. But the French artillery, firing three or four times a minute to the native once in fifteen minutes, put the host to speedy flight. The issue taught both French and English that they had nothing to fear from superior numbers in a native enemy, and the lesson was not lost. Artillery has always remained the strong arm of European power. The English in India have never stayed to count an enemy in battle.

After the departure of Labourdonnais Dupleix seized Madras, confiscated the property, and marched off the principal inhabitants as prisoners of war. He also tried to capture Fort St. David, another English settlement sixteen miles to the south of

---

* The Carnatic is the portion of the Madras coast between the rivers Kistna and Coleroon. It is about five hundred miles long by one hundred broad.

Pondicherry, and thus extinguish English power in South India, but failed. An English attempt, with new troops just arrived, on Pondicherry, was mismanaged and failed. In the end, Madras was restored to the English by the peace of Aix-la-Chapelle, 1748.

Dupleix now aimed at higher game. The result of endless intrigues and changes was that he placed one *protégé* on the throne of the Deckan, Mozuffer Jung, and made another, Chunda Sahib, Nabob of the Carnatic. Besides French influence thus becoming paramount in South India, Dupleix was made nominal governor of the Carnatic, the nabob being placed under him. The English now tried to recover the ground they had lost. Their candidate for the nabobship was Mohammed Ali, son of Anwar. They sent a force to the relief of Trichinopoly, which a few English troops were holding for him against Chunda Sahib. But a more daring plan for its relief was suggested by Clive, the future founder of the British empire in India, then a young captain. This was nothing less than to seize Arcot, the nabob's capital. His force for accomplishing this purpose consisted of two hundred Europeans, three hundred sepoys, eight officers, and eight guns. Arcot was taken, 1751, the garrison being so impressed by the hardihood of the assailants in marching through a thunderstorm that they made no resistance. The desired effect followed. Chunda Sahib at once detached ten thousand troops to recover his capital. Clive found the defence harder than the capture. The walls of the fort were a mile round and in weak condition. His troops were reduced by one-third, his officers by one-half. The besiegers were aided by one hundred and fifty Europeans. Fifty days the siege lasted, and the conflict on the last day raged eighteen hours; but every attack was repulsed, and the enemy withdrew. Amid the many daring deeds by which India has been won and kept, there is none more daring than Clive's capture and defence of Arcot.

The war went on with varying results. The centre of action was Trichinopoly, which the English held and the French tried to take. Every inch of ground was contested. Backwards and forwards the tide of victory rolled. Obscure as these conflicts

FRENCH DEFEATS.

were, they gave occasion to feats of strategy and valour on both sides as considerable as on larger fields. In them the fate of South India was decided. The palm of strategy and success remained with Major Lawrence, Clive's first commander in the field. Some idea of the character of the princes whose battles we were fighting, may be gained from the fact that Mohammed Ali, when he got his rival, Chunda Sahib, into his power, in spite of a promise of protection, had him assassinated and his head carried five times round the town on a camel's neck. But, of course, the native princes on both sides were mere puppets in stronger hands. Peace was arranged by the home authorities in 1754. The advantages gained by the French were more than counterbalanced by the recall of Dupleix, an unaccountable act on the part of the French government.

Dupleix's general, Bussy, afterwards carried the French power in the Deckan even to a higher point. The viceroy, Salabut Jung, answering to the present Nizam of Hyderabad, was his creature. Not only was Dowlatabad, the strongest fort in the Deckan, in his hands, but he obtained the cession of the four Northern Sircars, a district on the coast six hundred miles long, and yielding fifty lacs a year. Forts threw open their gates at the sound of his guns. But just as the whole Deckan was trembling at his name, to the astonishment of every one he was recalled by Count Lally, the new governor of Pondicherry, and at a stroke French power sank, never to rise again.

Lally was of Irish extraction, and possessed by an insane hatred of England. His fixed idea was to drive the English out of India by direct attack. Bussy entreated him to preserve the immense advantages gained in the Deckan, but in vain. At first his plans succeeded. He captured Fort St. David and Arcot, but an exhausting attack on Madras (1759) failed. After a two months' siege, just at the moment when a breach had been effected, an English fleet arrived in the roads, and the French had to retreat. From this time everything went against Lally. He was ill seconded by his officers and the civil authorities at Pondicherry; his troops were often starving. In 1760 he was beaten at Wandewash by Colonel Coote, a soldier only second to Clive, who had been summoned to the north; and in 1761 Pondicherry itself was taken and partially destroyed. Pondicherry was restored by the Peace of Paris in 1763, but the dream of a French empire vanished for ever. The brave but headstrong Lally returned home, and was foully executed as a traitor, with every circumstance of ignominy.

Meantime, greater events had been transpiring in the north. The Nabob of Bengal in 1756 was Suräja Dowlah, vicious, greedy and cruel beyond the usual measure, and in addition a hater of the English. One of the subordinate governors had sent his family and treasures to Calcutta to be beyond the nabob's reach. The nabob demanded their surrender, and forbade the English to add to their fortifications. The first order was not complied with, and as to the second, explanations were offered. This only enraged the nabob the more, and he marched at once upon Calcutta with fifty thousand troops. The defences, unfortunately, were in a neglected state. The repeated orders of the Court of Directors to strengthen the fortifications had been neglected by the local authorities, who were engrossed in trade. This would have mattered little, if those at the head of the community had acted worthily. But the governor and military commander were panic-struck, and took refuge with the women and children on board the ships, which at once moved lower down the river and left the rest to their fate. After a four days' siege the place surrendered, June 19th, 1756. The same night was perpetrated the tragedy of the Black Hole. One hundred and forty-six Englishmen were thrust into a guard-room eighteen feet square, with only two barred windows to the west. Even movement was next to impossible. There was just air enough to prolong life and suffering. While the nabob slept and could not be awaked, the poor wretches went mad with thirst and fever, begged for water or death, tried to provoke the guards to fire on them, raved, cursed, prayed, and gradually sank into stupor and death. The list of dead included three members of council, twenty-one company's officers, fifteen army and sea captains, five lieutenants, five ensigns, five sergeants, and others. Mr. Holwell, the acting governor, was one of the twenty-three survivors. When he was supported into the nabob's presence next morning, the only feeling of the latter was one of surprise and indignation at the small amount of treasure captured. Few tragedies have ever made a deeper impression on the European imagination than that of the Black Hole, but neither the nabob nor the people of India thought anything of it. Mohammedan historians of the period do not even mention it. No doubt on the scale of mere magnitude there have been far greater atrocities in history; the peculiar malignity of the Black Hole crime consists in the utter callousness of the perpetrators as well as in the special intensity of the sufferings inflicted.

It is a sign of the difference between those days and the present that news of the catastrophe took seven days to reach Madras. There was further delay about the preparations. But at last Clive was sent with nine hundred European troops and one thousand five hundred sepoys. On January 2nd, 1757, he retook Calcutta almost without a shot, and a week after, by way of further terrifying the nabob, captured the town of Hooghly. Surāja did indeed march towards Calcutta with forty thousand men. This time, however, he had different opponents to deal with. But for a dense fog he would have been routed at once, and the battle of Plassey anticipated by a few months. As it was, he was glad by treaty to concede to the English all their former rights and promise compensation. He only, however, yielded to force, and remained at heart as hostile to the British power as ever. With the French at Chandernagore near Calcutta and in the Northern Sircars, to the south of Bengal, all the elements of a combination as dangerous as that which threatened Madras were present. The nabob was in constant correspondence with the French, and a French officer, Law, and two hundred French troops were with him. Clive resolved to break up the confederacy. He tried to bind the French at Chandernagore to neutrality by a treaty, but the commander could not or would not enter into binding engagements. He then attacked Chandernagore, and took it after a brave defence of nine days. Clive had said, 'If we take Chandernagore, we cannot stop there.' This was soon realized.

The nabob's oppression and cruelty increased to such an extent that his own officers conspired to depose him and put Meer Jaffier, his finance minister, in his place. Clive entered into the plot. The nabob was compelled to dismiss the French in his service. The scheme was nearly ruined by the threat of one of the conspirators, Omichund, a wealthy merchant and banker, to divulge the whole unless he were bribed with thirty lacs of rupees and commission on all moneys paid. But Clive matched him in craft. By Clive's directions two treaties were prepared, one sham and one real. The former contained Omichund's stipulation, the other did not. However little sympathy is due to Omichund, nothing can justify the deception in Clive. Such treachery was habitual in native history; but the English empire would not have been what it is, if it had always adopted native ways. Clive defended his conduct to the last, alleging that a villain must be fought with his own weapons. Admiral Watson refused to put his hand to the sham treaty, and his name was forged. When everything was over, Omichund was told of the trick. It is said that he lost his reason, but this seems very unlikely in one of his wealth and character. Meer Jaffier swore an oath on the Koran to desert to the English on the field of battle, and a similar oath of fidelity to the nabob, intending of course to keep whichever oath was most convenient.

When everything was ready, Clive presented his list of grievances to the nabob, and moved towards Moorshedabad, the capital, to enforce it. The two armies met in the grove of Plassey: on one side fifteen thousand horse, and thirty-five thousand foot, and fifty guns; on the other one thousand Europeans, two thousand sepoys, and eight guns. No wonder even Clive hesitated. Failure meant destruction to his force and to the English power in Bengal. In the previous council of war Clive himself voted against fighting. He said afterwards 'that this was the only council of war he ever held, and if he had abided by that council, it would have been the ruin of the East India Company.' In the night, while musing in the mango-grove, Clive resolved to strike. The next day, June 23rd, 1757, after a harmless cannonade from the enemy, Clive led his troops to the attack. The opposing general was killed, Surāja Dowlah fled on his swiftest camel, and his great host instantly broke up. The loss in the battle which virtually made the English masters of India was seventy-two killed and wounded on the side of the victors, and not more than five hundred on the other. The nabob fled, was betrayed to his enemies by a man whose ears he had cut off, and was put to death. The victory of Plassey fell about a year after the capture of Calcutta. Exactly a century afterwards the Sepoy Mutiny occurred. Meer Jaffier paid the indemnity to the company, besides giving considerable presents to the English officers. Clive only stipulated for the fee simple of six hundred yards of land round Calcutta and the zemindarship of the country to the south; but practically the English were masters of Bengal. Their power was universally regarded as irresistible; they were without a rival alike in north and south India. Meer Jaffier was but a nominal ruler, and he felt it. Clive was omnipotent; he put down native rebellions; princes and people looked to him as the arbiter of their destinies. The emperor at Delhi proposed to make him *dewan*, or finance minister of Bengal, Behar, and Orissa, under Meer Jaffier, an offer which he declined; but he discerned the change which had come over the position of the English and the necessity of a military force sufficient for the maintenance of that position against all contingencies. He embodied these views in a letter to William Pitt. Pitt objected to the assumption of sovereignty by the English, because the conquests would belong, the judges had decided, to the company, and to transfer them to the Crown would constitute a danger to public liberty. Just a century afterwards the transference was made.

One of Clive's first acts was to send Colonel Forde, an able soldier, with a force into the Northern Sircars. Masulipatam, a strong place, was taken, 1758, and the district lost to the French. This, with the capture of Pondicherry by Colonel Coote, completed the ruin of French influence. Masulipatam with eight districts round it became English. In 1760 Clive returned a second time to England. The following is an illustration of Clive's decisive methods. Meer Jaffier, chafing under his insignificance, and having no French power to appeal to, invited the Dutch at Batavia to join him against the English. The Dutch sent a large force. As the English and Dutch were at peace, Colonel Forde would not attack without a written order. Clive was playing at cards when the request came. He wrote at once on the back of one of the cards, 'Dear Forde, fight them immediately; I will send you the order in council to-morrow.' Forde marched at once, came up with the Dutch near Chinsurah, and defeated them in half an hour, thus averting worse mischief. Seven thousand native troops under Meerun, Meer Jaffier's son, were waiting near, ready to join the Dutch if they had been victorious.

HYDER ALI.

CHAPTER III.

TO THE ADMINISTRATION OF WARREN HASTINGS, 1760 TO 1772—
SECOND ADMINISTRATION OF CLIVE—FIRST WAR WITH MYSORE.

N January 7th, 1761, was fought the great battle of Paniput, near Delhi, between the Afghan invader, Ahmed Shah, and the Mahrattas, in which the immense army of the latter was cut to pieces and their designs on the throne of India shattered for ever. This was the third time that the fate of India had been decided on the plain of Paniput. The first time was when Baber defeated the emperor in 1526; the second in 1556, when Akbar, or rather Akbar's general Beiram, defeated Hemu, the general of the rival Afghan dynasty. It is impossible for us to enter into the general history of India. The following extract from Mr. Marshman gives a bird's-eye view of the country at this time : 'The great empire of the Moguls was dissolved, and the emperor was wandering about in Behar, accompanied by a small band of mercenaries. In the districts around Delhi, the Jauts on one side, and the Rohillas on the other, were consolidating the power they had usurped. The Rajpoot rājas had been humbled during the encroachments of the Mahrattas, and manifested little of their former energy. The nabob-vizier of Oude possessed a rich territory and a large, undisciplined army, but was deficient in every military quality except courage. The Mahratta dream of universal empire in India under a Hindu sceptre had been dissipated by the recent defeat, and although the Peshwa was the head of the federation, its power was henceforth partitioned among the Guickwar, the Rāja of Nagpore, and Holkar and Scindia, who were seldom at peace with each other. The nizam at Hyderabad had been crippled by the surrender of some of his most valuable districts to the Mahrattas. The power of the

French was completely broken. In the south of the peninsula, the Nabob of the Carnatic had been seated on the throne by the English, and was maintained solely by their arms, and Hyder Ali was on the point of grasping the supreme control in Mysore. The power destined eventually to bring these various principalities "under one umbrella" * had recently subdued its European rivals in the south, and established its predominance in the valley of the Ganges, but was contemplating nothing so little as the conquest of India.'

The administration of Mr. Vansittart (1760—64) is not a pleasant subject of review to Englishmen. It was little more than one tissue of mistakes, peculation and corruption of every kind. Only the anarchy and weakness of the native powers saved the English rule from extinction. The governor himself was a man of honour, and he was ably seconded by Warren Hastings, then in unconscious training for his future career. But he was far too feeble to guide the course of a revolution such as was then running its course. From first to last he was thwarted and overruled by a majority in the council, whose original grievance was that he, a Madras civilian, had been made governor over their heads.

The general confusion was aggravated by an invasion of the Shahzada, son of the emperor, who presently, on his father's assassination, became emperor himself under the title of Shah Alum. He did not desist from his efforts, and the English found themselves at war with the emperor on whom nominally they depended. Shah Alum would only have been too glad for the English to escort him to Delhi, then in Afghan hands, and replace him on the throne, to so low a state was the great Mogul reduced; but the English did not see their way to comply. Otherwise, the problem of Indian empire might have received an earlier solution. The emperor's aim was the capture of Patna. Twice he was on the point of success. The first time he defeated the Hindu governor, who had foolishly engaged before the English force arrived; but, instead of

---

° The ensign of regal state in India.

following up his success, he lost time in plundering the district. Colonel Calliaud, a soldier of the school of Clive and Forde, came up and inflicted on him a severe defeat. Meerun, Meer Jaffier's son, was present, but hindered more than he helped the English. One day he would not fight, because the astrologers forbade it. The emperor then made a desperate effort, by a forced march, to seize Moorshedabad before Colonel Calliaud could follow him. Foiled in this, he doubled back on Patna, besieged it nine days, and was on the point of gaining possession, when Major Knox arrived with reinforcements. The major reconnoitred the enemy's position in the night, and next day put him to flight. Then, the Nabob of Purneah, with thirty thousand troops and thirty guns, took up the emperor's quarrel. With two hundred Europeans, a sepoy battalion, three hundred horse, and five guns, the major fell on this host under the very walls of Patna, which were crowded with excited spectators, and routed it. Just at this time, Meerun, as profligate and cruel a wretch as Surāja himself, was struck dead by lightning. In one of these conflicts the French officer, Law, was taken prisoner. When his men fled with the emperor, M. Law sat astride on a gun, and awaited the approach of the victors. Refusing to give up his sword, he was allowed to retain it. Nothing more astonished the natives than this honourable treatment of a vanquished foe.

In 1760 the English unmade the nabob they made in 1757. Meer Jaffier was old and feeble, and they replaced him by his son-in-law, the vigorous Meer Cossim, who ceded to his benefactors the provinces of Burdwan, Midnapore, and Chittagong, which yielded a third of the entire revenue, in addition to presents to the amount of twenty lacs of rupees. The council apparently did not dream that the vigour of the new nabob might be used against them, but so it was. Meer Cossim was no sooner established in his office than he bent all his energy to escape from the chains in which he was held, and render himself independent of the English. When he failed in doing this, he wreaked his vengeance in a massacre more cold-blooded than that of the Black Hole. His first step was to remove his court from Moorshedabad to Monghir, two hundred miles farther from Calcutta. Here he set to work to drill troops in European fashion, manufacture muskets, and cast cannon. He also obtained the confirmation of his nabobship from the emperor or promising an annual tribute of twenty-four lacs.* This made good his title in native eyes.

The dispute between the council and their nominee began in differences about the dues on merchandise. By imperial firman the goods of the company were to pass duty free. But the English claimed the same privilege for the private inland trade, by which they swelled their nominal incomes into immense fortunes. Not only the company's servants, but their servants again did the same. Any attempt on the part of the nabob's officers to levy duty was resisted by force. In this way, all the trade of the country was passing into English hands, the native merchants were being ruined, and the public revenue was robbed. But the council was inflexible. They would give up none of their claims; they would only consent as a favour, instead of the nine per cent. claimed on everything, to give two and a half per cent. on salt alone. The nabob met this by abolishing all duties whatever, thus placing his own people on the same level as the English. The council then peremptorily insisted on the duties being reimposed on native merchants. Anything more selfish and iniquitous it would be hard to conceive. A curious circumstance is that this private trade was carried on in defiance of express and repeated orders from the Court of Directors at home. But at the same time a great deal of the blame for the state of things that had arisen rested on the directors themselves, who gave their servants abroad inadequate salaries, and provided no substitute or compensation for the profitable trade on which they laid their veto. The same cause explains the large presents, each one a fortune, which the members of council and military officers were accustomed to receive from native princes. Every new appointment was the occasion of vast largesses. It is difficult not to believe that there would have been fewer depo-

---

* A lac of rupees=£10,000.

sitions and new creations but for this motive. Mr. Mill quotes from a statement of a Committee of the House of Commons in 1773, that the amount received in this way by individuals exceeded £2,000,000, in addition to nearly £4,000,000 to the company and individuals under the name of compensation. Clive himself after Plassey received about a quarter of a million, besides a *jaghire* worth three lacs a year. When this was made ground of accusation, he said that he only wondered at his own moderation in his position.

War at last broke out. The English, of course, were victorious, although in the battle of Gheria, August 2nd, 1763, the nabob's new discipline told heavily against them. Meer Cossim then turned round on his pursuers like a wounded tiger, and wreaked a savage revenge. Râmnarain, the wealthy and high-spirited governor of Patna, whom Mr. Vansittart had weakly and in violation of distinct pledges abandoned to the nabob's mercy, he threw into the Ganges, along with others supposed to be favourable to the English cause. More than this, he had in his power the whole of the English factory at Patna, numbering forty-eight officers, civil and military, and one hundred soldiers. These had actually seized Patna, and might have held it safely; but, scattering in different directions to plunder, they were driven out again. Cut off from Calcutta by Monghir, which lay between, they tried to make their way into Oude, but were obliged to surrender themselves prisoners. The nabob ordered them all to be put to death in cold blood. His officers refused to obey, saying that they were soldiers, not butchers. But a European adventurer who went by the name of Somru,* undertook the deed, and the unarmed prisoners were shot down or hacked to pieces to the last man. Meer Cossim takes his place for savage cruelty beside Surâja Dowlah and Nâna Sâhib. The two murderers then fled to the nabob-vizier of Oude, who invaded Bengal with a force of fifty thousand men. He was attacked at Buxar by Major Munro on October 23rd, 1764, and routed, his entire camp being

---

* Some accounts make him a Frenchman, and call him Walter Raymond; others a German, and call him Walter Reinhardt.

taken as it stood. The battle of Buxar is only second in importance to that of Plassey, seven years earlier. The last bulwark of native authority was now broken down, and north India lay at the feet of the English. Emperor, nabob, vizier had all been crushed. The vizier was anxious for peace, but the English insisted as the first condition upon the surrender of Meer Cossim and Somru. The first took refuge with the Rohillas. As to the second, the vizier's conscience would not permit him to surrender a guest; but he offered to invite him to a feast and slay him there before any one whom the English might depute as a witness, an offer which was declined.

Before the battle of Buxar Major Munro had to contend with a mutiny among his own sepoys. Their long course of victory had filled them with a sense of power, and, with arms in their hands, they demanded increased pay, which was refused. A battalion then deserted, intending to join the enemy. They were pursued and brought back. Twenty-four of the ringleaders were tried by their own officers and condemned to death. After four had been blown away from guns, the European officers of the sepoys reported that their men were determined to allow no more executions. Major Munro loaded his guns with grape, placed his European troops in the intervals of the guns, and ordered the sepoys to ground arms, threatening to fire if a single man disobeyed. The order was obeyed, the executions went on, and all danger passed away. It would have been well for India, if Major Munro's promptitude and firmness had always been imitated.

On Meer Cossim's defection the English again set up Meer Jaffier, 1764. He could do nothing but confirm all his predecessor's grants, adding gifts and compensation-money to the amount of fifty-three lacs, besides promising five lacs a month towards the expenses of the war. But his troubles did not last much longer; he died in January, 1765, at the age of seventy-five. Mr. Vansittart had retired from the scene; Clive was on his way out; but the acting governor, Mr. Spencer, without waiting for his arrival, at once appointed a new nabob, Nujum-ad-Dowlah, a youth twenty years old. It is impossible not to suspect that the haste had a mercenary motive. At the same time a deputy nabob was appointed, which formed a new occasion for presents, and the English took the military affairs of the country under their own direction. Naturally, the nabob looked upon his deputy, who wielded the substantial power, as his rival, and began to plot for his removal. It was time for a master to appear on the scene.

Lord Clive was appointed as the only man capable of dealing with the crisis, and arrived in May, 1765. He was armed with ample authority for the work expected of him. The ordinary council was superseded by a special select committee of five persons, in whom, along with the governor, supreme power was vested. Practically, Clive was dictator. In his letters home he gave a terrible picture of the disorganization and universal corruption prevailing. He first settled the external relations of the company. To the Nabob of Oude, whose wanton aggression had been rewarded by utter defeat, he restored his country with the exception of two districts reserved for the emperor. No one was more astonished at this generosity than the nabob himself; but Clive's course was dictated less by generosity than policy. In all his letters home he insisted earnestly that the English should not dream of extending their views beyond Bengal, Behar, and Orissa, just as formerly he had restricted them to Calcutta and its environs. As to the emperor, Clive formally accepted from him the *dewanship*, *i.e.*, financial administration, of the three provinces named. This had been repeatedly offered before, but declined. Now the time had come to consent. The formal investiture took place August 12th, 1765, and the ceremony was a strange parody on former memories. Clive's tent served for a palace, and a chair on two tables joined together for an imperial throne. In this sorry state Shah Alum, the heir of Akbar and Aurungzib, transferred to the English twenty-five millions of people and £4,000,000 of revenue. He could scarcely be so blind as not to see that he was virtually transferring his crown to the foreigner. To the Nabob of Bengal fifty-three lacs of revenue were assigned for his court and the judicial administration of the country. The worthless

D

youth danced for joy at the news. 'Thank God!' he said; 'I shall now have as many dancing-girls as I like.'

Clive next turned his attention to internal questions. The company's servants were all compelled to sign covenants* renouncing private trade; but Clive did not enforce this without providing compensation. He formed a company for carrying on the trade in certain articles, in the profits of which the company's servants were to share according to their rank, as in prize-money. This was manifestly a cumbrous arrangement which could not last long; but for the time it lessened the abuses which had so deeply dishonoured the English name.

He encountered greater difficulties in enforcing military reductions. The extra allowance made to officers on campaign in India is called *batta*. Since the battle of Plassey the nabobs had doubled the usual amount. As long as the expense fell on others, the company said nothing; but now that peace prevailed they insisted on double *batta* being stopped. The officers all united to resist, and resigned in a body. They thought that, with the Mahrattas threatening on the border, Clive must yield, and double *batta* be made permanent. Clive accepted the resignations, offered commissions to others, and sent for a supply of officers from Madras. The officers soon begged permission to recall their resignations. The danger was the greatest that had yet arisen, but Clive was equal to it. His iron will and dauntless courage were never more severely tested than on this occasion. The young nabob died in May, 1760, and another was appointed; but the change scarcely deserves record.

In May, 1767, Clive was compelled by ill health finally to return home; he was only forty-one. With one exception the British empire in India has produced no greater man than its founder. Pitt called him 'a heaven-born general'; it is just as true that he was a heaven-born ruler. On his return home he was ruthlessly attacked by those whose crimes and misdeeds he had exposed and punished. We are profoundly thankful to

---

* Hence the phrase, the Covenanted Service, as applied to the Civil Service.

be able to say that the House of Commons refused to endorse charges prompted by malice and revenge, and passed a resolution in recognition of his great services; but the malignity of his enemies so preyed on his spirits as to drive him to suicide in 1774. The difference between his fate and that of Lally is that the latter was the work of the government, while the former was the work of private enemies.

The interim governors of Bengal between 1767 and 1772 were Messrs. Verelst and Cartier, efficient administrators for the time. During this period the scheme of double government devised bore a crop of evil effects. The administration of justice was in one set of hands, the collection of the revenue in another. The English could not legally punish the excesses of their native officials, the nabob's officers durst not. It is easy to see what opportunity was given for injustice and oppression; but probably the blessing of peace was a compensation for the evils incident to this time of transition. Though Bengal was spared the ravages of war, in 1770 it was desolated by a terrible famine, in which, it is said, a third of the population perished.

Meanwhile, Madras passed through a period of mismanagement and weakness even more pitiable than Bengal had witnessed. The governors and members of council were well adapted for the management of a commercial establishment, but as little fitted to conduct affairs of State as some of the Bengal authorities just referred to. Directly that they had succeeded in establishing Mohammed Ali in the nabobship they found themselves in this difficulty, that while the defence of the Carnatic devolved on them the revenues were in the nabob's hands; they were therefore obliged to demand from the latter fifty lacs of rupees towards past expenses. His plan for raising the amount was intensely characteristic of the ways of native princes at that time. He had a standing dispute with the Rāja of Tanjore, and proposed that the English should join him in an attack on that country, which was wealthy and had suffered little from invasion. The English could not, and would not, agree to the proposal; instead, they offered themselves as arbitrators, and mulcted the Tanjore prince in twenty-two lacs for the past, four as a present, and four as tribute. This went to pay the nabob's debts to Madras. Gradually the revenues of the Carnatic passed into English hands; but for many years the English were in financial difficulty, and the interests of the country suffered.

By the Treaty of Paris, 1763, the French received back their old settlements in India, their nominee, Salabut Jung, was acknowledged Viceroy of the Deckan, and Mohammed Ali, Nabob of the Carnatic. But Salabut Jung had been deposed, and his place usurped two years before by his brother Nizam Ali, who, directly that he heard of the treaty, took care that his brother should gain nothing by it by having him put to death. Thus the treaty, made in ignorance at home, was the unwitting cause of Salabut's death. It is from this fratricide that the present ruler of Hyderabad derives his title of nizam.

But this period was especially memorable as having sown the seeds of enmity between the English and Hyder Ali, the new sovereign of the Mysore country, which from the Ghauts looks down upon the Carnatic. Hyder was the most dangerous and implacable enemy the English ever had in India. His career was only less extraordinary than that of Sivaji, the founder of the Mahratta power in the previous century. He was the son of a *peon*, or policeman. Entering the service of the Hindu Rája of Mysore, he gradually rose, by combined craft and force, to be the most powerful man in the kingdom, and then took his master's place. His resources of cunning and audacity were boundless. Once, when utterly defeated by the Hindu prime minister, Nunjirája, he suddenly presented himself unarmed and alone before him as a suppliant for forgiveness. Nunjirája fell into the trap, and soon Hyder was as powerful as ever. At another time, when hard pressed by the Hindu forces, he caused letters bearing Nunjirája's seal to fall in the opposing general's way, hinting at treachery among the troops. The general was so alarmed that he fled, whereupon Hyder attacked the troops left without a leader and won an easy victory. Afterwards, he invited Nunjirája to his capital under security of an oath on the Koran to do him no harm, and then threw him into prison for life, justifying the treachery by declaring that the book on which the oath was taken was not the Koran but a bundle of old leaves. It was in 1761 that he felt himself strong enough to sweep aside the Hindu dynasty. Presenting himself at the capital, he sent to the rāja to say,—that large sums were due to Hyder by the State, and ought to be liquidated; after the payment of these arrears, if the rāja should be pleased to continue him in his service, well; if not, Hyder would depart and seek his fortune elsewhere. The rāja understood the polite intimation, and was glad to escape with his life and a pension. Hyder's troops were scarcely inferior to the Mahrattas in the skill with which they plundered and devastated a country. Though their master could neither read nor write, his powers of mental calculation were such that it was useless for his officers to try to deceive him as to the amount of plunder. In his wars with the Mahrattas, who frequently overwhelmed him by mere weight of numbers, his affairs were often reduced to desperation, but he never failed to extricate himself and repair his losses.

It was this ambitious and able monarch whom want of knowledge, tact, and foresight in the Madras authorities, rather than design, converted into a bitter foe to the English name. It cannot be denied that Hyder had ground of complaint which, with a barbarian who only knows one way of settling a dispute, meant ground of war. In the treaty with the nizam made in 1766, in which the Madras government weakly promised to pay the nizam tribute for the Northern Sircars, although on the memorable August 12th, 1765, the emperor had given the English on Clive's demand the dewanship of those territories, as far as he could give anything, they also engaged to furnish the nizam with two infantry battalions and six guns, 'to settle, in everything right and proper, the affairs of his highness' government.' In dealing with European powers such a stipulation might matter little, but with a faithless Oriental prince it worked untold evil. At this very time the nizam was arranging with the Mahrattas an attack on Hyder, which took place, the English furnishing the promised contingent. Thus, the first attack was made by the English, not by Hyder, and it was wholly unprovoked. The only excuse which can be made for the Madras government is that they did not know what they were doing.

The moment Hyder had settled with his assailants he prepared to take his revenge on the English, and to make it complete he gained the nizam as his ally for a consideration of twenty lacs of rupees, and six lacs as tribute. Indeed, while the English were actually in the field helping the nizam, it was discovered that that worthy, while protesting fidelity, was arranging to go over to Hyder; whereupon the English officer, Colonel Smith, withdrew with most of his force. In 1767 Hyder and the nizam invaded the Carnatic together. Their force included forty-two thousand cavalry, twenty-eight thousand infantry, and one hundred guns. Colonel Smith commanded only one thousand and thirty cavalry, fifty-eight thousand foot, and sixteen guns. Against such odds in a battle at Changama, September 3rd, he held his own, but was afterwards obliged to retreat through want of provisions, of which Mohammed Ali had charge. At Trinomalee, however, he fought a two days' battle with the allies, and utterly routed them, taking sixty-four guns and inflicting a loss of four thousand men. The nizam at once retreated from the country, and Hyder was soon after recalled to the western coast. Two incidents illustrate Hyder's tactics The native guide employed with the officer sent in pursuit after the battle of Trinomalee led the troops into a swamp, and turned out to be a spy of Hyder's. At the same time Hyder sent his son Tippu, then a youth seventeen years old, at the head of five thousand light horse, to carry terror into the residences of the English near Madras. Had not the troops been so intent on plunder, they could easily have captured the President and Council in a body, and thus ended the war at a stroke.

It seems scarcely credible that in 1768 the English renewed the former treaty with the nizam, of whose treachery they had just had such conspicuous proof; but such is the fact. The nizam had been worsted, his capital was threatened by an English force sent from Bengal, he would gladly have agreed to anything; yet, with the exception of a slight reduction in the tribute from the

English, the treaty stood as it did before, even to the supply of an English contingent. The directors at home might well write: 'We cannot take a view of your conduct from the commencement of your negotiations for the Sircars, without the strongest disapprobation; and when we see the opulent fortunes acquired by our servants since that period, it gives but too much weight to the public opinion, that this rage for negotiations, treaties and alliances has private advantage for its object more than the public good.'

In the same year the Madras government resolved to carry the war into the Mysore country instead of waiting for the Carnatic to be devastated by Hyder. This was wise policy, if it had been wisely carried out. But the commissariat was again entrusted to Mohammed Ali, and failed; and still worse, two members of council were attached to Colonel Smith's force to control the operations, a fatuous course in face of a leader like Hyder. However, in spite of difficulties, Colonel Smith made such progress in capturing forts and passes, that Hyder sought peace; but the terms demanded by the President and Council were such that Hyder preferred to risk everything rather than accept them.

Victory now changed sides. The English were obliged, chiefly through the utter neglect of Mohammed Ali and the mistakes of the 'deputies,' to raise the siege of Bangalore, Hyder again carried fire and sword into the Carnatic; Colonel Smith was superseded, and almost immediately reappointed. Hyder saw his opportunity, and, repeating his former tactics, brought the war to an end by a bold and masterly stroke. The English force lay between Hyder and the Mysore; but this did not mean starvation to Hyder, as an Eastern force lives on the country it invades; it simply meant that Hyder was nearer Madras than Colonel Smith. He sent his infantry, guns and plunder by a circuitous route back to Mysore, the English not daring to pursue while Hyder remained behind. He then put himself at the head of six thousand select horse, marched one hundred and thirty miles in three days and a half, and on March 29th, 1769, appeared at St. Thomas, close to Madras. Hence he sent two demands: first, the instant despatch of an order to Colonel Smith, who was following hard in the rear, to halt, thus paralyzing the English force; secondly, that the governor should repair to his camp to conclude peace. Madras lay at his mercy; he could have plundered and destroyed the whole town outside the fort and departed before the arrival of help. The two conditions of the peace, dictated by the invader under the walls of Madras, were mutual restorations of conquests, and an offensive and defensive alliance. Colonel Smith had to lie inactive while the negotiations were settled. Victory and credit alike remained with the enemy. Few more humiliating treaties were ever signed by English officers.

WARREN HASTINGS.

CHAPTER IV.

ADMINISTRATION OF WARREN HASTINGS, 1772-1785—FIRST MAHRATTA WAR—SECOND MYSORE WAR.

ARREN HASTINGS had undergone a twenty years' training for the office to which he was called in 1772, having come to Bengal as a company's clerk in 1750, and climbed step by step to the governor's council. He was the only member in Vansittart's time who kept his hands clean of the presents by which the others quickly amassed enormous fortunes, in this respect comparing to advantage with Clive. He was the first and undoubtedly the greatest Governor-general India has ever had. The first: the office was created in 1770 by the act of Parliament which provided a new governing body for India, consisting of a Governor-general at a salary of £25,000 a year, and four councillors at £10,000. At the same time a Crown court was established at Calcutta, with a chief justice at £8,000, and three puisne judges at £6,000. The greatest: under his hands a trading company was organized into an imperial government, which has ever since proceeded substantially on the lines he drew. He had in a consummate degree the genius for ruling men, of which the Roman empire in ancient and the British in modern days have furnished perhaps the highest examples. He abolished the double government, which soon proved itself unworkable, and brought the real rulers face to face with the ruled. He was appointed to work out in detail the resolve of the Directors ' to stand forth as *dewan*, and to take on themselves the entire care and management of the revenues through the agency of their own servants.'

The treasury was removed from Moorshedabad to Calcutta. The office of deputy-nabob was abolished, and the allowance to the nabob himself reduced from twenty-two to sixteen lacs a year. The tribute to the emperor, who was a puppet in the hands of a Mahratta force at Delhi, was discontinued. It was Hastings who established the system of administration by English collectors, which is now universal in India. The collector is an officer with fiscal and judicial jurisdiction over a limited district, from whose decisions there is an appeal to superior courts. In India the government is the proprietor of land, the rent of which forms the chief source of public revenue. The rent is assessed to the ryot or farmer at the annual circuits made by the collector or his officers. The collector is the English substitute for the old zemindar,* who in Mohammedan days collected and often farmed the revenues, and was thus a sort of middle-man between the government and cultivators. Even during Hastings' days many changes were made, as new light was gained, in the mode of collecting the revenue and administering justice. The land question is even a more intricate one in India than in the west.

The mistakes in the endless controversy have mainly arisen from the application of European ideas to a different order of facts. Every one knows that the happiness and prosperity of a nation depend most on wise internal administration. But unfortunately these pages must be chiefly occupied with more exciting topics.

Warren Hastings had to contend with extraordinary difficulties in the council which was appointed to advise and help him. For many years a majority thwarted and outvoted him on every question small and great, administrative and imperial. The new councillors and judges arrived in 1774, and unfortunately brought with them the most violent prejudices against the Governor-general. Mr. Barwell was the only member who supported Hastings. The other three—Colonel Monson, General Clavering, Mr. Francis—bitterly opposed. The leader was Francis (generally supposed to have been the author of the *Letters of Junius*), the impersonation of implacable rancour, and a master of virulent invective. The qualifications of the oppo-

---

* A Persian term=landholder.

sition as against the governor's long and intimate knowledge of the country may be estimated from two facts. Before Francis had been two years in the country he recorded his opinions respecting the ancient customs of India and the measures necessary for its prosperity in a voluminous minute, the two main positions being : 1, That the opinion is erroneous which ascribes to the sovereign the property of the land ; 2, That the property in question belongs to the zemindars,*—positions as false of India as they are true of Europe. The other fact is, that when the new judges landed at Calcutta, one of them, observing the bare legs and feet of the natives who crowded to the sight, said to his colleague : ' Our court, brother, certainly was not established before it was needed. I trust we shall not have been six months in the country before these victims of oppression are comfortably provided with shoes and stockings.'† Meeting by meeting the controversy raged. Every question had to be referred to the home authorities, who, instead of removing one or the other party, distributed their praise and blame pretty evenly between the two sides. The impression made on the native mind was bad, and the weakness introduced into the action of government great. The opposition acted on the very principles which they blamed in Hastings. While condemning Hastings for 'letting out British troops for hire' to the Nabob of Oude, and interfering in politics outside the British limits, they continued the arrangement with the nabob, and gave to British territory the only addition it received during Hastings' administration, namely, the district of Benares. No one questions that all the dignity was on the side of the Governor-general. Francis and his friends wished to bring natives into the council to accuse the governor to his face of bribery. 'I know,' he replied, 'what belongs to the dignity and character of the first member of this administration, and I will not sit at this board in the character of a criminal,' and dissolved the meeting; whereupon the majority affected to try and condemn him in his absence. He was then accused of opposing inquiry ; but he only opposed

---

* Mill, vol. iv., p. 4. † Marshman, part i., ch. xiii.

inquiry in the wrong place. Pecuniary corruption was the last charge which should have been brought against him; the few gifts he did receive were applied to the necessities of the State.

The execution of Nuncomar in 1775 was long regarded as a dark stain on the fame of Hastings. Nuncomar, a Brahmin intriguer and peculator as unprincipled as Omichund, was one of those who were instigated to come forward as the governor's accusers. At the very time he was doing this he was arrested on a charge of forgery, tried, and hanged. The execution was certainly unjust, because forgery, though at that time a capital crime by English law, was not so by Hindu law. But, notwithstanding the coincidence in time, Hastings was never shown to have any connection with the case. The case was tried and the sentence passed by the royal judges, who on every occasion took pains to show their independence of the governor and company. The execution made an immense sensation in the country, as by Hindu law a Brahmin cannot be put to death even for murder. The judges must by this time have lost the tender consideration for native feelings which they professed a year before.

Nothing can be farther from our wish than to represent Hastings as always in the right. On the contrary, his proceedings were often high-handed, arbitrary, perhaps unjust. His action in the Rohilla war early in his administration looks very like letting out British troops for the sake of gain. By this means the Nabob of Oude, who had once invaded our territories, was able to crush out his enemies. We only say that allowance must be made for the difficulties in which he was placed. He was without precedents to guide him; he had great undertakings on hand, and was constantly at his wit's end for means to support them; he had no imperial credit upon which to fall back. A great deal of the blame belongs to the home authorities, who left the powers of the different factors in the government in such a loose, undefined state; the limits between the three Presidencies were left unsettled, which gave rise to much confusion and mistake. With trifling exceptions, the home authorities never went beyond verbal condemnation of any of Hastings' acts, they never gave back any advantage which his measures had gained for them. In 1776 Hastings obtained a majority by the death of Colonel Monson. This was disturbed for a brief period by a new appointment; but General Clavering's death in 1777, after an insane attempt to set himself up as a rival Governor-general, again threw the balance the other way. The personal hostility between Hastings and Francis issued in a duel in 1780. The latter was wounded, and returned to Europe. But we have anticipated the history.

It was at this time that the English first came into collision with the celebrated Mahratta power, whose capital was Poona, in the west. The history of the rise and growth of that power is one as full of romantic vicissitude as any in the world, but it lies outside our subject. We have already intimated that the Mahratta state grew and flourished by levying blackmail on surrounding states. The only question ever considered was its own power and the weakness of others; for it might was the only right. No state was ever so ready to attack and at the same time so difficult to injure in return as the Mahratta, and none consequently gave the English such trouble. When attacked, it yielded to the blow like the wave to the oar, and as quickly rose again. Sivaji's successor, the rāja, soon became a cipher, little better than a state prisoner in the hill fort of Satara, although everything was still done in his name; but the real power was in the hands of the peshwa, or prime minister, who played over again the part of the French mayors of the palace, and whose office was hereditary. At this time there was a civil war respecting the office of peshwa, for which there were two claimants: Raghoba, who was strongly suspected of having murdered his nephew, the last peshwa; and an infant, whose rights were maintained by a regency. Berar and Guzerat were in the hands of Mahratta families. Scindia and Holkar were Mahratta chieftains.

It must be admitted that the Mahratta war arose in the first instance from our interference in Mahratta affairs for our own ends. The Bombay Presidency was anxious to obtain the port of Bassein and the small island of Salsette, which faces Bombay. These were in the hands of the Mahrattas, and were as useless to them as they were important to us; but the Mahrattas attached a fanciful value to them, because they had been taken from a European power, the Portuguese. One would think that the right course was for us to wait till the places could be gained by peaceful means. But temptation came, and the Bombay government yielded to it. Raghoba sought their help against the regency. One stipulation made at Bombay was the cession of Salsette and Bassein. Even then Raghoba would not at first sign away Mahratta territory; but afterwards, having been defeated by the regency, he made the required cession by the treaty of Surat, March, 1775. Meanwhile, the English had taken Salsette by force to save it from falling again into the hands of the Portuguese, who were preparing to attack it. The Surat treaty was condemned and annulled by Mr. Francis and the majority in the Calcutta council, who, despite the protests of Bombay, negotiated a new treaty, the treaty of Poorunder, with the opposite party. The court of directors supported the Bombay government. The interference of Francis and his party did incalculable mischief, the Mahrattas being crafty enough to profit by this division of counsels. Hastings, while disapproving of the principle of the Surat treaty, thought that it should be upheld. When the directors heard of the second treaty, they enjoined the Bombay authorities to abide by it, unless the Mahrattas themselves infringed it. Such acts of infringement were easily found, and in the end a new treaty was made with Raghoba on the lines of the Surat one.

All that remained was for the English to perform their part of the contract, by establishing Raghoba in authority at Poona. In November, 1778, an expedition, consisting of four thousand men, was despatched under Colonel Egerton for this purpose; but the leaders were incapable, and the force was paralyzed by divided authority. Bombay followed the evil example of Madras in appointing 'field commissioners.' When the force came within eighteen miles of Poona, the leaders became panic-struck at the unknown dangers before them, and in spite of the protests of Raghoba and of their own subordinate officers, gave the order to retreat. No troops were ever better at harassing a retreating force than the Mahrattas, and but for the valour of a young officer, Captain Hartley, under whose orders the sepoys fought like heroes, the force would scarcely have escaped destruction. The only way of escape which the commissioners could discover was by signing the treaty of Wurgaum, promising to give up all the British acquisitions since 1773. Two English gentlemen were even given as hostages. Hastings might well call it 'an infamous convention, which it would be worth millions to obliterate.' Its authors were dismissed the service.

British honour found a vindicator in Colonel Goddard, who led a force of several thousand men from Bengal to Bombay, a march of one thousand miles through alien territories. He received the greatest hospitality from the Rāja of Bhopal, whose successors have ever been loyal allies of the English. The maharānee is a member of the order of the Star of India. At one point in his long march he received orders by letter from the Bombay 'field commissioners' to return to Bengal. He replied that he was under the orders of Bengal, and marched forward three hundred miles in nineteen days. Colonel Goddard was directed to negotiate a new treaty, and on the refusal of the Regency began war. He first attacked and defeated the forces of the guickwar in Guzerat, capturing the splendid city of Ahmedabad, February, 1780. He then inflicted two defeats on Scindia. The dominions of the latter were also attacked on the Bengal side by Major Popham, as brilliant a soldier as Goddard. It was on this occasion that he took Scindia's fort of Gwalior, which all India had regarded as impregnable. The height to be climbed by ladders was a scarp of sixteen feet, a rock of forty, and a wall of thirty. But Captain Bruce and twenty sepoys were on the battlements before they were discovered, and the garrison fled. The exploit filled all India, and the Mahrattas especially, with terror. Scindia was thus recalled from the west to defend his own dominions. Popham's successor in command began to retreat, and would have repeated the disaster at Wurgaum; but Bruce advised a night attack on Scindia's camp, which was perfectly successful, March, 1781. Just at the same time, Goddard had failed in a march upon Poona, the only failure in his career. Holkar, with twenty-five thousand horse, harassed his retreat, but did nothing more. The Mahrattas were not a little elated by their victory over a soldier like Goddard. Before this Colonel Hartley had cleared the Concan country, *i.e.*, the country below the upper western ghauts, of the Mahratta armies, after sustaining an attack from twenty thousand of their horse for two days, and Goddard had taken Bassein. Colonel Hartley's services were never rewarded.

Scindia's defeats had made him anxious for peace. Peace was also essential to the English, whose resources were strained to the utmost by the war with Hyder Ali in the south. On the seventeenth of May, 1782, the treaty of Salbye was signed, although the Mahrattas did not finally ratify it until December, when Hyder's death put an end to all their hopes of success in a united crusade against the English. The result of the first Mahratta war was that the English retained Salsette, a dear purchase, and Raghoba was not instated as peshwa.

The Mahrattas and Hyder had united to expel the English from India. The failure of the first was the result of their hopeless internal dissensions. Hyder had no such difficulty to contend with. For years he had been bringing his kingdom into order, fortifying his capital and training his army under the direction of French officers, forming leagues with French and Mahrattas; and then, when all was ready, he hurled himself upon Madras. The blow he struck was the most terrible hitherto dealt at the British power. The wonder still is that it failed. Technically, Hyder had some grounds of complaint. When called upon, in fulfilment of the offensive and defensive alliance, to help him against the Mahratta invaders, the Madras government always refused. An English force once threatened to march across a corner of his territories without leave. The Madras government, after capturing Pondicherry, in pursuance of a sentimental wish to extinguish French influence, sent a force to take Mahé, a small French settlement on the west coast, which Hyder regarded as under his special protection, and which was no doubt important to him as his only remaining link of connection with France. But these reasons were of course mere pretexts. His fixed idea was that the British power and his own could not coexist in India. A large French force, under the command of the veteran Bussy, was actually sent to Hyder's assistance, but was greatly delayed on its way. Had it arrived in time, the result might have been different. It only reached the Coromandel Coast in April, 1783, several months after Hyder's death.

The army with which Hyder burst upon the Carnatic in July, 1780, was the best appointed that south India had ever seen. It consisted of one hundred thousand horse and foot, many of them trained and led by French officers, and an equally well-trained artillery of one hundred pieces. He had, besides, a corps of four hundred Europeans under the command of M. Lally, who was also one of his leading advisers.

The invasion came upon Madras like a thunderclap out of a clear sky. Nothing was prepared. The governor, Sir Thomas Rumbold, and the commander, Sir Hector Munro, the victor of Buxar, knew nothing of Hyder's preparations and laughed at all warnings until the enemy had actually plundered Conjeveram, only fifty miles away, and sent his scouts as far as St. Thomas. The Madras council had been wasting its time in quarrels still less dignified and more violent than those in Calcutta. The former governor, Lord Pigot, had been arrested. The present governor, with two members of the council, were soon afterwards dismissed the service for corruption and disobedience to orders. What the country suffered during the two years that the invasion lasted, it would be impossible to describe. Strange to say, Hyder's cause was popular with the people of the country. The English could learn nothing of the movements of the enemy, while everything that went on in the English camp was well known to Hyder, our spies and guides being in his pay. No better proof could be given of the oppressive character of the government of the nabob, whom we supported.

At the time of the invasion one-third of the English force, two thousand eight hundred men, was actually away in the Northern Sircars under Colonel Baillie. Munro had with him five thousand two hundred men. Orders were sent to Baillie to join the main body at Conjeveram. Then began a series of mistakes on the side of both Baillie and Munro, which resulted in the annihilation of Baillie's force. The former, in his march southward to join Munro, unfortunately encamped on the northern side of a stream, which rose in the night and detained him nearly a fortnight. The latter, when Baillie was hotly engaged with a strong force under Tippu, Hyder's son, instead of moving his whole army to support him sent a detachment of one thousand one hundred men under Colonel Fletcher, which only weakened his own force and swelled the subsequent disaster. Munro indeed alleged that it was impossible for him to move for want of food and carriage; but afterwards, when Baillie and Fletcher had advanced to within a couple of miles of Conjeveram and were fighting for life with the whole of Hyder's army, Munro did nothing. By falling on the enemy's rear, he might have won an easy victory. Baillie's great error was in halting on the night of September 9th, instead of continuing his march. The result was that next day every man in his force was killed or captured within sight of Conjeveram, and Hyder won his only victory in the field. Our comfort is that every man of the devoted host, officer and private, English and sepoy, did his duty.

'Nothing ever exceeded the steadiness and determination with which this handful of men sustained the fury of their enemies. No effort could break their order, while sepoys as well as Europeans repeatedly presented and recovered arms with as much coolness and regularity as if they had been exhibiting on parade. When the heroic bravery of this little band presented so fair a prospect of baffling the host of their assailants, two of their tumbrils blew up, which, not only made a large opening in both lines, but at once deprived them of ammunition and overturned and disabled their guns. Their fire was now in a great measure silenced, and their lines were no longer entire; yet so great was the awe which they inspired, that the enemy durst not immediately close. From half after seven a.m. when the tumbrils blew up, they remained exposed to the fire of the cannons and rockets, losing great numbers of officers and men, till nine o'clock, when Hyder with his whole army came round the right flank. The cavalry charged in separate columns, while bodies of infantry, interspersed between them, poured in volleys of musketry with dreadful effect. After the sepoys were almost

HEROIC RESISTANCE OF BAILLIE.

all destroyed, Colonel Baillie, though severely wounded, rallied the Europeans who survived. Forming a square and gaining a little eminence, without ammunition, and almost all wounded, the officers fighting with their swords, the men with their bayonets, they repelled thirteen attacks, many of the men when desperately wounded disdaining to receive quarter, and raising themselves from the ground to meet the enemy with their bayonets. Though not more than four hundred men, they still desired to be led on, and to cut their way through the enemy. But Baillie, despairing now of being relieved by Munro, and wishing no doubt to spare the lives of the brave men who surrounded him, deemed it better to hold up a flag of truce. The enemy at first treated this with contempt. After a few minutes, the men were ordered to lay down their arms, with intimation that quarter would be given. Yet they had no sooner surrendered, than the savages rushed upon them with unbridled fury; and had it not been for the great exertions of Lally, Pimoran, and other French officers, who implored for mercy, not a man of them probably would have been spared. The gallant Fletcher was among those who lay on the field of battle. About two hundred Europeans were taken prisoners, reserved to the horrors of a captivity more terrible than death. The inhuman treatment which they received was deplored and mitigated by the French officers in the service of Hyder, with a generosity which did honour to European education.'* The next day Munro set out on his retreat to Madras, a body of the enemy pursuing and cutting off stragglers. Had Hyder acted with his usual vigour, a still greater disaster must have been the result.

Hastings saw that if Madras was to be saved, it must be by other hands. He suspended Mr. Whitchill, the acting governor. 'The creature,' Hastings said, 'made some show of resistance.' He despatched every soldier and rupee he could spare, and, above all, sent Sir Eyre Coote to the scene of his early triumphs. The treasure for the support of the troops was to be under the general's management. But these supplies were soon

---

* Mill, vol. iv., p. 134.

exhausted; and Coote's forces were always too few, ill provisioned and crippled for want of carriage. The nabob, whose country we were defending, did less than help. While our troops were on half rations, his officers sold the provisions collected for their support, and remitted the proceeds to his private purse. His own brother betrayed Chandrajiri Fort to the enemy for a consideration. 'The venality and political profligacy of the nabob's court, unmatched in India, was the constant theme of Coote's indignant remonstrances.'* At last he was compelled to resign the revenues to the company for a period of five years.

Early in 1781 Arcot was taken by the enemy, and Wandewash would have shared the same fate but for the skill and heroism of Lieutenant Flint, whose only reward was 'the applause of Sir Eyre Coote, whose admiration of the resources which had been employed knew no bounds.' Hyder's plan was to avoid pitched battles, and gradually get the forts and whole country into his hands, leaving the English nothing but Madras, which he would then besiege. Each party manœuvred, one to bring on, the other to avoid, a battle, and the stronger force generally succeeded. Aggression on Coote's part was out of the question; even the battles he fought were really defensive. His position in the presence of superior forces nearly resembled that of Wellington in the Peninsula, and his policy was the same. The battle of Porto Novo was fought July 1st, 1781. Coote had been sharply repulsed in an attack on the fortified temple of Chillambrum. Hyder was so encouraged by this that, despite warnings from Tippu, he marched towards Cuddalore to seek the English, and took up a strong position with a line of redoubts in front. The English, marching to the attack, had these redoubts in front, the sea on the right, and some sand-hills on the left. Presently an officer discerned a road through these sand-hills. It turned out afterwards that Hyder had cut this the night before, and intended while the English were attacking the redoubts in front to send his horse by this road and take them in the rear. Coote marched through this road,

---

* Marshman.

thus foiling Hyder's scheme. A six hours' severe conflict followed, in which Hyder was routed and obliged to withdraw from Wandewash and the south.

The battle of Pollilore followed, August 27th. Colonel Pearce had been on his way with a force from Bengal since January. Not only had his march been delayed by negotiations, but his force had been reduced one-half by cholera; yet in July he had reached Pulicat, forty miles north of Madras. Hyder sent Tippu to intercept him, hoping to repeat the tactics of a year ago; but this time he had to deal with Coote, who marched one hundred and fifty miles from Porto Novo to effect a junction with Pearce, and did so on August 2nd. The battle was fought on the scene of Baillie's defeat. Hyder claimed it as a victory; but it was only undecided, because he had taken up an impregnable position.

On September 27th Coote won a third victory at Solingur. Coote's object was the relief of Vellore, which was closely besieged and reduced to sore straits. Hyder's object was to prevent this. This time the enemy was taken by surprise, and only saved his artillery by the reckless sacrifice of his horse. The English loss was less than one hundred, the enemy's five thousand. Soon afterwards Coote again made three forced marches to relieve Vellore, and Hyder did not venture to interfere.

After this no considerable action took place. Owing to the treachery of guides Colonel Braithwaite's corps was cut off in the south as Baillie's had been in the north, after a resistance equally brave. The colonel had only one hundred Europeans, one thousand five hundred sepoys, and three hundred horse. He lay far away from Coote on the Coleroon for the purpose of shielding Tanjore. He was suddenly surrounded by Tippu, with ten thousand horse, ten thousand infantry, and twenty guns, beside four hundred Europeans under M. Lally, before he was aware of the enemy's presence. For two days, from February 16th to 18th, the English and sepoys held their own against such odds. 'They formed themselves into a hollow square, with the artillery interspersed in the faces, and the cavalry in the centre. Tippu laboured, by the fire of his cannon, to produce a breach in some of the lines, and as often as he fancied that he had made an impression, urged on his cavalry, by his presence, by promises, by threats, by stripes, and the slaughter of fugitives with his own hand. Repeatedly they advanced to the charge; as often were they repelled by showers of grape-shot and musketry; when the English cavalry, issuing from the centre, at intervals suddenly made by disciplined troops, pursued their retreat with great execution. After twenty-six hours of incessant conflict, when great numbers of the English army had fallen, and the rest were worn out with wounds and fatigue, Lally at the head of his four hundred Europeans, supported by a large body of infantry, covered on his flanks by cavalry, advanced with fixed bayonets to the attack. At this tremendous appearance the resolution of the sepoys failed, and they were thrown into confusion. The rage of barbarians was with difficulty restrained by the utmost efforts of a civilized commander. Lally is reported to have dyed his sword in the blood of several of the murderers, before he could draw them off from the carnage. It is remarkable, notwithstanding the dreadful circumstances of this engagement, that out of twenty officers only one was killed and eleven wounded.'* The survivors went to join their comrades in Hyder's dungeons in the Mysore. Mr. Mill, indeed, says that Tippu treated his prisoners with kindness. If so, it was a marked exception to his usual practice. Tippu also captured Cuddalore.

No one knew better than Hyder that isolated successes like these left him as far from the goal as ever. It is said that he bitterly lamented undertaking hostilities against the English. 'The defeat of many Braithwaites and many Baillies,' he said, 'will not crush them. I may ruin their resources by land, but I cannot dry up the sea; and I must be exhausted by a war in which I can gain nothing by fighting.' He had been obliged to detach Tippu to the west coast to resist an important diversion effected there by the Bombay army. On December 7th, 1782, his plans were cut short and his extraordinary career closed by

---

* Mill, vol. iv., p. 173.

his death at the age of eighty. The event was carefully concealed from the army, and the daily business carried on till Tippu's arrival, the body being embalmed, and sent to Seringapatam under an escort as treasure. Tippu at once withdrew nearly the whole of his force from the Carnatic.

Coote was obliged by ill-health to return to Bengal, and the command fell into the hands of Stuart, whom no efforts of the governor, Lord Macartney, could induce to take advantage of Hyder's death. Bussy had arrived at Cuddalore, and Stuart led to the attack a splendid force of fourteen thousand five hundred men, of whom three thousand were Europeans. Coote had returned to take the command, but died two days after his arrival at Madras, April 26th, 1783, idolized by the troops, whom he had so often led to victory. Stuart frittered away time and men, and would probably have ruined the whole expedition, if peace with France had not brought it to an end. Among the prisoners taken in one of the sallies from the town was Bernadotte, afterwards King of Sweden. Stuart, like Munro, had fought well under Coote, but miserably failed as a leader. So grave was his misconduct that he was put under arrest by the governor. As Stuart had formerly arrested a governor, Lord Pigot, a son of the nabob said sarcastically, 'General Stuart catch one lord; one lord catch General Stuart.' Since the various naval operations did not affect the result, we have passed them by.

On the west coast the English had occupied Tellicherry, Mangalore, Onore, and menaced Hyder's strong fort of Palghaut, commanding the chief pass between Malabar and the Mysore. General Matthews had even taken Bednore in the Mysore itself; but it was retaken, and the English officers and men marched off in irons, in violation of the terms of capitulation, to Tippu's dungeons in the Mysore. Tippu once nearly cut off Colonel Humberstone's force. It had come to a deep river; but Tippu, making sure of his prey, deferred the attack till next day. But in the night the English found a ford, and, though the water reached to their necks, crossed in safety. Tippu then sat down before Mangalore with a force of one hundred thousand men and one hundred guns. The garrison numbered only six hundred and ninety-six Europeans and two thousand eight hundred and fifty sepoys, under Colonel Campbell, of the 42nd Highlanders. Eight months the siege continued. Stones one hundred and fifty pounds' weight were hurled into the town. The garrison beat back every assault, and were reduced to eat horseflesh, dogs, jackals, frogs, snakes, kites, rats, mice. They only surrendered on condition of being allowed to march to Tellicherry with arms and all the honours of war. The siege of Mangalore and the name of Campbell should not be forgotten.

Tippu's willingness for peace had been increased by the success of a force from Madras under Colonel Fullarton, which had captured the renowned fortress of Palghaut, occupied Coimbatoor, and only waited the word of command to advance on Seringapatam. Instead of this, he was ordered to fall back. Lord Macartney, in ignorance of native character, on his own responsibility sent three commissioners to treat for peace. This was universally regarded in India as a suing for peace on the part of the English, and was so represented by Tippu, who kept the commissioners waiting for months, and would not admit them to his presence till Mangalore had fallen. By way of additional insult he even erected three gibbets in front of their tents. It was these commissioners who stopped Colonel Fullarton's advance, which, if persevered in, would certainly have brought Tippu to terms. The result was to inflame Tippu's arrogance the more and dispose him to another struggle. The peace of Mangalore was signed, March 11th, 1784, on the basis of mutual restoration of conquests. Mr. Marshman justly says: 'The treaty was not more disgraceful than those which the governors and council of Madras had been in the habit of making for the last fifteen years.' Tippu's own account was as follows: 'On the occasion of the signature of the treaty, the English commissioners stood with their heads uncovered, and the treaty in their hands for two hours, using every form of flattery and supplication to induce compliance. The vakeels of Poona and Hyderabad united in the most abject entreaties, and his Majesty, the Shadow of God, was at length softened into assent.' One hundred and ninety officers and nine hundred European soldiers were released from the tyrant's dungeons; but the most distinguished prisoners had been poisoned or hacked to pieces in the woods.

Much of our weakness and of the wretchedness of the country was owing to our subservience to the nabob, Mohammed Ali, whom a strong government like that in Bengal would have summarily swept aside. All the harm he did was done with the power derived from us. Nothing could be more unjust than our two attacks on the Rāja of Tanjore in 1771 and 1773, at the instigation of the nabob, who coveted his territories. He had suggested the attack once before to no purpose, but now he succeeded. It was an unworthy use of British power. So flagrant indeed was the wrong, that the Court of Directors insisted on restoration. It then appeared that the nabob had given a creditor a bond for £160,000 on the rāja's territories. The nabob's wild extravagance placed him at the mercy of usurers, many of whom were Englishmen, and even servants of the company, who made fortunes out of his folly and vice. When the English had paid his debts to the amount of five millions, they found that he had contracted thirty millions more. The nabob, as we have seen, had been compelled to make an assignment of his revenues to the company for a term of years, but he spared no effort to upset the arrangement. He appealed to Bengal and to the home authorities; and Mr. Dundas, President of the new Board of Control, ordered their restoration. They were restored, to the joy of his creditors and the loss of the country, although under honest management the sixth set apart for the nabob's use had produced more than he had previously received from the entire revenue. The incident shows how easy it is for governments at a distance to fall into error.

Hastings resigned in 1785. The opposition in the council at Calcutta culminated, as is well known, in the impeachment and trial in Westminster Hall, when the greatest ability and eloquence in England were engaged for the prosecution. The story may be read in the brilliant pages of Macaulay. The trial dragged on seven years, and resulted in an acquittal on all the twenty-two charges. It is said that Hastings felt nothing more acutely than being required at the commencement to kneel to the august assembly. Such a degradation might well have been spared one who for thirteen years had represented before all India the greatness of England. Nothing astonished the people of India more than his impeachment. Through the trial his dignity never failed. To the opening address of the Lord Chancellor, exhorting him to conduct his defence in a way worthy of his station and the court, he replied, 'I am come to this high tribunal, equally impressed with a confidence in my own integrity and in the justice of the court before which I stand.' The trial reduced him to honourable poverty. Pitt, who was prejudiced against him, refused to recommend him for a peerage; but a title would have added as little to Warren Hastings as to William Pitt. At the hands of posterity the two great commoners will never cease to receive equal honour.

SERINGAPATAM.

CHAPTER V.

LORD CORNWALLIS AND SIR JOHN SHORE—THIRD MYSORE WAR—
INTERNAL REFORMS, 1786-1798.

THERE was an interval of a year and half before the arrival of Lord Cornwallis in September, 1786. His was the first instance of the appointment to the highest office of one outside the company's service, a precedent which with two exceptions has been followed in every instance since. The arguments for and against such a practice are too obvious to need mention. One thing is certain, that it has been among the chief causes of the extension of British rule in India. A Governor-general, appointed by the ministry of the day, who had become practically the rulers of India, was far less amenable to restraint than a dependent of the company. Everything which could be done by acts of Parliament to prevent the extension of British territory had been done. Mr. Pitt's bill in 1784 expressly enacted 'that it should not be lawful for the Governor-general, without the express authority and concord of the Court of Directors, or of the secret committee, either to declare or commence hostilities, or to enter into any treaty for making war against any of the native princes or states in India, or any treaty guaranteeing the dominions of such princes or states, except when hostilities should have been commenced or preparations actually made for the attack of the British nation in India, or of some of the states and princes whose dominions it shall be engaged by subsisting treaties to defend.' Although this act was only two years old, Lord Cornwallis and one Governor-general after another proceeded as if it did not exist; and it would be hard to say that they could have done otherwise. The British empire in India would not have arisen if the act had been carried out to the letter.

The first three years of the new government were spent in reforming abuses among the company's servants. The directors still persisted in their system of giving inadequate salaries. They wrote despatches forbidding private trade, but steadily refused to apply the only effectual remedy. The old abuses therefore still continued. Public servants poorly paid, with the power in their hands of making large fortunes, were not likely to abstain from doing so in obedience to verbal orders from masters far away. Residents in receipt of one thousand rupees a month made four hundred thousand rupees a year. Happily, Lord Cornwallis possessed sufficient influence to enforce a system of more liberal payment on the directors, and the abuse gradually died out. No more necessary or beneficial reform was possible. We may observe that the popular mistake about the riches of India has proceeded on two fallacious grounds,—the fortunes made by the first Englishmen in India, and the lavish display of native courts, both ancient and modern. How the enormous gains of the first Englishmen were made we have seen, and the waste and show of native courts was the faithful reflection, not of the content and prosperity, but of the oppressed condition of the body of the people.

But Lord Cornwallis had to engage in another struggle with the Mysore power. The Sultan Tippu was born to lose the kingdom which his father had founded. Though not lacking in ability, he was inferior to his father in this respect, and far more arrogant, bigoted, rash and cruel. The last treaty had inflamed rather than lowered his arrogance. One of his first acts afterwards was to Mohammedanize thirty thousand Malabar Christians by force; Hindus shared the same fate; and two thousand Brahmins destroyed themselves rather than submit. From Coorg, one of his last conquests, seventy thousand persons of all ages and both sexes were ruthlessly driven off to Seringapatam.* Mr. Mill affirms that the English were too prejudiced against Tippu to do him justice. One of the proofs adduced is that Major Rennell speaks of Tippu as 'cruel to an extreme

---

° Marshman.

degree.' The question is, whether the allegation is true or not. Take a single fact stated by Mr. Mill. The little mountain-territory of Coorg had been subjugated by sheer treachery and atrocity combined. Directly that the third war broke out, the Coorg rāja, who had made his escape from captivity, struck boldly for independence, and rendered valuable service to the English, cause. Yet when Coorg was included in the territory to be ceded by the sultan, with his sons as hostages in the hands of the English, he was so determined to give a terrible example of the penalty of revolt, that he objected to the cession, and for a time risked the re-opening of the war rather than consent. Lord Cornwallis was equally determined not to leave Coorg at his mercy.

The origin of the war was this. The Rāja of Travancore, at the extreme south of the peninsula, was one of the parties to the treaty of Mangalore, and his state was under British protection. In December, 1789, Tippu attacked and sought to annex his kingdom. Success would have made the Mysore kingdom conterminous with Tinnevelly, the most vulnerable point in the Madras territory. Tippu's first attack failed. Though he led it in person, he afterwards disavowed it as unauthorized; and notwithstanding his disavowal, made another more successful attack in the following March, getting the northern half of Travancore into his power. Lord Cornwallis at once resolved to visit his infraction of the treaty with severe punishment. His first care was to form a league with Tippu's hereditary enemies, the Mahrattas and nizam, who were only too glad to enrich themselves at the expense of the English and Tippu. Nothing was effected in the first campaign of 1790. General Medows, the commander, though an excellent officer, was unequal to the conduct of large operations. The intention was to penetrate into the Mysore by the southern passes in the wake of Colonel Fullarton; but the force was split up into three sections, and the whole summer passed in a game of hide-and-seek with Tippu, neither side gaining any decisive advantage. The only redeeming feature was a victory of Colonel Hartley (the Colonel Hartley of the Mahratta campaign), who captured one of Tippu's generals with his force in Malabar.

F

In December Lord Cornwallis took the field in person, and while making a feint at one pass by another placed his entire force in February, 1791, on the Mysore plateau, within ninety miles of Bangalore. Tippu had barely time to rescue his harem and treasure from Bangalore before it was taken, March 21st. He allowed the British to advance so far without striking a blow to prevent them.

The army now advanced on Seringapatam, defeated the enemy in the battle of Arikeera, May 13th, and at once came within sight of the capital. But the English found it impossible to begin the siege for want of food; the cattle were too weak to drag the guns; the troops were starving and sickly. Tippu had taken care to reduce the country to a desert. To save his army, Lord Cornwallis was obliged, with the prize in view, to give the order to retreat, after destroying the heavy siege-guns and ammunition brought so far at such cost and with such difficulty. General Abercrombie, who was advancing from the west coast with the Bombay army, and who had dragged his guns with infinite labour over mountain passes, was directed to do the same. Tippu of course regarded this as a victory, and there was certainly want of foresight on the English side. On the very first day of the retreat, the Mahratta force came up with abundant stores of provision. So defective were the means of intelligence possessed by the English, that they had no idea of their allies being in the neighbourhood. The Mahrattas sold provisions to the English at an exorbitant rate. Their bazaar 'presented the greatest variety of articles: English broadcloths and Birmingham penknives, the richest cashmere shawls and the most rare and costly jewellery, together with oxen, sheep and poultry, and all that the best bazaars of the most flourishing towns could furnish, the result of long and unscrupulous plunder; while the carpets of the money-changers in the public street of the encampment, spread with the coins of every kingdom and province in the east, indicated the systematic rapine of these incomparable freebooters. But though the Mahratta sirdars had been enriching themselves with plunder from the day on which they took the field, they set up a plea of poverty, and demanded a loan of fourteen lacs of rupees. Lord Cornwallis had no time to examine the morality of the request; he had only to consider the consequence of refusing it—the transfer of their alliance to Tippu, who was ready to purchase it at any price.' We can imagine no other reason for seeking their alliance at all than the desire to keep them out of Tippu's hands. Down to the last they were intriguing with the sultan. Help they rendered none. All they did was to plunder and harry the country. Each of the two allies spent six months in reducing small forts in the north on their own account; yet they received an equal share with the English of the territory ceded and indemnity paid at the close of the war.

The English fell back upon Bangalore, and spent the rest of the year in collecting material and provision for another advance, and in reducing the numerous *droogs*, or fortified rocks, with which the Mysore country is studded, and which enabled the enemy to interrupt our communications. Convoy after convoy came up from the Carnatic, and Tippu made no serious attempt to cut them off. Among the principal agents in this work were tens of thousands of Brinjāris,—a nomad class, the immemorial carriers of the east, who travelled everywhere with impunity, even in time of war. The only droog not captured was Kistnagiri. But the capture of Nundidroog and Savandroog filled the country with wonder. Nature and art had done their utmost to render the positions impregnable. Nundidroog was taken in October. General Medows commanded the attack. The fort crowns the summit of a rock one thousand seven hundred feet high, which is only accessible on one side. Up this side guns and shot had to be carried, the very steepness of the ascent serving as a protection against the heavy guns of the fort. It took fourteen days to erect the batteries. When two breaches had been made, one in the outer wall and one in the outwork of the fort, the storming columns assaulted at midnight. The large stones rolled down the hill did more execution than the guns. The breaches were gained and forced with such rapidity that the defenders had no time to secure the gate of the inner wall, which after a little delay was carried. Savandroog was a far tougher task. The rock rises, from a base eight or nine miles round, two thousand five hundred feet, and is surrounded by a dense, feverish jungle several miles in depth, which ran up to the base of the wall. The only approach was by a narrow path, and the first thing necessary was to cut a road for the guns. The top of the rock is cleft by a chasm into two peaks, both of which were fortified and had to be attacked simultaneously. The jungle was of advantage in affording cover to the besiegers. On December 21st the storming party marched to attack the breach, the band playing *Britons, strike home*. The resistance was very slight, and the English had only one wounded. Several of the garrison fell over precipices in attempting to escape. We have mentioned these as instances of the exploits which threw a spell of invincibility around the English name.

By January, 1792, all was ready; and on February 5th a splendid army of twenty-two thousand men, with forty-four field-pieces, forty-two siege-guns, and innumerable stores of provisions, appeared a second time before Tippu's capital. The position of the enemy was a strong one. Seringapatam stands at the western end of an island formed by the river Cávery, which washes its walls on two sides, while the third side is defended by two massive walls a considerable distance apart, a deep ditch, drawbridges and outworks. Beside this, Tippu had formed an entrenched encampment outside the island, where he lay with his army. A strong-bound hedge, six redoubts, and one hundred guns added to the natural strength of the ground. In the island and fort were at least thrice as many guns. Lord Cornwallis reconnoitred the whole on the 6th, and resolved to attack that very night. The advantages of a surprise were thus secured to the fullest extent, as there was no time for the secret to reach the enemy, and the darkness rendered useless the guns of the fort and island. Our allies were aghast at the madness of the enterprise. To attack such a position without battery and bombardment seemed to them to be rushing on destruction, and the thought of the English commander fighting like a common soldier seemed still more preposterous. At half-past eight the army marched to the attack in three columns, that on the right

commanded by General Medows, that in the centre by Lord
Cornwallis, that on the left by Colonel Maxwell. The surprise
was complete; the enemy could do little but fall back, and the
English crossed to the island with the fugitives. The sultan
himself had barely time to escape to the fort. The details of the
attack were carefully arranged, and everything went well. The
right detachment somewhat missed its way; but even here the
great Mosque Redoubt, covering the west of the enemy's position, was taken. The great Sultan Redoubt on the east was
found abandoned. The morning saw the British firmly established on the island, and during this day and the next everything
outside the fort, including the line of redoubts, fell into our
hands. Three unsuccessful attempts were made to retake the
Sultan Redoubt,—which was bravely defended with considerable
loss, ammunition and water failing. A general attack on the
British position was easily repulsed. The entire English loss
was not more than five hundred and thirty. That on the other
side was reckoned at four thousand, and at least four times as
many more deserted in the night. On the 10th an attempt was
made on the life of Lord Cornwallis by a party of the enemy's
cavalry, who made their way into the English camp, being mistaken for allies, and asked for the tent of the *burra sahib*, 'chief
lord.' They were pointed to the tent of the artillery officer, but
on making towards it with drawn sabres, were recognized and
quickly dispersed.

On the night of the 18th, while the attention of the fort
was occupied by an attack on the south, the first parallel was
opened on the north side, and on the 21st a second. Tippu's
palace on the outside of the fort in the island was converted
into a hospital, and his pleasure-garden cut down to supply
material for the siege. But Tippu now despaired of successful resistance, and sent two English officers captured at Coimbatoor, and detained in spite of the capitulation, to treat of
peace. He saw that there was no fear of failure this time
through lack of supplies; it was the continuous stream of supplies both from the east and west coast which led Tippu to
remark, 'It is not what I see of the resources of the English

that I dread, but what I do not see.' The terms were severe; the cession of half his territories, an indemnity of £3,300,000, and two of his sons as hostages. The last condition was carried out with great ceremony. The fort saluted as the princes left, the walls were lined with people, and the sultan himself stood above the gateway. The procession consisted of camel outriders, seven standard-bearers with small green flags, one hundred pikemen with spears inlaid with silver, a guard of two hundred sepoys and cavalry. The princes rode on two richly caparisoned elephants in silver howdahs, and were attended by royal vakeels on elephants. They were received with a salute of twenty-one guns, and conducted through an avenue of sepoys, intended for their guard, to the Commander-in-chief, who showed them every courtesy and kindness and soon dispelled their fears. The head vakeel said : ' These children were this morning the sons of the sultan, my master; they must now look up to your lordship as a father.' The princes were Tippu's second and third sons, one about ten, the other about eight years old.

After many difficulties and delays the treaty was concluded on the terms dictated, March 19th, 1792. Once the sultan was reported to be erecting new works in the fort. On Lord Cornwallis remonstrating, Tippu proudly replied, 'His lordship was misinformed ; but for his satisfaction, if he desired it, he would throw down one of the bastions, to let him see into the fort.' It was Tippu's turn to complain next. The Mahratta commander had been plundering the country, notwithstanding the suspension of hostilities. Tippu requested that he might be called to give account, or, 'which would be a still greater favour,' said the sultan, 'that Lord Cornwallis would be pleased to permit me to go out and chastise him myself.' The territory taken by the British included the Baramahal and Lower Ghauts on the east, the district of Dindigul in the south, and Tippu's Malabar possessions in the west, and was worth forty lacs a year. Both the Governor-general and General Medows declined their share of the prize-money.

Lord Cornwallis' period of rule was as celebrated for internal measures of reform as for its external operations. He completely reorganized the financial and judicial system. What is known as the 'permanent land settlement' is his work. More praise is due to the intention than to the principle and method of the measure, which was based upon the false notion that the zemindar is the proprietor of the soil in the English sense. What the zemindar received, the government and cultivator lost. From being a mere agent or middleman the zemindar was made a landed proprietor. The Governor-general applied English ideas to Indian customs, and went altogether astray. He argued that it would be more convenient for government to have to do with a single proprietor, and that the latter would have the strongest motive to improve his holding, if his obligations were fixed at once and for ever. All interest of the government in the increase was sacrificed. As to the cultivators, it would be the interest of the owner to act justly and generously to them. Thus they were left to the enlightenment and sense of justice of the zemindars. It is true that the latter were required to give leases to the cultivators; but this was evaded in numberless ways. The measure was as defective in detail as in principle. The government had power of summary recovery as against the zemindar, but the zemindar had to proceed against the ryot by slow course of law. When the zemindar was left without means to discharge his dues, government stepped in, and sold as much of his land as was necessary to pay the amount. By this means numbers were soon brought to ruin. When in course of time the power of summary recovery from the ryot was bestowed on the zemindar, the power was fearfully abused. It is to be remembered that the 'permanent settlement' only affected the province of Bengal.

A regular series of civil and criminal courts was established with supreme courts of appeal in Calcutta. Mr. James Mill in his chapter on this subject exposes with merciless severity the defects and abuses of the British judicial administration. It is unfortunate that a singular prejudice against everything British makes his able *History of British India* read like one long indictment of everything the English did and left undone in India;

and in nothing is this prejudice more evident and more unreasonable than in his comments on the present subject. The inevitable mistakes and defects of a period of transition are represented as designed and inherent; the improvement in comparison with former days is never mentioned; the English are condemned for not giving India at once a perfect code of law and a cheap, simple, expeditious and certain administration of justice,— things which even England does not possess at the present time. We quote a single specimen of the pervading exaggeration. The system of criminal law in India is spoken of as 'a sort of mixture of the Mohammedan and English systems, and so contrived as to combine the principal vices of both,'* as if any nation was ever demented enough to contrive such a system. Strange to say, while recommending such impracticable measures as European colonization and the establishment of Jeremy Bentham's *panopticon* penitentiaries, or hospitals for the mind, he does not once hint at the one real defect of these arrangements; viz., the exclusion of natives from the higher offices under government, a blot which has only been removed in comparatively recent days. It should also be observed that the witnesses whose evidence he quotes against the English government are the very servants of that government. It may surely be presumed that defects, so well known to the highest official authorities, would be gradually removed. Besides, we need to remember the material with which the government had to work. No one has said stronger things than Mr. Mill on this subject: 'In India there is no moral character. Sympathy and antipathy are distributed by religions, not by moral judgment. If a man is of a certain caste, and has committed no transgression of these ceremonies by which religious defilement or degradation is incurred, he experiences little change in the sentiments of his countrymen on account of moral purity or pollution. In employing the natives of India, the government can, therefore, never reckon upon good conduct, except when it has made provision for the immediate detection and punishment of the offender.'† What

---

* Vol. v., p. 395.   † *Ibid.*, p. 408.

would have been the fate of an ideally perfect government in such hands?

Lord Cornwallis was succeeded in 1793 by Sir John Shore, afterwards Lord Teignmouth, a distinguished servant of the company. Sir John Shore was of a pacific temperament. He was anxious to keep within the lines of the 1784 Act. But we cannot allow, as Mr. Marshman in his excellent History plainly intimates, that his policy implied anything ignoble or inconsistent with engagements. The only colour for the latter charge is derived from the Governor-general's conduct to the Nizam of Hyderabad. Directly that Tippu's power was broken, the Mahrattas prepared to carry out their long-cherished purpose of plundering the nizam. Pretexts were always forthcoming in the claims for the *chout* levied upon the nizam's territories. The nizam was naturally anxious for the English protection, and would have done anything to secure it. But it is a mistake to suppose that the treaty of 1790 gave him any claim to this. That was simply a treaty for a specific purpose, namely, against Tippu. If the latter had attacked the nizam, there might have been some ground for a claim. It may be open to argue that a bolder policy would have been wise in the Governor-general; but there was nothing like breach of faith in the course pursued. Lord Cornwallis had always declined to give the pledge for which the nizam was anxious. The case was altogether different from that of the Travancore rāja in 1790, as the latter was distinctly under British protection. For Sir John Shore to have given the pledge desired would have been to stand forth ostensibly as the arbiter of India, a character which suited Sir John Shore less than those who preceded and followed him. No doubt it would have prevented future complications; but these it was not easy to foresee. Another result would have been to extinguish the independence of Hyderabad. The British resident with the nizam advocated intervention on the express ground that the country would thus be brought under British control. It is perhaps owing to Sir John Shore's abstinence that Hyderabad is to-day the only independent state in South India.

The English, however, held aloof. The English resident

and English battalions in the nizam's service were ordered to remain neutral. The Mahrattas, therefore, easily defeated the nizam's forces and dictated their own terms, March, 1795. But in the complications and intrigues which arose on the death of the Mahratta peshwa in the same year, and the succession of another, the nizam easily recovered the territory which he had been compelled to cede. Of course the nizam was chagrined at the English refusal of help, and showed his anger by transferring his favour to the French, who were only too glad to improve the occasion. M. Raymond, an old comrade of Lally, tried to play the part of a second Bussy. He was commissioned to increase his force, and received a grant of territory for its support in the neighbourhood of the company's dominion. But Sir John Shore peremptorily insisted on the removal of the force to other quarters.

In 1795-6 there was a mutiny on the part of the English military officers in the company's service similar to the one which Clive quelled with such vigour. Reductions had been pressed on them as on the civil officers, but without like compensation. They therefore leagued together to demand their own terms, and threatened to seize the Governor-general and Commander-in-chief to hold as hostages. Such a conspiracy was full of peril for British rule. Its branches were everywhere. It had an active committee in London. Sir John Shore was not the man to cope with the emergency, and in the end the officers gained all their demands. But whatever blame may attach to concession belongs to the directors and ministry at home as well as to the Governor-general.

Sir John Shore displayed greater firmness in dealing with the affairs of Oude. The province of Oude in the north stood in much the same relation to us as the Carnatic in the south. Ever since the restoration of the country to the nabob by Clive, a British resident and British force had been stationed in it as a protection against the Mahrattas, who were always casting covetous glances over the border. A subsidy was paid for the British force, which was responsible for the defence of the country. This was the general course which the extension of

British rule took, protection led to annexation. The process ran its course quickly in Bengal, more slowly in the Carnatic, more slowly still in Oude. We doubt whether the method was a merciful one to the people. The British power secured the native rulers against the only dangers they feared, and removed the sole checks upon their tyranny, namely, internal rebellion and external invasion. The consequence was that they gave themselves up to oppression and indulgence with impunity. Perhaps no other course was open to us, but it was hard for the people. This was the case in Oude. The nabob, who died in 1797, cared for nothing but cock-fighting, opium, buffoons, and the like. Some English adventurer suggested to him a new pleasure,—old women racing in sacks. The nabob declared that after all the lacs he had spent on amusements nothing had yielded him so much delight. His successor, Vizier Ali, was, if possible, still more degraded, besides being averse to English influence. It was alleged that he was illegitimate and without right to the throne. Sir John Shore examined the matter, and, finding the charge true, resolved to depose him and instal Saadut Ali, the late nabob's brother. To carry the decision into effect required no little nerve. Vizier Ali had a large force at command. The vast population of Lucknow was ready for any mischief, as recent history has sadly proved. But Sir John Shore went to Lucknow, and replaced one nabob by the other. With Saadut Ali a new treaty was made, fixing the amount of subsidy, forbidding him to increase his own force beyond a certain number, or to enter into alliance with foreign Powers without British consent. Sir John Shore returned to England immediately after the conclusion of this arrangement in the early part of 1798.

On October 13th, 1795, died Mohammed Ali, 'our nabob of the Carnatic,' at the age of seventy-eight, after a rule of fifty years. He was succeeded by his son Omdut-ul-Omrah.

CHAPTER VI.

LORD WELLESLEY—FOURTH MYSORE WAR—SECOND MAHRATTA WAR—AFFAIRS OF OUDE, ETC. 1798-1805.

LORD WELLESLEY* arrived in Calcutta May, 1798. As member of the Board of Control, and in other ways, he had become thoroughly informed on Indian matters. In consequence of the neutral policy of Sir John Shore, when Lord Wellesley assumed the reins the English power was weaker and the native states were stronger than they had ever been. Tippu had a thoroughly equipped army of at least sixty thousand men, trained in great part by French officers. The sepoys in the nizam's service, commanded by Raymond, and after his death by Piron, numbered fourteen thousand. Scindia, who had risen to be the chief of the Mahratta powers, had a similar force of forty thousand men, commanded by General Perron. It only needed a combination of these to put in peril the very existence of the British power. The Governor-general set himself at once to anticipate the danger.

There could be no doubt as to the design of Tippu's preparations. As soon as Lord Wellesley reached Calcutta he heard of a proclamation by the French governor of Mauritius, mentioning a proposal of Tippu to the French for an alliance against the English, and inviting volunteers for the service. The fact of the issue of the proclamation was confirmed by a letter of Lord Macartney's from the Cape. It was also reported that a French frigate had landed at Mangalore a number of French officers, who, on reaching Seringapatam, dubbed the

---

* We anticipate Lord Mornington's title. He was created Marquis Wellesley on the fall of Seringapatam.

MARQUIS WELLESLEY.

sultan Citizen Tippu, set up trees of liberty, and indulged in other like fantastic freaks. It is certain that Tippu intrigued at Poona for the same object, received letters of encouragement from Bonaparte in Egypt, and even wrote to the Afghan ruler Zemaun Shah, at that time threatening to invade India, urging him to join in a crusade 'against the infidels, idolaters and heretics.' As the negotiations were cut short by Lord Wellesley's prompt interference, it is hard to judge what they amounted to and impossible to say what issue they would have had. We can only assume that the grounds on which the Governor-general acted were as good as he believed them to be, and, on this assumption, the wisdom of not waiting for the attack to be made is self-evident. The whole war in its reasons and results received the unanimous and emphatic approval of the home authorities. It is certain that Tippu never explained the ambiguous points in his conduct. His replies to the Governor-general's letters were curt and evasive. He saw no need for any fresh arrangements, and only gave permission for an envoy to come to 'the presence' when it was too late.

Lord Wellesley would have struck a blow at once, but, as usual at Madras in those days, nothing was ready. He urged on warlike preparations with the utmost speed, and meanwhile turned his attention to Hyderabad and Poona. The latter declined, the former accepted proposals for an alliance against Tippu. The condition was the dismissal of the French force and the substitution of English troops. Through the influence of the nizam's able minister, Mushir-ul-mulk, like Salar Jung in our days a steady friend of the English, the alliance was concluded. When the time came for its execution both nizam and minister shrank and temporized; but Captain Kirkpatrick, the resident, and Colonel Roberts, the commandant, were firm, and the proclamation, disbanding the force, was issued. The suddenness of the stroke paralyzed resistance. The British guns surrounded the French encampment. The officers surrendered, and the men were pacified by the tact and management of Captain Malcolm. Most of the troops engaged in the English service and fought against Tippu. The affair was well managed, and made a great impression on other Powers. This was in October, 1798.

In February, 1799, the Madras army was ready to start. It was the finest ever assembled under the English flag in India, numbering twenty-one thousand, of whom six thousand were Europeans, with forty siege and sixty-four field guns, besides the nizam's contingent of twenty thousand horse and foot. The latter was commanded by Colonel Wellesley (brother of the Governor-general and afterwards Duke of Wellington) and Captain Malcolm. The Governor-general sent a letter to Tippu, informing him that instead of an envoy he was sending General Harris at the head of an army, to whom all proposals of peace must be made. The Bombay force under General Stuart, six thousand four hundred strong, marched from the west coast to join the invading force under the walls of Seringapatam. On this occasion, as on every subsequent one, Lord Wellesley showed his wisdom, not only in selecting able leaders, but also in entrusting them with full military and political power. His practice was to supply them with different terms of peace calculated for different stages in the operations, with power to modify at discretion.

Tippu's conspicuous inferiority to his father was never more clearly evinced than in his last stand for independence and life. There was never a feebler defence. General Harris may be said to have had a clear march over the ground. During a march of one hundred and fifty miles through an enemy's country, with enormous *impedimenta* and no communications, he met with no opposition worthy of the name. The sultan seemed paralyzed by indecision and vacillation. Instead of bending all his strength against the main army under General Harris, and hurling his splendid cavalry on his train, he marched first with the flower of his army against the Bombay force, which he succeeded in surprising. Our trusty ally, the Rāja of Coorg, was the first to announce the enemy's presence. The advanced guard, under General Hartley and Colonel Montresor, bore the attack of Tippu's whole army for six hours. When General Stuart came up and turned the scale of victory, they had scarcely a cartridge left. Tippu wasted other precious days in irresolution before marching against Harris. Then the only thing he did was to take post, against all advice, at Malvelly, half-way between Bangalore and Seringapatam, where, on March 27th, he was easily defeated. He seemed to be utterly destitute of resource. For every emergency he had but one plan of operation, and baffled in this had nothing to fall back upon. He concluded that the British would take the same road that Lord Cornwallis had done, and had the country laid waste. But General Harris took a more southerly route through a country rich in pasturage, and crossed the Cāvery while Tippu was looking for him twenty miles farther north. Tippu was wild with rage, and, assembling his chief officers, said, 'We have now arrived at our last stage; what is your determination?' 'To die with you,' was the reply.

With a European foe, or any spark of foresight or enterprise in Tippu, General Harris's march would have been impossible. He might easily have been delayed, and delay meant ruin for the present; for it was essential that the issue should be decided before the breaking of the monsoon, and this was a question of a few weeks. But it is precisely by recognizing the difference between European and Oriental armies that all our victories in India have been won. Tippu's officers and men had some idea of strategy, but Tippu himself had none. Hence his ruin.

On April 6th, the British force broke ground before Seringapatam. On the 17th the first parallel was formed, and on May 3rd the breach was reported practicable. One incident of the siege has become memorable from the share which Colonel Wellesley took in it. A night attack, led by Colonel Wellesley, was made on a part of the hostile position. It failed, owing to the severity of the enemy's fire, the darkness of the night, and the roughness of the ground. Next day the attack was renewed, and succeeded. More than once Tippu applied for a conference to be held; but he was told that the terms were fixed beyond discussion: the cession of half his dominions, an indemnity of £2,000,000, four of his sons and four of his chief officers as hostages. The mention of the terms threw him into a fury of passion. 'Better,' he cried, 'die like a soldier, than live a miserable dependent on the infidels, and be placed on the roll of their pensioned rájas and nabobs!'

May 4th was fixed for the assault, the hour noon. Sir David Baird, who had worn chains three years in Tippu's prisons, led the storming party at his own request. It was the very height of the hot season, and most of the garrison were taking their usual mid-day repose. Tippu, surrounded by boys and flatterers, and putting more faith in astrologers than in his officers, who told him that the final moment was near, persisted in saying that it would not come till night, and refused to take even such precautions as cutting off the breach by new entrenchments, which might easily have been done. He was at his meal when word was brought that the attack had begun. At one o'clock the British force, four thousand four hundred strong, sprang from the trenches, rushed across the broad, rocky river-bed, and, after a desperate struggle, in seven minutes planted the British colours on the breach. Then, dividing right and left, the attacking force slowly swept the walls until they met over the eastern gate. A fierce resistance was made at certain points, especially where the sultan himself fought, but at last the enemy's troops broke into general flight.

Tippu, instead of escaping, as he might easily have done, through the water-gate, made for the arched gateway leading into the fort, intending apparently to go to the palace. This gate was choked with fugitives coming both ways, and a heavy fire was being poured into the struggling mass by English troops from both sides of the gateway. The sultan received several wounds. His horse was also wounded and fell. He was then placed in a palanquin by his faithful attendants, but it was impossible to make any progress. Some English soldiers coming into the gateway, one of them made a snatch at the sultan's rich sword-belt. The sultan with a sabre wounded his assailant in the knee, when the soldier shot him through the temple.

A portion of the British force arrived at the palace, and the officers, after long hesitation and delay on the part of the inmates, were admitted. The princes were assured of protection, and taken to the Commander-in-chief; but Tippu was not to be found. Informed at last of the occurrences at the gateway, General Baird, Major Allen, and others proceeded there, and by the aid of a lantern, for it was now night, found the still warm body of the sultan under heaps of slain. The breach where the British force entered, and the gateway where the sultan fell, may still be seen in the decaying walls of the almost deserted capital. Tippu was only forty-six years old. He was buried with military honours in his father's splendid mausoleum a few miles from Seringapatam. His family was pensioned, and Vellore in the Carnatic assigned as their residence. His chief officers also were treated generously. Of his territories, some outlying portions were annexed to the British dominion, and an equal portion given to the nizam. But the bulk was formed into a new kingdom, over which the heir of the old Hindu dynasty, displaced by Hyder, was set. The new rāja was then a child five years old. He reigned over the Mysore under British protection till within recent years. The present rāja is his adopted son, and is shortly to receive the country back in full sovereignty. The disposition of the conquered territory sufficiently disproves the allegation of Mill's history that Lord Wellesley's motive was lust of conquest. By subsequent arrangement with the nizam the territory which he had gained from the Mysore was given over to the British for the support of the English contingent in his service. In contrast with the conduct of Lord Cornwallis and General Medows at the former siege, General Harris and the other general officers on the present occasion took a double share of prize-money.*

Lord Wellesley's changes in the Carnatic and Oude were not less radical. In 1801 the former was taken entirely into British management. Under Omdut-ul-Omrah, as under his father,

---

* In 1800 a corps of five thousand volunteer sepoys was sent under Sir David Baird to cooperate in the expulsion of the French from Egypt. By the time they arrived, however, the need had passed away, and the corps returned to India. Mr. Marshman observes that this concentration of troops from Europe and Asia on the shores of the Mediterranean is a wonderful illustration of the resources of the British empire.

there was ceaseless controversy about finance, the English demanding, the nabob refusing, help towards war and other expenses. Proposal after proposal was made by the English and rejected. The nabob was really in the hands of merciless creditors. Some correspondence, alleged to be of a treasonable nature, between the nabob and Tippu, was found in Seringapatam, and made the pretext or occasion for annexing the Carnatic. The death of the nabob in 1800 postponed the measure a few months. When his successor refused, under advice, to accede to the arrangement, he was set aside, and another appointed to receive the empty title and the pension. The change was no doubt inevitable and essential for the wellbeing of the country, which was all but utterly ruined under the divided government. But it would have been more straightforward to put the measure on its true ground—that of absolute necessity, and to have said nothing of a correspondence, which, whatever its character, had exploded harmlessly. The small Tanjore kingdom had been already extinguished. Thus was formed, with the annexations from the Mysore, the Madras Presidency as it now stands.

Oude was very little better than the Carnatic. The country suffered all the misery of a double rule; but in addition there were great external dangers. Scindia had a well-appointed army on the frontiers, which was only kept from action by the presence of the British force. An Afghan invasion was threatened. The nabob's troops were reported to be utterly useless. The Governor-general therefore called upon Saadut Ali to disband them and pay an increased subsidy for a proportionate addition to the British troops. The nabob was more manageable than some of his predecessors, but his avarice and pride alike rebelled against the demand. The correspondence went on two years. Saadut Ali fenced, protested, offered to abdicate, withdrew his offer, said he would go on pilgrimage to Mecca, to which the Governor-general raised no objection. But in the end the weak had to submit to the strong. In ceding half his territories in perpetuity to the company in lieu of subsidy (November, 1801), the nabob was careful to let it be known that he yielded to superior force. Undoubtedly the measure was substantially right. In what he did, both in the Carnatic and Oude, Lord Wellesley had the hearty support of the home authorities. But his manner was imperious, not to say harsh. Opposition and remonstrance irritated him. His was the iron hand without the velvet glove.

His quarrel with the directors, which in the end became irreconcilable, arose in the first instance from more petty transactions than those already referred to. Lord Wellesley, in 1800, sent a magnificent and useless mission to Persia under Captain Malcolm, established a college at Fort William, in which the young civilians were to be trained for their work as governors and administrators, advocated greater freedom in trade, to meet the growing trade between India and England, in opposition to the old policy of close monopoly. The directors, on the other hand, were constantly nominating persons to important posts in India with no regard either to fitness or the Governor-general's wishes. These were the points round which other matters of controversy gathered. More important grounds of difference soon appeared. The ideas of the directors and of Wellesley diverged farther and farther, until they reached the point of diametrical opposition. The company were merchants still; Wellesley was an emperor. He could do nothing on a small scale. The board of the students at his college was to cost £500 per month. The college was ruthlessly cut down by orders from home to very modest—as the Governor-general thought to very insignificant—dimensions. The directors accused their servant of reckless ambition and waste. The servant was stung at last into speaking of his masters as 'the cheesemongers of Leadenhall Street.' In 1802, Wellesley resigned, but at the request both of ministers and directors consented to remain till January, 1804, at least. That period was destined to supply tenfold more matter for controversy of the same kind. Lord Wellesley had destroyed Tippu's power, neutralized the nizam, annexed the Carnatic. There only remained the Mahrattas, whom he next sought to bring under British influence, and he would have undoubtedly succeeded, if he had been allowed to finish his plans.

The peshwa at this time, the last of the line, was Baji Rao, son of 'the luckless Raghoba.' It does not belong to this history to recount the intrigues by which his succession was secured. Even among the Mahrattas he had no master and few equals in craft and duplicity. But the office had lost all substantive power, which had passed into the hands of the three Mahratta chieftains,—Scindia, Holkar, and the Berar rāja. The peshwa barely maintained his position by playing off one chief against the other. Each was anxious to get the peshwa into his power and rule in his name. Sometimes one, sometimes the other got the upper hand at Poona. There never were princes more utterly faithless and unscrupulous. Until united by common hatred to the English, they were engaged in ceaseless plots and wars against each other. The country was given up to anarchy and strife.

Dowlut Rao Scindia was the most powerful of the three. His kingdom was a splendid one, including rich territories both in Hindostan and the Deckan. His army, trained by French officers, was the finest at this time in India. General Perron governed for him in Hindostan, where he was master of Delhi and the person of the emperor, Shah Alum. The poor emperor had been blinded by a Rohilla chief, but his name was still a power. The career of Jeswunt Rao Holkar had been a most romantic one. Of illegitimate birth, by force of daring and ability, and by the usual Mahratta cunning and violence, he had gained all his father's territories, which he governed nominally for a nephew. He was a genuine Mahratta. As a dashing horseman he had no equal in his day. There was no hope of either of these chiefs accepting a position of dependence on the British. The only chance was with the weakness of the peshwa; but even he would not part with the shadow of independence until reduced to the sorest straits. He rejected overture upon overture of this tenor. In October, 1802, Holkar defeated the combined forces of Scindia and the peshwa under the walls of Poona.* The latter had to flee, and at once accepted the

---

* The last circumstance which roused Holkar's wrath against Baji Rao was, that the latter had seized a brother of his, and had him trampled to death with elephants, himself gloating over the horrid spectacle.

proposed treaty on condition of the English restoring him to power. In December, 1802, Colonel Close, a prince of diplomatists, concluded with the peshwa the celebrated treaty of Bassein, by which he resigned his independence to the English, whom he constituted arbiter in all his disputes. A British force of six thousand infantry was to be stationed near Poona, and territory worth twenty-six lacs a year assigned in the Deckan for their maintenance. All foreigners were to be excluded from his service. He was to make no war or treaty without the consent of the English. Lord Wellesley had gained his end. But the same reasons which commended the treaty to the English rendered it hateful to the other Mahratta powers, who saw themselves checkmated and their occupation gone. The peshwa was secured against their attacks, and could no longer be used like a king of chess. The treaty was an excellent instrument for giving peace to a distracted country, if Scindia and the rest would respect it. But as they were not likely to do this, it became the occasion of wars, which were only brought to an end by the entire subjugation of the Mahratta power. The peshwa obtained safety and enjoyed a quiet which he had never known before, but it was at the price of dependence and eventual extinction. The ink of the treaty was scarcely dry before he began to encourage the chiefs to disregard it. He wanted the benefits without the condition.

Scindia, Holkar, and the Rāja of Berar, Raghoji Bhonsla, who saw not only the peshwa but the nizam snatched from their grasp, began at once to league against the treaty. Scindia said, 'The treaty takes the turban from my head.' To all inquiries of the Resident respecting the meaning of the communications, he merely replied that the peshwa had no right to enter into engagements apart from the other Mahratta powers, that he was about to confer with the Berar rāja, after which it would be known whether there was to be peace or war. From this point there was a rapid drifting into war. The forces of Scindia and the Berar rāja, reckoned at one hundred thousand men in fine order and with a powerful artillery, took up a menacing position on the nizam's frontier. To meet this the British forces, fourteen thousand infantry and thirteen thousand horse, under General Arthur Wellesley and Colonel Stephenson, were moved up from Hyderabad and Mysore. The Resident, Colonel Collins, left Scindia's camp, August 3rd, 1802. General Wellesley called upon Scindia to withdraw his forces, but no agreement could be come to. The British plan of campaign was an extensive one. Scindia's territories were to be attacked simultaneously at all points. The troops were ready, and in three months every part of the programme was carried out.

On August 12th, General Wellesley captured the wealthy city and fort of Ahmednuggur, Scindia's chief arsenal in the Deckan. He then went in search of the enemy, and after much marching and countermarching came up with him at the village of Assaye, east of Ellore, September 23rd. He had agreed with Colonel Stephenson, who took a different route, to make a joint attack on the 24th, but hearing that the enemy were likely to retire he resolved not to wait. The odds were great. The Mahrattas numbered fifty thousand, a fifth of them trained sepoys, with one hundred guns. Their position was a strong one. General Wellesley had but four thousand five hundred men. The British artillery was soon silenced by the superior fire of the enemy, and the force had to advance without guns through such a storm of shot as no Indian troops had ever before encountered. The execution was so severe that a body of the enemy's cavalry attempted a charge, but were repulsed with slaughter. One-third of the British force was killed or disabled; but the victory was complete. The enemy left ninety-eight guns, seven standards, and all his camp to the conquerors. Lieutenant-colonel Maxwell fell in the action. The Mahrattas resorted to a favourite device of theirs. Their gunners fell down as if dead, and when the British had passed on, began playing upon them. General Wellesley was obliged to proceed with a regiment of European infantry and one of native cavalry to stop this, and had a horse shot under him. The battle of Assaye broke Scindia's power in the Deckan. On October 15th, Colonel Stephenson entered the great city of Boorhanpore in Indore, and on the 21st the fort of Asseerghur, the key

BATTLE OF ARGAUM.

of the Deckan. Scindia had nothing more in the Deckan to defend.

Berar was next attacked. The outlying province of Cuttack was occupied by Colonel Harcourt and added irrevocably to the British possessions. The acquisition was important, as it completed the communication by land between Bengal and Madras. On approaching the famous temple of Jagannath the colonel was told by the Brahmins that they had asked the god whether he preferred the protection of the English or the Mahrattas, and he had replied, the English. The news was sent by express to Bengal. The Rāja of Berar was utterly defeated in the battle of Argaum, near Elichpore, November 29th. It was late in the day before the battle began, the British having had a long march on a hot day. There was very little resistance, the enemy retiring and leaving behind all his guns and ammunition. The attack was still farther delayed by a panic which seized upon three native regiments who had fought nobly at Assaye. General Wellesley rallied them with difficulty. He says: 'If I had not been there, I am convinced we should have lost the day. As it was, so much time elapsed before they could be formed again, that there was not daylight sufficient for effecting all that might have been performed.' On December 15th, Colonel Stephenson took the rāja's strong fort of Gawilghur. The fort is situated on a lofty point of a mountain-ridge between the rivers Poorna and Tapti. Guns and ammunition had to be dragged by hand over mountains and ravines by roads made for the purpose. A breach was soon made, the outer fort carried, then the inner fort escaladed by Captain Campbell and troops of the 94th regiment. General Wellesley was covering the siege. 'Vast numbers,' he says, 'were killed, particularly at different gates.' The province of Bundelkund was occupied by Colonel Powell. Scindia's port of Baroach and his Guzerat possessions were occupied by Bombay troops under Colonel Woodington.

The Rāja of Berar was anxious for peace, which was concluded on December 18th, 1803, by the treaty of Devagaum, the negotiator on the English side being Mountstuart Elphinstone.

General Wellesley was invested with full power to act. At his dictation the rāja ceded Cuttack to the English, and a rich cotton district west of the Wurda to the nizam, and engaged to exclude all foreigners from his dominions and submit his disputes with the nizam and peshwa to the decision of the English. His vakeel, or representative, at first protested against the severity of the demands. General Wellesley replied that 'the rāja was a great politician, and ought to have calculated rather better his chances of success, before he commenced the war ; but that having commenced it, it was proper that he should suffer before getting out of the scrape.'

The campaign against Scindia's Hindostan possessions was equally rapid and decisive. His deputy, General Perron, had a force of twelve thousand foot and five thousand horse with one hundred and forty guns, all in the highest state of efficiency. The English Commander-in-chief, General Lake, was one of the most dashing leaders the English ever had in India. Brave as a lion, he lacked General Wellesley's foresight and strategic skill. His victories were won by hard fighting and at unnecessary cost. His failures were due to impetuosity and want of forethought. In a forced march or a charge straight on the muzzle of the guns he was ever foremost, and his name is still cherished by the Bengal army. Like General Wellesley, he was invested with full powers in the field.

His first feat was the capture of the great fort of Alighur, August 29th, 1803, Scindia's chief arsenal in the north, with a store of two hundred and eighty-one guns. It was as strong as art could make it, being provided with ten bastions, a fine glacis, a ditch one hundred feet wide, thirty deep, with ten feet of water, and the country levelled for a mile round. All India looked on it as impregnable. General Lake in his impetuous way proposed, instead of the slow labour of a siege, to blow open one of the gates. By half-past four the storming party, under Colonel Monson, arrived within a hundred yards before they were discovered. They then crossed the ditch by a narrow causeway, and Major Macleod of the 76th with two grenadiers tried to mount the wall by ladders, but saw that it was useless. It was twenty

BATTLE OF DELHI.

minutes before the outer gate could be blown in, and during this time the party was exposed to a destructive fire and suffered severely. A long, narrow, winding passage, raked by the enemy's fire, led to the inner gate, upon which it was difficult to bring the gun to bear. The gate was too strong for the gun, and Major Macleod with his grenadiers pushed through the wicket and ascended the ramparts. The garrison broke and fled, many leaping into the ditch. About two thousand perished. The British loss was fifty-nine killed and two hundred and twelve wounded, six of the former and eleven of the latter being officers. General Wellesley regarded this as one of the most daring exploits in the annals of war.

A week after this Scindia sustained a great loss in the withdrawal from his service of General Perron. His position and talents made him a constant object of jealousy and envy to Scindia's officers, and by his retirement he merely anticipated dismissal. His predecessor was another adventurer, De Boigne, who founded Scindia's disciplined force.

General Lake next moved towards Delhi, near which, on September 11th, he came upon the Mahratta force under Perron's successor, Louis Bourquin, drawn up in an impregnable position, a swamp on either hand and entrenchments in front. They were nineteen thousand against the British four thousand five hundred. The latter were wearied with a hot march of eighteen miles. It was eleven o'clock. The British cavalry were about a couple of miles in front and exposed for an hour to a heavy fire. The Commander-in-chief had a horse shot under him. As the infantry approached, he ordered the cavalry to fall back as if retreating. The enemy fell into the snare, and left his entrenchments. At the right moment the cavalry opened and let the infantry pass through. They were received with a tremendous cannonade; but forming in line they advanced, the general at their head, delivered a single volley, and then charged with the bayonet. The enemy gave way in every direction, on which the infantry fell again into columns of companies, and let the cavalry pass through in pursuit. Great numbers of the enemy perished in the Jumna at the rear of their position. All their guns, sixty-eight in number, treasure, and ammunition were taken. Of the British loss, which was four hundred and nine, one-third fell on the 76th Highlanders. Three days afterwards Bourquin and three of his officers surrendered to General Lake.

Not only did the battle of Delhi break in pieces Scindia's force in Hindostan, but it gave the English the imperial city and the person of the emperor, who was only too glad to exchange Mahratta for British protection. Native chroniclers said that he recovered his sight from excess of joy. Whatever legitimacy the imperial name conferred in native eyes henceforth belonged to the English. The Commander-in-chief was conducted in state by the heir-apparent into the emperor's presence. The streets were blocked with wondering crowds. Sir Thomas Roe came in 1615 to Jehanghir as an ambassador; General Lake came as conqueror. In Lord Wellesley's words, he 'found the unfortunate and venerable emperor oppressed by the accumulated calamities of old age, degraded authority, extreme poverty, and loss of sight, seated under a small, tattered canopy, the remnant of his royal state, with every external appearance of the misery of his condition.' The emperor gave his visitor the second title in the empire, *Sumsum-u-dowla, ashgar-ul-mulk, Khan dowran Khan, General Gerard Lake bahadur, futteh jung*: 'The sword of the state, hero of the land, lord of the age, victorious in war.' The Governor-general wished to transfer the imperial family to Monghir, but the emperor was so unwilling that he desisted. The change would have prevented a great tragedy in our own days.

General Lake captured the fort and town of Agra on October 17th, and rewarded the exertions of his troops with the treasure there taken. He had then to face a new danger. Scindia had sent fifteen battalions, the flower of his troops, known as the Deckan Invincibles, to assist in the defence of his important possessions in Hindostan. These united with the remains of Perron's force and made for Delhi. On the 27th General Lake left Agra in pursuit, and on the 31st was within a march of the enemy, who were encamped near the village

BATTLE OF LASWAREE.

of Laswaree, sixty miles north-west of Agra. To prevent them escaping he set off at midnight with his cavalry alone, ordering the infantry to follow, and after a ride of twenty-five miles came up with the enemy at sunrise, November 1st. Seeing a cloud of dust, which he took as a sign that they were breaking up camp in preparation for their morning's march, without waiting to reconnoitre he ordered the cavalry, unsupported as they were by infantry, to charge. The enemy were simply changing position, their left resting on the village, their right on deep jungle-grass and a rivulet, and their front covered by powerful artillery. None knew better than the Mahrattas the art of strong positions. In order to increase the difficulty of the ground, they had broken the embankment of a tank. The British advanced guard and first brigade, under Colonel Vandeleur, forced the enemy's left and entered the village; but the withering fire made it impossible for them to form for a second charge, the leader had fallen, and there was nothing but to retreat. The right flank was attacked with equal valour and like results. On account of the deep grass the first sign of the entrenchments was a tremendous shower of grape and double-headed shot. Against this and a galling fire of musketry from behind deep entrenchments, mere cavalry could effect nothing, and there was sad sacrifice of life. The general himself led the charge. The cavalry was withdrawn to save it from annihilation.

The mistake was in attacking at first on mere surmise instead of ascertained fact. Had he reconnoitred, the general would have done what he had to do at last, wait for the infantry, which arrived at eleven o'clock, and after an hour's rest was formed into two columns for the attack of the enemy's right. The cavalry was thrown into three brigades: one to support the infantry, one as a reserve in the centre, and one to watch the enemy's left. Owing to the roughness of the ground, the 76th Highlanders, with a battalion and five companies of sepoys, advancing rapidly, became separated from the body of the infantry, and were exposed to a fearful hail of canister-shot and a cavalry charge. The British cavalry had to be brought up sooner than was intended to repel the attack, which they did, though at considerable loss. The advanced troops carried the first line of the enemy before the rest of their comrades came up. The second line was then carried after fierce resistance. The enemy next made a stand near a small mosque in the rear, but were cut up by a simultaneous charge of the three cavalry brigades. Another column, trying to escape, shared the same fate. The remainder, to the number of two thousand, laid down their arms. The whole force was thus broken up. Laswaree was the hardest battle yet fought by the English in India. Of the loss of eight hundred and twenty-four killed and wounded, one-fourth fell on the 76th regiment, which the general himself led through the day. Major Griffiths and Major-general Ware were among the slain. General Lake had two horses killed under him, and his son wounded by his side. Just as the latter fell, the general had to lead a charge. The enemy showed to the full the advantage of their French training. They had no French officers with them. Left to themselves, they disputed every step of ground and resisted till resistance was hopeless. The temper of British troops was never more severely tried. Laswaree completed the destruction of Scindia's power.

As Wellesley and Lake could now easily march on Oujuir, his capital, Scindia had no choice but to submit. By the treaty of Sirji Anjengaum, December 29th, 1803, he ceded half his territories, viz., all his territories to the north of the Jumna and of Jeypore and Jodepore, the fort and territory of Baroach and Ahmednuggur, and his possessions to the south of the Adjunti Hills. He renounced all claims on the nizam, peshwa, and guickwar, and engaged to exclude foreigners from his service. He also acknowledged the independence of minor Rájpoot states, formerly his tributaries, now English allies. Asseerghur and Boorhanpore were restored. Scindia's negotiator was Wittul Punt, whom General Wellesley called the Talleyrand of the east.

Holkar alone remained. He had not joined his confederates, pleading poverty. He spent the time in wholesale plunder, with the results of which he succeeded in collecting a force of sixty thousand horse and fifteen thousand foot, which was increased by all the wild spirits set free by Scindia's defeat. He then deliber-

THE WAR WITH HOLKAR.

ately provoked a conflict with the English, sending both to General Lake and General Wellesley to demand the cession of certain lands, belonging, he said, to the Holkar family, and also free permission to levy the Mahratta *chout* as heretofore, accompanying the demands with the threat that otherwise 'countries many hundred miles in extent should be plundered and burnt, the English general should not have time to breathe, and calamities should fall on myriads of human beings by a continued war, in which his armies would overwhelm them like waves of the sea.' He also harried the territory of our ally, the Rāja of Jeypore. In April, 1804, therefore, Generals Wellesley and Lake were ordered to act against him.

Holkar was easily driven out of Jeypore. His strong fort of Rampoora in the north was also taken. Then came the blunder which wrecked the whole campaign. General Lake withdrew into cantonments for the rainy season, but left Colonel Monson with a small force to watch the enemy. Colonel Murray was advancing from Guzerat on the other side, but retired, while Monson advanced much farther than General Lake intended. Hearing of Colonel Murray's withdrawal, and that Holkar was about to attack, he completely lost his head and determined to retreat. The retreat began on July 7th. On the 10th he was attacked by Holkar in force at the Mokundra Pass, but repelled him. Even in the retreat there was no lack of bravery, but every step was a blunder. He reached Rampoora on July 27th, and instead of marching on did not leave it till August 22nd, the second grand mistake. Every rivulet was flooded. Boats, rafts, elephants were brought into use. The enemy's cavalry charged fiercely at every opening. Guns, baggage, ammunition were abandoned, and the remains of the force straggled into Agra as best they could. The influence of the disaster was far worse than that of Baillie's defeat in 1780. Holkar was highly elated, and the confidence of India in British power was shaken. A native ballad said: 'Putting the elephant's *howdah* on the horse, and the horse's saddle on the elephant, Colonel Monson fled away in haste.'

In October Holkar's southern possessions were subdued by

the capture of the strong forts of Chandore, one hundred and thirty miles north of Poona, Dhoorb, twenty miles north-west of Chandore, and Galna, thirty-five miles north-east of Chandore. All were surrendered, without resistance, to Colonel Wallace.

Encouraged by the mishap to Monson, Holkar advanced with his whole army to Muttra, which he took. On October 1st General Lake marched against him. Holkar now planned an enterprise of characteristic audacity upon Delhi. Leaving most of his cavalry to employ Lake, he marched with his infantry and guns to seize the capital and the emperor, arriving there on the 7th. There were only eight hundred men with eleven guns to defend ten miles of wall in a ruinous state against twenty thousand assailants and a hundred guns. But under the Resident, Colonel Ochterlony, and the commandant, Colonel Burn, wonders were done. Mutinous symptoms in some of the native garrison were severely repressed. A sortie led by Lieutenant Rose destroyed one of the enemy's batteries. A breach was cut off by an inner entrenchment. A general assault on the Lahore Gate on the 14th was repulsed, and the same day the enemy retreated. The defence of Delhi is not unworthy of being ranked with Clive's defence of Arcot.

Holkar's next move led to the ruin of his force. Leaving his infantry under the protection of the guns of Deeg, he set off at the head of his cavalry to ravage the rich British territories of the Dooab in true Mahratta style. General Lake at once followed, leaving General Frazer to deal with the infantry. Holkar managed to keep twenty miles ahead, burning everything he could not carry off. For thirteen days Lake made a march of thirty miles a day. On November 16th, by a double march through the night he thoroughly surprised Holkar's camp, which lay at Futtyghur dreaming that the English were forty miles away. Holkar galloped off with a few troopers, leaving his troops to shift for themselves. The force was utterly broken up. The British must have ridden in the forced marches and pursuit almost seventy miles without drawing rein.

Holkar now made for his infantry, near Deeg, but this had been crushed four days before by General Frazer. The enemy was, as usual, strongly posted, and had no fewer than one hundred and sixty guns. His position was in fact a series of batteries, which the British force had to storm in succession for a distance of two miles. The 76th distinguished itself as usual. Eighty-seven guns were taken, among them being fourteen of those lost in Monson's retreat. This was a satisfaction to Colonel Monson, who had to command in the battle of Deeg after General Frazer was wounded. The general died three days afterwards, greatly lamented. The remnant of the enemy's force took refuge within the walls of Deeg.

Holkar was now without army or territory. The Bombay army under General Jones, after subduing Malwa, had joined Lake. But the results of the campaign were to a great extent thrown away by General Lake's unfortunate determination to besiege Bhurtpore, the rāja of which had joined Holkar. Deeg belonged to the Bhurtpore rāja, and its garrison had fired on the British force during the battle. Bhurtpore was eight miles round, and defended by a mud wall of immense height and thickness and a deep, broad ditch. General Lake was little fitted for the slow operations of a siege; his battering-train was ludicrously inadequate, and his engineers incompetent. It is said that he wished to use his favourite device of blowing open a gate, which would probably have succeeded, but he was overruled. The siege dragged on from January 4th to April, 1805. Two breaches were made, and no fewer than four desperate assaults delivered. The baffling obstacle was the deep water in the ditch in front of the breach. Some of the men did even creep round the water by a narrow path to the breach, but had to retire. Others in another assault clambered up the face of one of the bastions and planted the colours on the summit, but the few who penetrated the embrasure were instantly cut to pieces. The small climbing parties were received with grape, logs of wood, and pots filled with fire. The loss in these useless efforts against insuperable physical obstacles was no less than three thousand two hundred in killed and wounded. It is singular that the only fort which ever successfully defied British troops in India was one of earth. Though his town was not taken, the rāja was tired of the war, and glad to

H

make peace by a payment of twenty lacs of rupees. The British reputation suffered not a little from the repulse at Bhurtpore. In distant places might be seen on walls rude pictures of British soldiers hurled from the bastions of Bhurtpore.

Worse than this was the circumstance that the delay over a minor operation in the war caused the transference of the final negotiations from Lord Wellesley's hands. Disputes had arisen with Scindia over the execution of the treaty. He was in active intrigue with Holkar, and indeed the two chiefs moved about the country together. Lord Wellesley had tenfold more reason for treating him as an enemy than ever existed in the case of Tippu; but, while making dispositions in the last resort to overrun Scindia's remaining territories, he was exceedingly anxious to avoid hostilities. In July, 1805, the Marquis Cornwallis arrived in Calcutta as Governor-general, and Wellesley returned home to be censured by directors and proprietors, and thirty years later to receive a grant of £20,000 and a statue from the same hands. His policy and Lord Lake's sword added northern India to the British empire.

Lord Cornwallis was sent out at the age of sixty-seven to reverse the policy of Lord Wellesley. He started for the northwest to settle affairs in person; but he had only time in a letter to Lord Lake to sketch his intended policy when he was carried off by death at Ghazipore, October 5th. That policy was to concede the points in dispute to Scindia, and to reinstate Holkar in the possession of the territories which he held before the war. He disagreed entirely with Lord Wellesley's system of native alliances, and was resolved to bring it to an end. The British were to retire to their own territories, and leave the native powers to themselves. On his death, Sir George Barlow, the senior member of council, succeeded to power, and resolved to carry out the new system at any cost. Strangely enough, Sir G. Barlow had agreed with Lord Wellesley in all his measures. The concessions made to Scindia were unimportant, and about them little need be said. But the course to be pursued with respect to Holkar was extraordinary in the highest degree. That chief had fled with all the forces he could collect to the Punjab, in the hope of obtaining help from Runjeet Sing, the new ruler of that country. But Lord Lake pursued him from place to place and gave him no rest. It was now for the first time that British troops encamped on the banks of the Sutledge. The sepoys, from superstitious fears, refused to cross, when Colonel Malcolm rode into their ranks, and exclaiming, 'The city and shrine of Umritsir, with the water of immortality, is before you, and will you shrink from such a pilgrimage?' overcame their fears. The troops advanced as far as the Beeas, the ancient Hyphasis, near the spot where Alexander the Great, coming from the opposite direction, had once encamped. The young chief, Runjeet Sing, is said to have visited the camp in disguise. Holkar, now reduced to despair, sent vakeels to sue for peace, and was astonished to learn that his dominions were to be restored to him. Sir George Barlow even went beyond the terms fixed by Colonel Malcolm, and made concessions which the latter officer had positively refused, the fort of Rampoora being one of them. Thus, by the stroke of a pen the advantages gained by the war with Holkar were thrown away. The river Jumna was fixed as the boundary of British influence. Beyond this Sir George Barlow would undertake no responsibility. This could not be done without positive breach of faith with the Rājas of Jeypore and Boondi, who had good cause for dreading Holkar's vengeance for the help they had given our troops, and to whom our word was pledged. But the Governor-general was immovable. The two rājas were abandoned, in spite of Lord Lake's most strenuous protests.

However foolish the deliberate sacrifice of territory so dearly purchased, there was nothing dishonourable in it. But this cannot be said of our renunciation of express alliances. Nothing we ever did in India stained the English name so deeply as our conduct to these Rājpoot allies. Lord Lake threw up his political authority in disgust, and limited himself to his military duties. The Rāja of Jeypore's vakeel justly taunted us with making our faith subservient to our interests. From that prince Holkar extorted eighteen lacs of rupees. As to Holkar's subsequent career, we need only say that, after putting his nephew and brother to death, he gave way to reckless intemperance, and died raving mad in 1811. The result of the hasty, ill-considered policy now carried out, in obedience to orders from the home authorities, was that central India was surrendered to twelve years of strife, plunder, and desolation, after which the English were obliged in self-defence to interfere, and at the cost of another war regain what was now given away. Professor H. H. Wilson justly says: 'What was done in 1817 might have been accomplished, with quite as much reason, with more ease, and still less cost, in 1805.'* Mr. Metcalfe, afterwards Governor-general, characterized the policy as one of 'disgrace without compensation, treaties without security, and peace without tranquillity.'

° Mill's *History*, vi., 470, note.

TEMPLE AT ELEPHANTA.

PALACE OF VELLORE

CHAPTER VII.

SIR GEORGE BARLOW AND LORD MINTO. 1806–1813.

EVEN Sir George Barlow could not maintain a policy of absolute neutrality. When the new nizam, Secunder Jah, showed a disposition to get rid of the British alliance, and the peshwa tried to regain some of the independence which the treaty of Bassein had given up, the Governor-general held them firmly to their engagements. He argued that whatever ground we gave up would be used against us.

In 1806 occurred the sepoy rising at Vellore, a miniature of the mutiny half a century later. It arose from similar causes and was attended by similar circumstances. Both were occasioned by fears on the part of the sepoys that the English were about to interfere with their religion. From inadvertence or ignorance new regulations had been issued about dress and accoutrements, which seemed to aim at Europeanizing, and this to native minds was equivalent to Christianizing, the sepoys. A new form of turban, resembling a hat, was especially obnoxious.* The orders were unquestionably a mistake, and they were enforced in a harsh, arbitrary way. Objections on the part of the men, instead of being listened to, were severely punished. Regimental discipline had become loose, else the conspiracy must have been discovered. There was the same blindness to warnings in 1806 as in 1857. One of the sepoys revealed the fact of the conspiracy, but the denial of his assertions by the conspirators themselves was accepted as sufficient. He was actually put on his trial as a slanderer before these very conspirators, and, of course, condemned. But the regulations were simply a spark to a train already laid, and a spark designedly applied. Vellore

---

* *Topi wallah*=hatman, is a common Indian term for European.

was full of combustible matter. Here, within forty miles of the Mysore frontier, Tippu's family were located. The place swarmed with their adherents, as well as with Mohammedan fanatics. One regiment was composed of Mysore Mohammedans. Many of the servants and dependents of the palace were most active in encouraging the disaffected. The Mysore ensign was hoisted on the flagstaff. But there was no evidence to connect any of the princes themselves with the conspiracy. Method or aim in the rising, beyond massacre, there was none. The mischief was done and the danger over in a few hours. At three o'clock on the morning of July 10th the sepoys, who numbered one thousand five hundred to the three hundred Europeans, having first secured the main-guard and powder-magazine, surrounded the European barracks and poured in volley after volley through the venetians, until eighty-two of the soldiers were killed and ninety-one severely wounded. A gun was planted opposite the door, and musketry fire directed on any who attempted to rush out. How any escaped seems strange. But the soldiers protected themselves with beds, and the sepoys dared not enter the building. Detachments were told off to the officers' houses, and thirteen of the officers fell in this way. A few of the officers, who had managed to defend themselves in a house, made their way to the barracks, and, putting themselves at the head of the men, led them through a murderous fire to the ramparts, where they found cover above the main gateway and in a bastion. There, with nothing but their bayonets, they beat off the assailants until help arrived.

News reached Arcot, nine miles off, at six o'clock. Colonel Gillespie at once galloped off with some of the 19th Dragoons and 7th Native Cavalry to the rescue. There were four gates. Two were open, one was opened by the English within, but the fourth was commanded by the mutineers. But when the guns arrived at ten o'clock the gate was blown open, and simultaneously Colonel Gillespie, who had been drawn up the rampart, put himself at the head of the survivors and charged the mutineers. Between three and four hundred were slain, and of the rest many escaped over the walls. In the end, the native regiments were broken up. The rising was an immense shock to feeling both in India and England. Hitherto no suspicion had breathed on the loyalty of the sepoy troops. Two remarks are suggested. First, the neutrality and reticence of our government with respect to Christianity and its kindly attitude towards idolatry had egregiously failed. The Hindus always suspect a policy of silence and secrecy. Secondly, it is not sufficiently remembered that British rule in India has most to fear from Mohammedans, inasmuch as it was from them that we took the empire of India. The Mahrattas were the only considerable Hindu power in the country, and their internal dissensions effectually prevented their reaching the supremacy which they coveted. The Mohammedans can never forget that they were once masters. In 1857 it was the Mohammedan standard at Delhi round which mutiny rallied, as in 1806 at Vellore.

With singular injustice and inconsistency the Vellore mutiny was visited on Christian missionaries. On the ground that missionary work tended to unsettle and alarm the natives, Sir G. Barlow interdicted the Serampore missionaries from preaching, and ordered two newly-arrived missionaries out of the country. As to the perversity of this course we need only say that it would be impossible for the Hindus, if they understood the real nature of Christianity, to suppose that it could ever be imposed on them by force, and that the most effectual means for making Christianity understood by the Hindus is missionary labour.

The same Governor-general who forbade Christian preaching took the great temple of Jagannath in Cuttack under British management, not excepting even the three hundred dancing girls. The tax paid by pilgrims from all parts of India went into the company's exchequer. Lord Wellesley had refused the alliance of a Christian government with a great centre of idolatry and evil of every kind, and the Court of Directors disapproved of it. But the Court of Proprietors approved, and the connection continued until abolished by Lord Dalhousie.

Lord Minto's appointment in 1807 was a compromise between the Cabinet and the directors, the former wishing to appoint

Lord Lauderdale, the second to continue Sir G. Barlow. As President of the Board of Control, Lord Minto had gained an insight into Indian affairs. He was not without ability and force of character, but he was hampered by instructions from home. Lord Wellesley was held up before him as a beacon; Lord Cornwallis in his old age as a model. When he reached Calcutta he said jocosely that the two points about which the directors expressed anxiety were,—the policy of intervention in native states, and the great consumption of pen-knives by their clerks. Nothing of special moment marked his administration, but in more than one instance Lord Minto found destiny, we should rather say Providence, stronger than instructions from directors at home.

One of his first tasks was the pacification of Bundelkund, which had been ceded by the peshwa in lieu of a subsidy for the troops. It lay near the British provinces and was worthless to the peshwa. The country was very much broken by hill and jungle, in which a swarm of petty chieftains had established themselves, who lived at the expense of the people. Sir G. Barlow had winked at their lawlessness, saying that 'a certain extent of dominion, local power, and revenue would be cheaply sacrificed for tranquillity and security within a more contracted circle.' Lord Minto felt that such a state of things could not be allowed to continue in British territory, and sent a force under Colonel Martindell to capture the strongholds of the chiefs. One chief, Gopal Sing, kept the field and baffled all the troops sent against him for four years, and in the end received a full pardon and a jaghire of eighteen villages. The two chief forts were Ajighur and Kalinja. The first surrendered on a breach being made. The chief earnestly begged that his lands might be restored or that he might be blown from a gun, saying that life without honour was not worth having. On being refused, he secretly departed for Calcutta to press his request, but without effect. When he disappeared, it was thought wise to keep his family as a kind of hostage, and his father-in-law was requested to take charge of them. But, instead of doing this, he put them all to death,—his own wife, daughter-in-law, grandchild, and four female attendants,—and then stabbed himself. Native opinion in those wild districts commended the deed. The capture of Kalinja was more difficult. The fort had never been taken before. Seven centuries previously, Mahmud of Ghuzni had tried and failed. In the last century one of the peshwa's officers had besieged it two years in vain. As a sign of his determination to succeed, he had a house built near the fort. Not to be outdone, the commander of the fort sent him some mango-seeds to sow in the garden with an intimation that when the seeds had grown to a tree and the tree borne fruit, he might succeed. The fort crowned the summit of a rock, which rose abruptly nine hundred feet from a marshy plain, the base of the rock being from ten to twelve miles round, the summit a plateau four miles round, and the sides dense jungle. A breach was made from a somewhat lower hill; but when the storming-party had made good their ascent, they found that to reach the foot of the breach a precipitous rock had still to be scaled, which defied all their efforts. After losing many in killed and wounded, the force retired. The next day the fort was surrendered, the chief receiving an assignment of land.

At this time there were apprehensions of an invasion of India by Napoleon, as very a chimera as ever troubled English brains. To bar the way splendid embassies were sent to the Punjab, Afghanistan, and Persia, conducted by Charles Metcalfe, Mountstuart Elphinstone, and Colonel Malcolm, three of the ablest of the company's servants. The Punjab had just been united under the rule of Runjeet Sing, who, like Hyder Ali in the south, with equal skill and sagacity had founded a kingdom. He next tried to extend his sway over the Sikh * principalities to the east, between the Sutledge and Delhi. These had formed part of the Mahratta province subdued by the English. When Mr. Metcalfe stated the object of his mission, Runjeet demanded as an equivalent the cession of this territory, to which Mr. Metcalfe had no power to consent. Runjeet then broke off the conferences and tried to carry the envoy with him in an expedition

---

* *Sikh*=disciple, alluding to Nanuk, the founder of the Sikh faith.

into the disputed province, but Mr. Metcalfe refused to accompany him. Runjeet had formerly merely hinted at his claims on the territory. Now that he formally put them forward, Lord Minto as formally took the country under British protection, and sent Colonel Ochterlony with a force to the banks of the Sutledge to carry the proclamation into effect. Runjeet was foiled in the projects of years. He stormed, affected compliance, promised, threatened; but in the young civilian he found his match. With greater wisdom than Hyder he foresaw the consequences of resistance, and on April 25th, 1809, a treaty of perpetual amity was signed between the two powers, which for thirty years, up to the time of Runjeet's death, was faithfully observed on both sides. British power was now extended from the Jumna to the Sutledge, Lord Minto thus treading in the steps of Wellesley rather than of Cornwallis.

Mr. Mountstuart Elphinstone found the Cabul ruler, Shah Soojah, at Peshawur, March, 1809. He, like Runjeet Sing, did not see the necessity of an alliance, the advantages of which were to be all on one side. Besides, he wished to hear the French state their case before coming to a decision. Soon afterwards disaster overtook an expedition sent by him into Cashmere. His brother Mahmud at once seized Cabul. Shah Soojah then asked for an equivalent in the shape of ten lacs of rupees to enable him to march against his brother. But the dread of invasion had passed away, and Lord Minto refused the gift. Mr. Elphinstone urged its being granted. In all probability, if his advice had been followed, our expedition thirty years later to establish Shah Soojah on the throne would have been unnecessary, and the greatest disaster that ever befell British arms in India avoided. With the fall of Shah Soojah the treaty came to nothing.

The Persian embassy gave rise to a curious conflict of jurisdiction, little creditable to the British name. The Cabinet nominated Colonel Malcolm as ambassador, but the directors objected to a disciple of Wellesley, and appointed Sir Harford Jones, who reached Bombay, April, 1808. Lord Minto, however, had already despatched Colonel Malcolm, who took very high ground in his communications with the Persian court, and, on being requested to confer with the heir-apparent, quitted the country without reaching the capital. At Calcutta he urged an expedition to punish the insult. Sir Harford Jones now started on his mission, in which he perfectly succeeded. Lord Minto wrote to the Persian court disavowing Sir Harford Jones. Sir Harford Jones represented Lord Minto as a servant of the Crown like himself. Lord Minto, however, could do nothing else than ratify the treaty which had been concluded; but he now sent Malcolm again for the sole purpose of vindicating the honour of the company. The Persians hoped to profit by the dissensions of the two ambassadors, but the latter had too much sense to give them an opportunity. The king, who had known Malcolm as Wellesley's ambassador in 1800, and who looked on him as the greatest of Englishmen, received him with every honour. 'What induced you,' he asked, ' to hasten away from Shiraz, without seeing my son?' 'How could I,' replied Malcolm, 'after having been warmed with the sunshine of your majesty's favour, be satisfied with the mere reflection of that refulgence in the person of your son?' 'By Allah,' cried the king, 'Malcolm Sahib is himself again!' The treaty was duly ratified, French influence excluded, the British demand granted; but nothing came of it. The Persian embassies cost thirty-eight lacs (£380,000), and the only tangible result was the order of the Lion and the Sun instituted in honour of Colonel Malcolm, of which he was the first member. Ever since those days English diplomacy in Persia has been carried on by the Crown.

In 1809 there was a dangerous mutiny on the part of the English officers in the Madras army, similar in origin and character to the two already mentioned in Bengal. In Bengal double *batta* was in question; in Madras the tent contract, a monthly allowance to officers, nominally to enable them to equip their regiments, really a part of their pay. The officers were undoubtedly in the wrong; but they were sorely provoked by the arbitrary way in which Sir George Barlow, now Governor of Madras, sought to carry through the reductions. The danger was great, nothing less than civil war being threatened. But the Governor was firm in refusing to concede anything to threats, and when the officers were brought face to face with rebellion they gradually gave in. Seringapatam was the only place in which a collision occurred, a regiment commanded by disaffected officers being fired on by the king's troops and many killed and wounded. Many of the highest officers were involved. Some were cashiered, some dismissed, though all were afterwards restored. Sir George Barlow, always unfortunate, was recalled.

Advantage was taken of the war in Europe to conquer the French islands in the Indian Ocean, Mauritius, and Bourbon, from which fleets were always issuing to prey on our commerce. During the present war alone vessels and property had been taken worth £2,000,000. Lord Wellesley had been anxious to put down the nuisance, but was baffled by the perversity of the English admiral. Lord Minto effected the conquest in 1810. A footing had already been gained in Bourbon by a small force under Colonel Keating; but in November, 1810, General Abercrombie arrived with a force which the French had no means to resist. General Decaen surrendered, and the Mauritius became British territory. The isle of Bourbon was restored to France at the peace.

Upon the conquest of Holland by Napoleon, the Dutch islands in the East came into the possession of France. It was resolved to undertake the conquest of these. The smaller islands of Amboyna and Banda were soon occupied, and in August, 1811, a considerable force under Sir S. Auchmuty, Commander-in-chief at Madras, arrived at Batavia for the conquest of Java. Lord Minto accompanied the expedition, and with him was Mr. Stamford Raffles. The island was defended by seventeen thousand troops under General Jansens; but in less than a month it was completely overrun, chiefly through the enterprise of Colonel Gillespie, of Vellore fame. The chief position was Fort Cornelis, eight miles inland, situated between two rivers, one of which was impassable, and the other defended by redoubts and batteries. Colonel Gillespie stormed and took the redoubt at the head of a slight bridge, which communicated with the enemy's position, rushed across the bridge and took another redoubt. One by one the redoubts fell. In one of them the powder-magazine blew up, burying defenders and assailants in the ruins. The colonel then put himself at the head of the dragoons and horse artillery, and pursued the enemy for ten miles. A position, as nearly impregnable as nature and art could make it, was thus captured in a few hours. The British loss was nine hundred in killed and wounded, of whom eighty-five were officers. Colonel Gillespie was afterwards made commander of the troops in the island, and Mr. Raffles governor. But in 1814 the home government agreed to restore Java to the Dutch, and the results of the expedition were thrown away.

On his arrival in India Lord Minto was under the influence of the party in the government opposed to missionary operations, and issued an order for the removal of the Serampore press to Calcutta, where it would be under the control of officers, many of whom were bitter enemies of Christian missions. But the blow was averted by the firmness of the Danish governor of Serampore, Colonel Krefting, and the temperate conduct of the missionaries, Carey, Marshman, and Ward, who sought an interview with the Governor-general, and gave him such an account of their mode of working as led him to rescind the order. In 1812, eight missionaries were ordered to quit the country as unlicensed, and one was actually deported. Many Anglo-Indians in those days became thoroughly Hindu in their opinions and morality, and attacked missions as dangerous to the stability of British power. At home, Mr. Twining, son of a wealthy tea-dealer, and Major Scott Waring were the leading prophets of this school, and Sydney Smith lent them the shafts of his wit. In India, Colonel Stewart wrote on the same side. He had become a Hindu by profession, went down daily with flowers and the usual paraphernalia to perform his ablutions in the Ganges, and was generally known as 'Hindu Stewart.' He spoke in raptures of the virtues of Hinduism and Hindus, concluding his pamphlet with a solemn appeal to the company 'by the most prompt and decisive interposition of their authority to obviate the menaced consequences of that current of indignation now raised in the minds of our Indian subjects by the impolitic, unwise, and improper conduct of these misguided missionaries.'

But these restrictions were soon to be swept away. In 1813 the company's charter was renewed for another term of twenty years, with two important relaxations. The monopoly of trade was abolished. Outsiders were admitted within certain limits. The company, of course, stoutly opposed any alteration. It is a striking illustration of the narrowing influence of special interests and experience even upon powerful intellects, to find men like Warren Hastings, Lord Teignmouth, Charles Grant, Colonels Malcolm and Munro coming forward as witnesses against freedom of trade. When Warren Hastings appeared at the bar of the Commons, bending under the weight of eighty years, the whole house rose spontaneously to receive him. The wonderful development of the trade in recent years has singularly falsified the predictions of ruin which were heard on every side.

The missionary question was too delicate for the government to touch. Lord Castlereagh did not at first include it in his measure. It was forced upon the government and the House by the public opinion which Mr. Wilberforce's efforts called forth. Directly that he proposed the removal of all restrictions upon the dissemination of Christianity in India, the whole country spoke in a way which the government could neither misunderstand nor resist. The House was deluged with petitions. Once, as they were rained upon the table, Lord Castlereagh said, 'This is enough, Mr. Fuller,' alluding to Andrew Fuller, of Kettering. Here again the whole weight of Indian experience was on the side of restriction. Sir H. Montgomery, who had been twenty years in the Madras army, thought that the Hindu religion was pure and unexceptionable. A Mr. Prendergast, a well-known duellist, told a story from his own experience of Dr. Carey standing on a tub in the streets of Calcutta, and abusing Hinduism to such an extent that the mob would have killed him but for the police. Andrew Fuller wrote to Mr. Prendergast, denying the statement, and asking him to withdraw it. Mr. Prendergast, instead of doing this, would have sent Mr. Fuller a challenge, if he had not been dissuaded by Mr. Wilberforce. Mr. Marsh, an old Madras

INDIA OPENED TO MISSIONS.

barrister, was the most outspoken in his denunciations of missionaries and their ways. It was not for shoemakers and weavers and blacksmiths to encounter subtle philosophers like the Brahmins. 'Calvinism and gin' would be poor substitutes for the treasures of Hindu civilization. Mr. Prendergast repeated his tale of a tub. Mr. Robinson 'in pathetic terms prayed that the House would not sanction that clause of the Bill which gave full toleration to missionaries to convert the Hindus from a religion to the doctrines of which they were so much attached.' 'Mr.—afterwards Sir Charles—Forbes affirmed that it was the opinion of ninety-nine out of every hundred of those acquainted with India that Christian Missions would be attended with the worst possible effects.'* The clause passed by a majority of twenty-two. Mr. Wilberforce's speech of three hours on the first reading was one of his best efforts. It should not be forgotten that the cause of free trade and a free Gospel was carried by English against Anglo-Indian opinion.

* Marshman's *Life of Carey, Marshman, and Ward.*

CHAPTER VIII.

LORD HASTINGS—NEPAL WAR—PINDĀRI WAR—EXTINCTION OF
THE MAHRATTA POWER, ETC. 1813–1823.

THE first part of Lord Hastings' administration was spent in warfare on the greatest scale and with the most momentous results. The elements of disturbance had long been gathering, and needed to be dealt with in the most decisive manner. The Nepal War is one of the few wars as to which there can be no doubt on which side the right lay. It was an aggressive war in pure self-defence. For a quarter of a century the Nepalese government had been slowly encroaching on Hindostan. They then boldly laid claim to two districts of Oude belonging to the British. There were negotiations without end. Investigation on the spot thoroughly established the British right. In this state affairs stood when Lord Hastings came to power. The Nepalese government and chiefs deliberated on the question, and distinctly refused to concede the disputed territory. The Commander-in-chief, Amar Sing, a brave and skilful leader, counselled peace, saying, 'We have hitherto been hunting deer; but if we engage in this war we must be prepared to fight tigers.' The war-party, however, carried the day. The recent policy of rigid abstention had created a general belief in British weakness. 'Hitherto,' they said, 'no power has been able to cope with us. The small fort of Bhurtpore was the work of man, yet the English were worsted before it, and desisted from the attempt; our hills and fastnesses are the work of the Deity, and are impregnable.' The Nepalese declared war May, 1814, by attacking a British police-station, where they killed the chief officer and eighteen of his men. The officer was tied to a tree, and shot to death with arrows.

The kingdom of Nepal lies in the very heart of the Himā-

RANGOON.

layas, consisting of a valley left between the highest ranges on the north and the lower on the south. Its defences are forests, snow-clad mountains, the roughest passes and ravines. The Ghoorkas* are a Rājpoot race who emigrated from Hindostan several centuries back, and founded a dynasty in Nepal about the time of the battle of Plassey. Without any discipline, they fought with the utmost recklessness of life. Repulse after repulse did not daunt them. In every conflict they would march up to the very muzzle of the muskets, over which they tried to cut down the British with their peculiar short swords. Single combats between British officers and Ghoorka leaders often took place. The Ghoorkas were especially clever in making stockades, —rude but strong fortifications made of a double row of palisades filled up with earth and stones. They were thrown up very quickly, and the materials were abundant everywhere. These defences gave the British troops more trouble and inflicted more loss than many regular fortresses. But, of course, the chief difficulties were caused by the nature of the country to be invaded, as to which the English knew next to nothing.

The campaign was skilfully planned. Instead of waiting to be attacked, the English resolved to attack in four columns at four different points. General Ochterlony commanded in the west, Generals Gillespie (of Java and Vellore fame), J. S. Wood, and Marley led the other columns. The last three all miscarried. General Gillespie was killed in the first onset, and his command fell into incompetent hands. Gillespie's attack on Kalunga, October 31st, gave the English an example of the new kind of enemy they had to do with. The fort was simply an open space surrounded by stone walls, with additional supports of stockades. When summoned at night to surrender, the Ghoorka leader replied that the hour was too late for correspondence, which must be deferred till next day. General Gillespie, no doubt influenced by his experience farther south, unwisely determined to carry the place by assault without first employing artillery. When the storming-party were driven back by the fire, the

---

° *Goraksha*=cowherd.

general, with characteristic impetuosity, put himself at their head, to lead them on again, and was shot through the heart. His death was a great loss to the British army. On November 27th, after the place had been breached, another assault was made. But on reaching the breach, the assailants found a sheer descent of fourteen feet, and at the foot a mass of spears and arrows and matchlocks waiting to receive them. Nothing could induce them to proceed, and after a two hours' exposure to a destructive fire they withdrew. The place was then bombarded; and, as the besieged had no shelter, the commander at length withdrew, leaving five-sixths of his force of six hundred dead. This was equivalent to a Ghoorka triumph, and gave earnest of the sort of resistance to be expected. General Martindell, who succeeded the brave Gillespie, quite failed in an attack on the fort of Jytak. It is true that hill and jungle warfare presented special difficulties, but there were also mistakes in timing the two simultaneous attacks. One column fled in disgraceful panic, pursued by hooting, yelling Ghoorkas with their sharp swords; the other had to retreat with difficulty and loss.

General J. S. Wood's imbecility has seldom been surpassed. In January, 1815, he attacked the stockade of Jitpur; but just as the enemy were on the point of retreating, he was smitten with some undefinable dread of stockade and jungle fighting, and gave orders to retreat. He never struck another blow, but after marching about for four months withdrew. The enemy took advantage of his cowardice to ravage our territories.

General Marley did no better. His division was intended to march on the Nepalese capital, Katmandu; but it can scarcely be said to have started. Two detached posts, which he left without support, were attacked and cut to pieces; and this seems to have satisfied the general that the British could not conquer the Ghoorkas, for he soon after secretly abandoned his force. Two defeats inflicted by subordinate officers on Ghoorka divisions showed what the British troops would have done if they had been properly led. There was never a clearer case of lions led by deer. The generals were chosen not by fitness but length of service.

English honour was redeemed and the objects of the campaign were secured by General Ochterlony's brilliant operations in the west. The enemy were here led by Amar Sing himself, and both leader and troops proved themselves not unworthy of British steel. The English general's plans were marked by as much wisdom as daring. He did not commit the mistake of flinging his troops in masses on strong positions, but first cleared the way by artillery. Dragging guns and ammunition over mountains was no easy task. The points to be taken were the forts of Nalagerh, Ramgerh, and Maloun, situated on as many different ranges of hills, and each higher and stronger than the other. The first was surrendered on November 6th. The second stood at a height of four thousand six hundred feet above the level of the sea, and was rendered unassailable in front by a network of stockades. General Ochterlony resolved, therefore, to turn its left flank and get in the rear. But the difficulties of the ground were such that this was not effected, and the way cleared for an advance on Maloun, till April 1st.

Here the final stand was made. The fort of Maloun occupied one end of a long hill, the whole of which bristled with strong posts. Under the walls of the fort the Ghoorka forces were encamped. Two important posts, Ryla and Devathal, were carried by the British, the attention of the Ghoorkas being distracted by feigned attacks on their lines. In one of these latter attacks a single combat took place between Captain Showers and the Ghoorka leader. When the latter fell, his troops fired a volley and killed Captain Showers, whereupon the British force fled, and were rallied with difficulty. As the loss of Devathal was fatal to the enemy, he made a desperate effort to recover it. Amar Sing sent one of his best captains, Bhakti Sing, with a select force to the attack. Bhakti Sing, before setting out, told his two wives to prepare for suttee on the morrow, as he was determined to conquer or die. The Ghoorkas attacked fiercely. Mowed down by grape-shot, repulsed again and again, they charged to the muzzle of the guns. All the British soldiers were killed or wounded, save three privates and as many officers. The two field-pieces were also disabled. When the strength of the enemy began to flag, Colonel Thompson ordered a bayonet-charge, which was successful. Bhakti Sing's corpse was delivered up, and next day his two wives burnt themselves with it in sight of the two armies. Amar Sing now retired to the fort, on which heavy guns began to play. On May 8th the bulk of his force, overcome as much by hunger as superior force, gave themselves up, and on May 11th Amar Sing came to terms. The country west of the Jumna was to be ceded, and the Ghoorka leaders to be allowed to depart.

The power of the Ghoorkas was now broken, and negotiations commenced. The condition to which the Nepalese objected most was the cession of the *terai*, a fertile plain five hundred miles long and twenty broad, lying at the edge of the forest bounding Nepal, and on this war broke out again. But it was of short duration. In February, 1816, the British force again entered Nepal at different points. The Ghoorkas had stockaded the Chiriaghati Pass, but a ravine was discovered on the left, up which the general led his force in single file. The ravine was a mere torrent-bed between high banks with overshadowing trees. The ascent took from midnight till eight a.m. The Ghoorkas at once quitted the pass. A sharp action was fought on February 27th near Makwanpur, in which victory lay with the English. The other columns also were successful. The government at Katmandu now yielded, and a treaty was signed on March 2nd, which has been faithfully observed ever since. The territory ceded includes the hill retreats of Simla, Mussoorie, Landour and Nynee-thal. The Ghoorkas, who had no more than twelve thousand men at the beginning of the campaign, made an excellent defence. They have since furnished great numbers of excellent troops to the British army, troops whose loyalty has proved equal to their courage. In later days Sir Henry Lawrence was Resident at Katmandu. At the time of this war Nepal paid annual tribute to China, and appealed to the emperor for assistance. But the assistance was limited to the writing of a letter to be delivered to the English, in which his Imperial Majesty, whose heart is 'as pure as the sun and enlightened as the moon,' expresses his unbelief in the reported conduct of the English, and asks for an explanation to be sent.

A far more important war was that undertaken for the extirpation of the Pindāris, who, after desolating central India for long years, began to extend their raids into British territory. Out of this war grew the Mahratta complications which ended in the extinction of the peshwa's power and the annexation of his territories to the British dominion. The Pindāris were armed robbers, who in time of war sold their spears to any purchaser, and in time of peace lived by plunder. During the disorders of the last century, they had grown very much in numbers and power. In mere wantonness of destruction they were many degrees worse than the Mahrattas. Fire and flood were not more destructive or more cruel. Their practice was to assemble in the fall of the year, at the time of the great Dessera feast, arrange the forays for the coming cool season, and then disperse to carry them out. The best-mounted carried a spear twelve or fifteen feet long, the rest any sort of weapon. Without bag or baggage, they swept over the country like a whirlwind. In order to compel the people to discover their treasures they resorted to all sorts of tortures; such as, pouring boiling oil over the naked body, tying straw round the limbs and setting it on fire, suffocation by bags of ashes tied on the head, etc. The impartiality which marked their ravages may be seen from the fact that once, on the Rāja of Bhopal declining to employ them in plundering the Nagpore territories, they plundered the Bhopal territories for the Rāja of Nagpore, and did it so effectually that it was twenty years before the country recovered. They did not always spare their chief protectors, Holkar and Scindia, but were far too serviceable to be interfered with by those chiefs, who often repaid themselves by compelling the Pindāris to disgorge their booty. Scindia once squeezed six lacs out of Kurim Khan, one of the leaders. The other leaders were Dost and Wassil Mohammed and Cheeto. Their headquarters were at Nimar, among the Vindhya fastnesses.

After having exhausted central India, the Pindāris essayed fresh fields and pastures new in the unravaged British territories. In 1812, in Lord Minto's days, they made a raid into Bundelkund and Rewah, alarmed the rich merchants of Mirzapore, and got off with an incredible amount of plunder before any force could be organized for resistance. In October, 1815, and again in February, 1816, immense bodies swept through the nizam's territories and fell upon the Northern Sircars, sacking the town of Guntoor, and carrying off booty to the amount of twenty-five lacs, *i.e.*, £250,000. On the latter occasion three hundred and thirty-nine villages were destroyed, one hundred and eighty-two persons killed, five hundred wounded, and three thousand six hundred put to torture. Women destroyed themselves rather than fall into their hands.

Lord Hastings early saw the necessity of striking at the root of the mischief; but it was long before he obtained permission to act. Two members of his council opposed all interference. In September, 1816, he was expressly prohibited by orders from home 'from engaging in plans of general confederacy and offensive operations against the Pindāris, either with a view to their utter extirpation, or in anticipation of an apprehended danger.' Even Mr. Canning, when he became President of the Board, endorsed these views. The directors feared a war with Scindia more than the Pindāris. But the last two irruptions greatly modified opinion at home, and fresh ones at the close of 1816 and beginning of 1817 removed the opposition in the council at Calcutta. A later despatch in September, 1816, expressly declared that the previous orders were not intended to forbid measures against actual invasion : ' We think it due to your lordship not to lose an instant in conveying to you an explicit approval of any measures which you may have authorized or undertaken, not only for repelling invasion, but for pursuing and chastising the invaders.'

The Governor-general at once began to form alliances and prepare for action. The offer of British alliance and protection was eagerly embraced by the numerous Rājpoot states, which, during the abeyance of British influence, had been remorselessly victimized by Holkar, Scindia, the Pindāris and other freebooters. Jeypore, Boondi, Udaypore, Jodhpore, Kotah, Bhopal and many other states were thus taken under the British wing. The old Rāja of Nagpore had always refused a British alliance;

but on his death in 1817 the power fell into the hands of a regent, Appa Sahib, who, to support himself against his rivals, eagerly sought such an alliance. Even Scindia was forced to promise help against the Pindāris, though his heart was with them. The Pindāri envoys said to him, 'If we are' destroyed, what will become of you?' boasting that they would outdare the feats of Holkar, and carry fire and sword to the gates of Calcutta. But Scindia remembered Assaye and Deeg and Laswaree, and made his wishes wait on his fears.

The military preparations were on a vast scale. Lord Hastings called out the whole strength of British India. The three armies of Bengal, Madras and Bombay were to converge on the Pindāri haunts, and with the native contingents numbered one hundred and sixteen thousand horse and foot with three hundred guns. Such a force was out of all proportion to a raid on Pindāri robbers; but it was altogether uncertain how the Mahratta powers would act, and the result showed that there was good ground for apprehension. The Governor-general himself was Commander-in-chief. Among the subordinate commanders were Sir Thomas Hislop, General Donkin, Sir John Malcolm, General Lionel Smith.

Just as the Governor-general took the field in November, 1817, his camp was decimated by cholera. In a single week seven hundred and sixty-four fighting men and eight thousand camp-followers perished. Lord Hastings had fears for himself, and directed that in the event of his death he should be buried in his tent, and his death concealed until the negotiations pending with Scindia were settled. On removing the encampment to a new site, the epidemic disappeared.

It would have been useless to attack the Pindāris in a single body. No horse or man could have come up with them. They were therefore surrounded, the fords and passes all guarded; in fact, they were shut up in a trap. It would be tedious to follow the chase which went on for the next few months. The Pindāris found themselves hemmed in on all sides. To flee from one pursuing force was to rush into the arms of another. They were hunted down like herds of wolves or tigers, and thoroughly dispersed. Most of the leaders submitted, and were sent into Bengal, far away from their old haunts. The most daring of them all, Cheeto, refused to accept the terms offered him, eluded the pursuers, and, gradually forsaken by his followers, at last took refuge in a tiger-jungle, where his remains were found, with his horse, saddled and bridled, quietly grazing near.

The Mahratta affairs were less easily settled. The peshwa, Baji Rao, had come thoroughly under the influence of Trimbakji, a favourite of low origin and low character, who encouraged his master's vices and fanned his jealousy of the English. This Trimbakji had instigated the assassination of a Brahmin, who had come under promise of British protection as envoy from Guzerat. The Resident, Mr. Elphinstone, therefore demanded his surrender. The peshwa refused as long as he could, but at last, in September, 1815, gave him up on condition of his life being spared. Trimbakji was imprisoned in the fort of Tanna in the island of Salsette, but a year afterwards effected his escape. The plan devised for his deliverance was communicated to him in the words of a song sung under his window by a Mahratta groom in the service of an English officer. Baji Rao professed to know nothing of Trimbakji's whereabouts, whereas the two were busily engaged in raising troops, ostensibly to act against the Pindāris, really to act against the English. On May 6th, 1817, Mr. Elphinstone presented an ultimatum, demanding the surrender of Trimbakji, and of three fortresses as security. Many advised the peshwa to refuse, among others Gokla, his commander-in-chief; but at the last moment Baji's courage always failed. It was known that he had been endeavouring to engage the other Mahratta powers—Scindia, Holkar, Nagpore—in an alliance against the English. Lord Hastings therefore determined to deprive him, as far as this could be done by treaty, of all power to do harm. By the treaty of Poona, June 15th, 1817, the peshwa formally renounced his position as suzerain of the Mahratta states, and ceded territory to the value of twenty-four lacs of rupees in lieu of former engagements. This treaty superseded the treaty of Bassein, and reduced the peshwa to a state of helpless vassalage. It is hard to see what the Governor-general hoped to gain from treaties extorted by force. The peshwa, it was well known, was intriguing right and left to shake off the bonds of the Bassein treaty, and the present one was far harder. If the object had been to drive him to desperation, no more effectual measures could have been adopted. He undoubtedly deserved his fate, but this does not excuse harshness on the other side. Directly after signing the treaty, he withdrew from his capital in order to push on warlike preparations away from the Resident's observation. To Sir John Malcolm and the Resident he professed that he was arming against the Pindāris. The former, always friendly to native princes, believed him, but not so the latter. No one will blame Baji Rao for desiring independence. His guilt lay in the wholesale falsehood and perfidy by which he sought to compass it. It is said that he suggested the assassination of the Resident, but Gokla, a brave and honourable soldier, refused to be a party to the plan. It is quite certain that he tampered with the native officers and soldiers of the British force at Poona, and that in commencing hostilities he relied confidently on the British sepoys deserting during the battle.

His negotiations with the other Mahratta powers all took effect, except in the case of Scindia. However little these powers would brook the peshwa's interference in their own affairs, they still looked to him as the head of the Mahratta name and race. Scindia would have joined the league but for the presence of two British divisions, one under Lord Hastings, within two marches of his capital. In these circumstances, on November 5th, he had no choice but to sign a treaty which placed his forces absolutely at the British disposal. Two of his strongest fortresses, Asseerghur and Hindia, were to be surrendered. It is characteristic that while he gave the British an order for the surrender of Asseerghur, he wrote to the commandant ordering him to resist. The commandant showed the letter to the British, and the fort had to be taken by siege. A letter was also intercepted from Scindia to the Rāja of Nepal, in which the latter was urged to attack British territory on the north. The letter was delivered to Scindia in open durbar. How he looked or what he said is not recorded.

On the very day on which Scindia bound himself to neutrality by the treaty, the peshwa broke out into hostilities. At the time General Smith had gone with the bulk of the troops to join in the operations against the Pindāris, and not more than three thousand infantry were left. The British had no cavalry. The peshwa's force amounted to eighteen thousand horse and eight thousand foot. At noon on November 5th Baji Rao sent Mr. Elphinstone a sort of ultimatum, which was of course rejected. Directly that the latter left the residency for the camp, the residency was invaded by cavalry and burnt to the ground. Both Mr. Elphinstone and Colonel Burr thought that a bold policy was wisest, and the small British force marched out to the attack. It was soon enveloped by clouds of cavalry. A strong cavalry charge, led by one of the peshwa's best officers, was repelled, and the commander killed. An attack by a choice body of three thousand infantry on the 7th native regiment was also repulsed; but the victors, pursuing too eagerly, were taken in flank by six thousand Mahratta horse and thrown into confusion. Colonel Burr, however, led up two companies of Europeans and restored the day. The Mahrattas now retired on every side. The peshwa, who watched the conflict from a neighbouring height, looked in vain for desertions. The battle of Kirklee, which finally extinguished the peshwa's power and the Mahratta name, cost the British only eighty-six in killed and wounded.

General Smith at once returned and occupied Poona on November 17th, 1817. He then started in pursuit of Baji Rao. For three months the chase continued. North, south, east, west, hunters and hunted marched and countermarched. At last on the morning of February 20th, 1818, General Smith surprised the Mahrattas near the village of Ashti, just as they were mounting for the march. The peshwa fled with all expedition; Gokla and the cavalry stayed to hinder pursuit. A sharp cavalry action followed, in which the brave Gokla fell, covered with wounds. It is said that Baji Rao blamed him for the surprise, and he was no doubt weary of constant flight. He charged the British cavalry at the head of his troops, and found the death he sought. In former days he had fought by General Wellesley's side. In turning against the English he was animated by genuine patriotism, and never listened to any but honourable counsels. At Ashti, Baji Rao's camp and effects, and even his household gods, were taken. It is a curious illustration of the nature of Hinduism, that while Baji Rao was steeped in vice and duplicity, he was not merely devout but superstitious. He was a munificent patron of Brahmins and temples, lavishing on them a large portion of his diminished revenues. At Ashti was also taken the Rāja of Satara, nominally the peshwa's master, really his prisoner. The English reinvested him with the title and some territory.

Even Baji Rao became at last weary of his fugitive life. Every way of escape was closed by a line of bayonets. One and another of his chiefs deserted at every step. In May he addressed himself to Sir John Malcolm as his 'oldest and best friend,' and the two met at the foot of a mountain-pass in the neighbourhood of Mhow. The peshwa was anxious to preserve his place and title, but he was told that his abdication was inevitable, and that all he could hope for was generous treatment as a pensioner. Sir John Malcolm's generosity went far beyond the Governor-general's intentions. He promised the fallen sovereign a pension of eight lacs (£80,000), as well as the continuance of grants to adherents, Brahmins and others. Some, like Mr. Elphinstone and Sir T. Munro, thought the terms not excessive, as the peshwa might still have given great trouble. Baji Rao was settled at Bithoor, near Cawnpore. Nāna Sahib, the evil genius of the mutiny, was his adopted son. It was the refusal of the English to continue the large pension which inspired the latter with the desire for a fiendish vengeance.

A brilliant episode which occurred during the pursuit deserves mention for its own sake rather than for any results. At one point in his flight the peshwa was nearer to Poona than General Smith, and threatened an attempt upon his old capital. This induced Colonel Burr to recall the corps at Seroor, north-east of Poona. Captain Staunton set off on the night of December 31st, 1817, at the head of six hundred sepoys, three hundred irregular horse, two six-pounders, and twenty-four European artillerymen. On reaching Korygaum, a village on the banks of the Beema, within sixteen miles of Poona, he saw his way on the other side barred by the whole army of the peshwa, nearly thirty thousand strong. He made at once for the village, an Arab force of the enemy made for the same point, and the village was jointly occupied. A fierce contest then took place, which lasted the whole day. The peshwa's generals did their utmost to exterminate the force. The overwhelming numbers of the enemy made it impossible for the British force to drive them out; the steady heroism of the sepoys and the example and energy of the officers repelled every onslaught on the other side. Lieutenant Chisholm, commanding the artillery, was slain, with many of his men. Lieutenants Pattinson, Conellan, and Swanston, and Surgeon Wingate, were wounded. Captain Staunton, Lieutenant Innes and Surgeon Wylie only were left. One of the two guns was captured, when Lieutenant Pattinson, though mortally wounded, rose from the ground, seized the muzzle of a musket, and at the head of a band of sepoys fell upon the Arabs and retook it. He was shot a second time in the attempt. The Arabs forced their way into a choultry, where our wounded were lying, and massacred many of them, but were driven out. Some in the British force were for surrender, but Captain Staunton told them that this meant their destruction. About nine at night the whole village was abandoned by the enemy. The troops had suffered most from thirst, but in the night water was procured. A similar attack next day must have crushed the little band of heroes; but happily the peshwa heard of General Smith's approach, and marched away. Captain Staunton returned to Seroor in triumph. Beyond the Governor-general's thanks he received no reward for an exploit which contrasted nobly with the defeats of Baillie and Monson. This was too often the fate of mere company's officers. The little force lost nearly a fourth of its strength in killed and wounded.

Ever since Jeswunt Rao Holkar's death, his dominions had been in the most distracted condition. At the head of the regency was Tulasi Bai, his favourite mistress, a beautiful but profligate woman. She wished to remain at peace with the English, but the military leaders determined to aid the peshwa with the whole strength of their army, which numbered twenty thousand men. Sir Thomas Hislop came up with it on December 21st, 1817, at Mahidpore, near Oujein. The Mahrattas were as usually admirably posted and commanded seventy guns. The British troops had to cross the river Sipra by a single ford in face of the enemy's batteries. This was done, and the batteries carried. Both cavalry and infantry then fled. The British loss was considerable, amounting to seven hundred and seventy-eight men, owing to the tremendous artillery fire encountered. The Holkar resistance was broken. On December 20th the army leaders had beheaded Tulasi Bai and thrown her body into the Sipra. By the treaty of Mandeswar, January 6th, the young raja was mediatized; *i.e.*, a British Resident and British force were stationed at his court.

Of the Mahratta confederacy only the Nagpore state remained. Appa Sahib proved himself quite the equal of Baji Rao in faithlessness. As Regent he needed British support, and remained loyal. But in February, 1817, the young raja was found dead in bed, as was ascertained afterwards, strangled by order of Appa Sahib, who succeeded to the throne, and at once became anxious to get rid of the British connection. He was in close alliance with the peshwa, from whom he received the dignity of Commander-in-chief in the Mahratta empire. He even invited the Resident, Mr. Jenkins, to witness his assumption of the title. This was on November 25th, 1817. On the 26th a determined attack was made on the British force, in the hope of crushing it at a blow. To the eighteen thousand men of the raja's army, four thousand of whom were Arabs of reckless ferocity, the British could only oppose thirteen hundred men, consisting of two battalions of Madras sepoys, two companies of the Resident's escort, three troops of Bengal cavalry, with four six-pounders. The residency, on the west of the town

K

of Nagpore, was covered by a low range of hills, the northern and southern extremities of which were held by the British. All through the night the attacks of the Arabs on the northern hill went on with little effect. But in the morning a heavy fire was directed on it from nine pieces, one of the two British guns was disabled and withdrawn, a tumbril exploded, and the Arabs, charging in the confusion, carried the hill. They then advanced against the southern hill, fired the sepoys' huts, and began to close in the position on every side, when victory was turned by one of those daring strokes which have so often worked wonders in India. Captain Fitzgerald had again and again requested Colonel Scott to allow him to charge with the cavalry, but was refused. At last Colonel Scott sent word, 'Tell him to charge at his peril.' 'At my peril be it,' replied Fitzgerald; and, leading the cavalry to the attack, swept all before him, taking two guns. The example inspired the sepoys with new courage, and the enemy were chased off on every side. The fight had lasted eighteen hours. The civilians of the residency staff were forced to bear part in it. The ladies took care of the wounded. But for the happy genius which at the critical moment suggested the cavalry charge, destruction would have fallen on all. As it is, the defence of Seetabaldi ranks with the brightest achievements of the English in India. The Madras sepoys who had made so noble a stand occupied the place of the regiment which was struck off the rolls for its part in the Vellore mutiny. The only reward they asked was to be allowed to resume the old number and facings.

Appa Sahib hastened to disown the conduct of his troops. He was required to disband them and give himself up to the English. This after some hesitation he engaged to do. But the troops refused to obey, and were only overcome after a sharp conflict. Even then five thousand Arabs and Hindostanees threw themselves into the palace in the city, which they defended with great obstinacy. A siege was necessary to dislodge them. But Appa Sahib continued to intrigue with the peshwa, and left no stone unturned to circumvent the English. He was then ordered to be deposed and sent to Allahabad, and the next heir enthroned in his place. But on the way he escaped from his guard by the connivance of some sepoys in the escort, and took refuge in the Mahādēva Hills, where for nearly a year he hid in security. Many of the chiefs and people befriended him, Force after force was baffled in its attempts to penetrate the rocky jungles which served him as a shelter. An offer of £20,000 and an estate of £1,000 a year failed to induce his friends to betray him. Eventually he fled to Runjeet Sing in the Punjab, then to the Himālayas, and last of all returned to Jodhpore, in Rājputana, where he was allowed to remain in obscurity. This was the last scene in the drama of Mahratta history.*

After the storm a calm. The latter part of Lord Hastings' government was as illustrious for the victories of peace as the former part had been for the victories of war. It was characteristic of his largeness of mind that he encouraged native education, which great numbers in authority opposed. Ignorance, it was maintained, was the mother of obedience. On the contrary Lord Hastings wrote: 'This government never will be influenced by the erroneous position that to spread information among men is to render them less tractable and less submissive to authority. . . . It would be treason against British sentiment to imagine that it ever could be the principle of this government to perpetuate ignorance in order to secure paltry and dishonest advantages over the blindness of the multitude.' A native college was founded for the study of English. The Serampore missionaries pushed on their educational schemes with energy. On May 31st, 1818, the first native newspaper issued from the Serampore press, under the title of *Samāchūra Durpana*, 'Mirror of News.' Out of this seed has grown a mighty harvest of universities, English and vernacular schools and newspapers, which more than anything else are profoundly affecting native life and thought.

We have already mentioned that in Bengal the *zemindary*

---

* It has been impossible for us to enter into the details of the innumerable petty actions and sieges by which the whole Mahratta territory was subjugated.

system of land assessment was established. In Madras, on the other hand, the *ryotwary* system was established. Under this the government settles with each *ryot*, or cultivator, instead of with the *zemindar* in the lump. The merits of the two schemes are eagerly debated in India between rival schools. The great champion of *ryotwary* was Sir Thomas Munro, through whose influence it was finally sanctioned in Madras in 1820.

Like Clive, Warren Hastings and Wellesley, Lord Hastings incurred the displeasure of many of his employers at home. Narrow views respecting British policy in India still prevailed in many quarters, but in the altered state of opinion it was impossible to arraign Lord Hastings on the broad features of his administration. It was therefore determined to do so on narrower grounds. The Governor-general had given his approval to a banking firm at Hyderabad,—Palmer and Co.,—with which a relative of his was connected. No allegation of corrupt motives was made. But the law forbade financial transactions between native princes and British subjects, and the Governor-general's sanction contravened this law. His action was imprudent, and was probably abused, but the motive was the public good. However, the whole transaction was condemned in despatches from home, and the despatches were formally approved by the Court of Proprietors after a six days' discussion by a large majority. The petty slight rankled deeply, and was an unworthy return for great services. While Lord Hastings is not to be ranked with his greatest predecessors, his period of rule made an epoch in Indian history. He completed the work of Warren Hastings and Wellesley. By the annexations from the territories of the peshwa, Holkar, Scindia, and Nagpore, the trunk of the British empire in India was completed and rounded off. Subsequent additions were simply branches. Arriving in India at the age of fifty-nine, for nine years he laboured seven and eight hours a day without a break. His native courtesy and kindliness of bearing conciliated all classes. The inhabitants of Calcutta owe to him some of the greatest improvements made in the city. Of him it may be said emphatically that he deserved well of the commonwealth.

TROOP OF MAHRATTAS.

CHAPTER IX.

LORDS AMHERST AND WILLIAM BENTINCK—FIRST BURMESE WAR—
SIEGE OF BHURTPORE—INTERNAL REFORMS, ETC. 1823–1835.

THE first task awaiting Lord Amherst, who had served as ambassador in China, was a war with the semi-Chinese state of Burmah. It is singular that the reigning dynasty in that country, like most of the powers we found in India, dates no farther back than the middle of the last century. Alompra, its founder, originally a hunter, flourished about the time of the battle of Plassey. Aracan, which adjoined British territory, was conquered by the Burmese as late as 1787, Assam and Munipore in 1822. It cannot be denied that the Burmese had some slight ground of complaint. Their oppressive rule drove thousands of the Aracanese across the border into Chittagong, and the refugees often made raids into the country they had left behind. The British did their best to repress these raids, but gave a firm refusal to the demand of the Burmese for the surrender of the fugitives. They also sent three several embassies to Ava to explain how matters stood. But these embassies were regarded as proofs of weakness. The fact is, the Burmese, having conquered up to the borders of Bengal, longed for Bengal itself, and were thoroughly convinced of their ability to drive out the English. The English, they said, had only defeated the timid Hindus. In the Burmese they would find their masters. The king actually sent a letter to the Governor-general claiming the districts of Chittagong, Dacca, and Moorshedabad. The Burmese struck the first blow by driving off a guard from the small island of Shahpuri, at the mouth of the river Naaf, which separates Aracan and Chittagong. To the Governor-general's letter the answer was the despatch of a large army into Aracan under their best general, Maha Bandoola, with orders to expel the English from Bengal and golden chains in which to send the Governor-general prisoner to Ava. Lord Amherst therefore had no choice but to declare war, February 24th, 1824.

The British plan was to penetrate the country by the river Irrawaddy, taking Rangoon at its mouth, and thence advancing upon the capital. For this purpose an army of eleven thousand European and native troops was assembled under the command of Sir Archibald Campbell. The native troops were all from Madras, as the Bengal sepoys objected to go by sea. Lieutenant Havelock and Major Sale were among the officers. There can be little doubt that the plan was a wise one, the Irrawaddy supplying the easiest mode of access. The mistake was in the season of the year selected, just before the breaking of the rains which converted the country into a reeking swamp. To this all the delay and losses of the campaign are to be traced. The moment the army was able to advance into the country, the war was decided. The forces arrived at Rangoon May 11th. The city was at once deserted by troops and people alike, and the British took possession. Within a week the rains commenced, and the invaders could only stand fast where they were. Two miles north of Rangoon stood a great Buddhist pagoda, with a tower three hundred feet high, elevated on an immense terrace thirty feet high. Here the 69th regiment was posted, and here Havelock often held services with his men. The pagoda formed one of the strongest points in the line of English works. The two roads connecting the pagoda with the town were occupied by other portions of the force. It was not till the following February, 1825, that the British were able to start for the capital. During this long halt two-thirds of the troops were disabled, and great numbers perished from fever and dysentery. Their sufferings were greatly aggravated by the utter failure of the commissariat, which supplied mouldy biscuits and putrid meat. But for the exertions of Sir Thomas Munro, Governor of Madras, the force must either have perished or been withdrawn.

One effect of the capture of Rangoon was to withdraw Maha Bandoola and his army from Aracan, where he had succeeded in destroying a British detachment and filling Bengal with alarm. Most unwisely Captain Noton with a small force had been pushed forward to Ramoo, on the extreme border of our territories, a hundred miles from the nearest support. Here he was attacked by overwhelming numbers; the irregular troops fled, and the regular troops were all killed, captured or dispersed in the retreat. The commander, with four other officers and the surgeon, was slain. But the theatre of decisive conflict lay elsewhere.

The incessant rains which reduced the British to inaction were no hindrance to the Burmese, who displayed the utmost activity in their attempts to hem the invaders in and prevent them getting supplies from the country. This they succeeded in doing to a great extent. But they failed altogether in relaxing the British grasp on the country. One general after another was sent down from Ava to drive away the English, but was either killed or returned to report his failure. The Burmese were most expert in the art of stockading and entrenching. A hoe or spade was as essential to a Burmese soldier's equipment as a knapsack to that of an English soldier. In a few moments he threw up a mound which yielded excellent protection. The Burmese also sent fire-rafts down the river in the hope of damaging the British vessels. The country was a most difficult one for military movements. The British troops in their expeditions often found it impossible to get any guns across the swamps and through the dense jungle. At one or two of the stockades they met with temporary checks; but this was generally owing to unwise dispositions. Thus, in October, the Madras sepoys begged to be allowed to attack a strong stockade at Kykloo, and the general humoured them. Of the three columns of attack one was unable to penetrate the dense thickets, another withdrew without either gain or loss, and the third was repulsed and pursued in headlong flight, after losing several officers. When a combined European and native force marched to repair the mistake, they found the corpses of their fallen comrades mutilated and hung on trees, but no enemy. The entrenchment was abandoned. Even when the Burmese had successfully resisted an assault, they seldom awaited a second.

In August an expedition was sent to reduce the province of Tenasserim. In Martaban, the capital, a large arsenal was captured, and, more welcome still, the province supplied bullocks and vegetables for the troops.

After many petty attempts, the Burmese made a grand effort in December to get rid of the invader. A large army under Bandoola himself invested Rangoon. The enemy were allowed to take up their position without interruption. They came so near the great pagoda that our soldiers watched them busily at work entrenching. Three hundred men of the 38th with twenty guns occupied the pagoda, and easily repulsed every attack. On December 6th and 7th the British force sallied out and thoroughly beat up first their left, then their right flank, taking possession of all the entrenchments on which so much labour had been spent. The Burmese contrived by means of incendiaries to set fire to the town, half of which was reduced to ashes. They next retired to strong positions at Kokien, four miles away. Two stockades on either flank bound together six lines of circular entrenchments three miles in extent. On December 15th the British stormed in front and rear at the point of the bayonet, and inflicted great slaughter. Thus faded away the last hope of taking Rangoon. The Burmese fell back on Donabew, a strong position which they had prepared forty miles up the river.

In the beginning of 1825 Assam, the tea-province, was occupied with little difficulty by Colonel Richards. Two divisions were also organized for the purpose of penetrating into Burmah from the north, but the only result was to prove that the route was impracticable. It was argued that as the Burmese had always invaded from this direction, they could be reached in the same way. But the great difference between a native army and one encumbered with all the appliances of western warfare was overlooked. One force, seven thousand strong, under Colonel Shouldham, was to march through Cachar and Munipore; but after struggling about forty miles over hills covered with forest and valleys reduced to bog by rain, it was compelled to return. Cattle, camels, elephants sank in the mud, and could not be got out. Cachar and Munipore were afterwards occupied. The expedition to Aracan, ten thousand strong, under General Morrison, took the coast route, and met with even greater difficulties. They found the country cut up by countless streams and rivers, all swollen into floods by the rains. In three months they only accomplished two hundred and fifty miles. After infinite difficulty, the town of Aracan was taken at the end of March, 1825, but it was a costly purchase. The site of Aracan is unhealthy at any time, but in the rains it is a den of fever. One-fourth of the whole force perished, and of the rest two-thirds were in hospital. 'Aracan fever' was long a name of terror in the army. The seat of government has since been fixed in a more healthy spot. Thus forces were wasted on useless enterprises which would have made victory at Rangoon sure, rapid and decisive.

In February, 1825, General Campbell was ready for a forward move on Ava, five hundred miles distant. Again he fell into the error which worked so much mischief in this campaign, that of dividing his force. The three divisions were to converge by different routes upon Prome: one, under General Cotton, proceeding by the river; one, under Colonel Sale, round by Bassein; and one, under the commander, marching all the way by land. But the scheme came to nothing. Colonel Sale took Bassein, but for want of carriage could advance no farther, and speedily rejoined General Campbell at Rangoon. General Cotton found the entrenchments barring the passage of the river at Donabew too strong for his column. They consisted of one large stockade and two smaller ones, constructed of solid teak beams, fifteen feet long, and protected by ditches and every contrivance for annoying an enemy. The garrison numbered twelve thousand, and was commanded by Bandoola. For the attack General Cotton had no more than six hundred men. Even with these he carried the outer works, but the column of two hundred men sent against the larger one was repulsed with loss. General Campbell, who was considerably in advance, had to return, and valuable time was lost. The passage of the river alone, on extemporised rafts, took five days. On March 27th the garrison made a strong sortie, which was driven back. In the bombardment the great Bandoola himself, the pride and hope of the Burmese, was killed by a shell, whereupon Donabew was at once evacuated by the enemy. Prome was occupied on April 25th.

The next few months were consumed in negotiations. The British were tired of the conflict, and would have been glad to make peace; but the Burmese were not prepared to accept the terms insisted on—the cession of Assam, Cachar, Munipore and an indemnity of two millions. They quoted for the imitation of the English the conduct of the Chinese, who, after invading the country, went away as they came. In November the enemy took up a strong position at Watigaum, twenty miles in advance. The British attack failed from the old cause—division of forces. Three columns were to march through a country of which they knew nothing, and meet at a certain point at a certain time. Of course they never met. One reached the enemy's position, found itself unsupported, bore the whole brunt of the conflict, and at last found itself retreating and pursued with heavy loss. The success encouraged the Burmese to close in on Prome, but they were again attacked and in a series of conflicts driven back on the town of Mellown, whither they were pursued by the British. They now professed to be eager for peace, and a conference was held in a boat moored in mid-stream. The same terms were insisted on as before, save that the indemnity was reduced to one-half. On January 3rd, 1826, the treaty was signed, and an armistice agreed on till January 18th. But the ratification never arrived, and on the 19th Mellown was attacked and taken. The Burmese made another effort to retrieve their fortunes. A general boasted to the king of his ability to drive off the English, and was allowed to try. At Pagham, on February 9th, the last battle of the campaign was fought. The Burmese could only bring sixteen thousand troops into the field. To meet these General Campbell had thirteen hundred men, but of these nine hundred were European. He advanced fearlessly to the attack and routed the enemy. In the beginning of the conflict, an incident occurred which showed the temper of the troops. The advance division had become separated from the main body by a considerable interval. The enemy threw a strong force into the gap. But the advanced troops retired with such order and precision that the enemy saw they could gain nothing, and soon gave up the battle. The next march was to Yandaboo, within sixty miles of Ava, and here, on February 24th, the treaty was signed by which the Burmese gave up Assam, Cachar, Munipore, Aracan and Tenasserim, engaged to pay an indemnity of a million and to receive a British Resident in the capital. The last was the most humiliating stipulation of all.

If it cannot be said that the Burmese had fought well, they had taken full advantage of the natural difficulties of the country and the ignorance of the English, and succeeded in prolonging the conflict. The chief cause of the delay, however, was the lack of ability in the direction of the British expedition. The cost of the war was great, amounting to thirteen millions. The provinces taken were in a miserable condition, but they have since become valuable. Assam is one great tea-garden. 'The desolate and pestilential swamp of Aracan has become the granary of the Bay of Bengal, and hundreds of vessels are annually employed in conveying its produce from the port of Akyab to India, China, and Europe. Moulmein, the capital of the Tenasserim provinces, which contained only half a dozen fishermen's huts when it was first occupied, has become a flourishing port, with a population of seventy thousand souls and a trade of more than fifty lacs of rupees a year.' *

As we have seen, Bhurtpore was the only Indian fortress that had successfully defied the British arms, and the natives of India had not forgotten the fact. Its turn now came. The new rāja was a minor, and in 1825 was set aside by an ambitious cousin called Darjun Sal. Sir David Ochterlony, Political Agent in the north-west, who had installed the rāja, promptly collected an army to chastise the usurper. But the

---

* Marshman.

Governor-general, with the Burmese war lingering in his hands, was in no mood to undertake a new conflict. He sharply interdicted all interference and disavowed any obligation to support the rāja. Sir David Ochterlony at once resigned his post and retired to Meerut, where he died two months after, the end being no doubt hastened by the rebuff he had received. He was sixty-eight years old, had been fifty years in India, and was equally eminent in diplomacy and in the field. He was the first company's officer to receive the distinction of the Bath. Sir Charles Metcalfe succeeded him, and speedily induced Lord Amherst to sanction the policy which had just been condemned. It was soon evident that force must be employed. Bhurtpore became the resort of all the disaffected spirits in India, who hoped to see a repetition of the former triumph.

On December 10th, 1825, the Commander-in-chief, Lord Combermere, appeared before the city at the head of a well-appointed force of twenty thousand men with a powerful battering-train. The strength of the defences had been increased, one new bastion being vauntingly called 'The Bastion of Victory.' The natives said it was built of the skulls and bones of those who had fallen in the former attack. The tank, from which in the previous siege the ditch had been flooded, was seized by the English in time to prevent its being used for the same purpose again, and thus the chief cause of the former defeat was obviated. Nothing can more clearly show the utter inadequacy of the means formerly employed than the fact that the present powerful armament made little impression on the massive, earthy ramparts. Thirty-six mortars and forty-eight heavy guns played on them for days to little purpose. Mining had to be resorted to. Several small mines were exploded, and on January 18th, 1826, an immense one, with a charge of ten thousand pounds of powder, was sprung with deadly effect. Not only many of the defenders, but some of the assailants, who in their eagerness to be first in the storming pressed too near, were buried in the explosion. Two strong columns, under Generals Reynell and Nicolls, assaulted the main breach. One column clambered over a shattered rampart, while another forced one of the gates.

FALL OF BHURTPORE.

There was much severe fighting before the town was really won. The loss of the defenders amounted to thousands, that of the victors to about six hundred. When the town fell, the citadel surrendered. Parties attempting to fly were intercepted. Darjun Sal was taken, and sent prisoner to Allahabad. The state treasure found in the city, to the amount of forty-eight lacs of rupees, was seized by the military authorities and distributed as prize money. Lord Combermere's share amounted to six lacs. Sir Charles Metcalfe, who was present, indignantly condemned the spoliation, writing: 'Our plundering here has been very disgraceful, and has tarnished our well-earned honours. Unless I can get rid of the prize agents, I cannot establish the sovereignty of the young rāja, whom we came professedly to protect, but have been plundering to the last *lotah* (waterpot) since he fell into our hands.' The fort was dismantled, and a British Resident established at the court. The effect of the victory on British prestige received a curious illustration. The Calcutta government had been forced to issue a loan, but it hung fire. Little native money was offered. But one morning in January, to the astonishment of the officials, thirty lacs of rupees poured in. This was the first intimation the government received of the fall of Bhurtpore, of which the natives had heard by secret and more expeditious channels. In the last mutiny it was often the case that the bazaar received important news before government.

On July 6th, 1827, Sir Thomas Munro died of cholera. He had resigned the governorship of Madras and was anticipating rest and ease in his native land. He was one of a band of eminent administrators who adorned those days—men who disposed of crowns, ruled kingdoms, led armies. Munro, Ochterlony, Mountstuart Elphinstone, Malcolm, Metcalfe were examples of an order of men whose talents for organization and government have never been surpassed.

In March of the same year passed away, at the age of forty-seven, a prince who had been brought into intimate relations with the English, and whose rule of thirty-three years had been marked by great vicissitudes—Dowlat Rao Scindia. He had lived through the great days of Wellesley and Hastings, and seen the British empire expand, largely at his own expense. His once splendid kingdom had shrunk to a mere principality, which he held by the favour of the English. His easy temperament adapted itself to the change, and in his later years he became a close friend of the conquerors.

After the fall of Bhurtpore Lord Amherst made a progress to the north-west, calling at Cawnpore, Lucknow, Agra, Bhurtpore and Delhi, and holding interviews with the native princes or their envoys. His durbar at Delhi was an imposing one. He then made a considerable stay at Simla, which from this time became the official retreat during the height of the hot season. He returned to England in February, 1828, and was succeeded by Lord Bentinck, formerly governor of Madras.

Lord Bentinck's administration was honourably distinguished, not for any great war or sweeping annexation, but for unexampled activity in internal legislation and improvement. On this ground it ranks with the best Indian administrations. We notice in the first place the reforms which bear chiefly on the interests of the government.

One of his first tasks was the ungrateful one of retrenching expenditure and reducing salaries. There was ample scope for this in the civil service. Mention is made of an opium agent, whose routine duties were remunerated at the rate of £7,500 a year; one-third was cut off. Some offices were abolished, some combined. Lord Bentinck incurred still greater obloquy by a measure for the reduction of the military officers to half-batta. But his action was purely ministerial. The question had been referred home twice already, and he had no choice but to obey an order thrice repeated. The discontent was deep and loud, and there seemed every prospect of a repetition of former scenes of violence. But the local authorities, civil and military, while sympathizing with the aggrieved officers in the substance of their complaint, steadily discountenanced all insubordination. The reduction only applied to regiments stationed within the old territories of the company, and the distinctions thus created aggravated the bad feeling. The home authorities were only too ready to issue orders, the execution and odium of which devolved on others. The saving effected did not amount to more than two lacs a year.

Another question dealt with was that of *Enām* lands; *i.e.*, lands granted rent-free by former native rulers to individuals and temples. These represented an enormous loss of revenue. No question of the kind existed under native rule, as native princes never respected the acts of their predecessors more than was convenient, or scrupled to resume grants at any time. But the British had promised to leave undisturbed grants made prior to their assumption of power. This was taken advantage of on a large scale, and the manufacture of title-deeds became a lucrative business. Various remedies were tried with little effect. But just before Lord Bentinck's arrival a special Board of Commissioners was established to investigate and settle such matters, and Lord Bentinck confirmed the measure. Lands were resumed and rents imposed. There was considerable outcry, but no doubt justice was done. Thirty lacs a year were added to the revenue.

But the reforms by which Lord Bentinck's name will be longest remembered are those bearing on the welfare of the people. He greatly simplified the proceedings of courts of justice, established a new Appeal-court and new Board of Revenue at Allahabad for the north-west provinces, and substituted the vernacular languages for Persian in all judicial proceedings. The latter change alone was an invaluable boon. Persian was the official language in Mohammedan days, and hitherto the English had continued it. The conservative instincts of the old civilians resisted the change, but the people rejoiced.

Another great measure was the permanent settlement of the land-assessment for the north-west provinces. The labour involved was enormous. An area of seventy-two thousand square miles had to be surveyed, village by village and field by field. The interests of twenty-three millions of people were involved. But the work was carried through, agreements made with *ryot*, landholder or village, and the settlement fixed for thirty years. The credit is mainly due to the energy and skill of Mr. Robert Bird, one of the ablest of the civilians.

L

In throwing open the public service to natives Lord Bentinck repaired the cardinal error of Lord Cornwallis's policy. As to the wisdom and justice of the new policy there cannot be two opinions. Even Mohammedans had never excluded Hindus from all share in the government of their own country, and had found among them some of the ablest of their servants. The Brahmin Purnia governed Hyder's and Tippu's territories with signal ability. The Hindus are excellent financiers; and there can be no doubt that the presence of natives in all departments has given no little stability to English rule.

One of Lord Bentinck's very earliest acts was the bold one of abolishing the ancient practice of *suttee*.* The home authorities had long counselled the measure, and the doubts of local officials only concerned its expediency or safety. Directly on his arrival Lord Bentinck addressed inquiries on the subject to the chief civil and military officers, and the great majority being favourable to his views, on December 14th, 1829, he issued an order declaring the practice 'culpable homicide.' The decree was at once enforced by the police without difficulty or disturbance of any kind. According to official returns, in the Calcutta division alone five thousand one hundred cases of *suttee* occurred between 1815 and 1828. The British interference before simply aimed at preventing compulsion, but this of course wore the appearance of sanctioning the practice in all other cases. Happily, Lord Bentinck was bold enough to prefer humanity to cruel custom.

By Hindu law an apostate from Hinduism was disinherited, and as the Hindu and Mohammedan codes were acknowledged in British courts, a convert from Hinduism to Christianity lost all claims of inheritance. In remodelling the laws, Lord Beninck quietly introduced a clause to the effect that 'the Hindu

---

* 'The term *suttee*, or *sati*, is strictly applicable to the person, not the rite, meaning "a pure and virtuous woman," and designates the wife who completes a life of uninterrupted conjugal devotedness by the act of *saha-gamana*; *i.e.*, accompanying her husband's corpse. It has come in common usage to denote the act.'—H. H. WILSON.

and Mohammedan law of inheritance should apply only to those who were *bona-fide* professors of those religions at the time of its application.' This effectually remedied the injustice. From fear of offending native prejudices, native Christians had been expressly debarred from government service. This disqualification was removed, caste, creed and nation being pronounced no barrier to office.

Another great reform was the suppression of Thuggism. The Thugs* were a caste of murderers and robbers in one. Professing to live by agriculture, they really lived by waylaying, murdering and robbing travellers. They joined a party of travellers, got into their confidence, and watching their opportunity strangled them with a cloth or turban. They then plundered and buried the bodies. All this was done as a trade and under religious sanctions. Durga, or Kāli, a form of Pārvāti, the wife of Shiva, was their favourite goddess. To her they made offerings after every murder. A Thug leader, when asked whether he never felt any compunction for his crimes, answered, 'Does any man feel compunction in following his trade? and are not all our trades assigned us by fate?' The children were regularly trained to the art. 'The boy was at first employed as a scout, and not permitted to witness the proceedings of his seniors; as he grew older, he was allowed to see and handle the corpse of the victim, and assist in the interment; and when he attained manhood, and displayed adequate strength and resolution, he was entrusted with what had then become to him an object of ambition, the application of the noose. Previous to the murder, he went through a form of mysterious initiation by one of the elders, whom he chose for his *guru*, or spiritual guide.' Thousands perished every year in this way. Many of the criminals had already been caught, but detection was difficult. The Governor-general's plan was to form a special department for the purpose of extirpating the evil. Major Sleeman, a most capable officer, was placed at its head, and in a few years he succeeded in accomplishing his task. Between 1830 and 1835

° *Thug* means 'a cheat.'

two thousand Thugs were taken, of whom fifteen hundred were punished in various ways. An industrial school was established at Jubbulpore for training the children in useful trades.

Another momentous change was the substitution of English for Sanscrit in the higher education of the people. Opinion was sharply divided, and controversy ran high. Orientalized Englishmen fought for the old ways, but Mr. Trevelyan, Macaulay and Dr. Duff advocated the adoption of English. Mr. Macaulay, who was legal member of the supreme Council and President of the Board of Education, said : 'We are at present a board for printing books which are of less value than the paper on which they are printed was when it was blank, and for giving artificial encouragement to absurd history, absurd metaphysics, absurd physics, and absurd theology.' On March 7th, 1835, the Governor-general in council decided that 'the great object of the British Government ought to be the promotion of European literature and science among the natives of India, and that the funds appropriated to education would be best employed on English education alone.' It is impossible to estimate the issues of this decision. The higher Hindu mind has proved most receptive of Western thought on every subject and of every kind. Anglo-Hindus know English history as well as educated Englishmen know Indian history, and know English literature better than educated Englishmen know Indian literature.

Lord Bentinck was the first to advocate steam communication between England and India by the Red Sea. The *Hugh Lindsay*, a steamer of four hundred tons, was the first of its class to reach Suez from India, the pioneer of innumerable fleets. The Court of Directors objected to the cost, and the enterprise was left to be taken up afterwards by a private company.

Such a list of wise, beneficent measures does equal honour to the mind and heart of the author, revealing as it does the best qualities of a ruler. It would not be easy to name any other country in which so much progress has been made in a like period. Nothing but the most resolute determination could have sufficed for carrying out so many and such great reforms in the teeth of prejudice, interest and difficulties of all kinds. It is easy to see why the name of Bentinck has always been an honoured one among Hindus.

Lord Bentinck's policy with respect to the native states was not marked by the same consistency and firmness. He did his best to carry out the instructions from home enjoining non-interference. Probably they accorded with his pacific disposition, but he was not always able to preserve absolute neutrality. In the states of central India and Rājputana—Bhopal, Jodhpore, Jeypore, the Scindia territories—court dissensions rose to a high pitch. A word from the Governor-general would have restored peace, but he refused to say it. It is curious that in three of these cases the disturbances arose from female ambition. In Bhopal the widow of the last nabob was regent, and adopted a nephew as heir to the throne, but steadily refused him any share in the power after he reached his majority. Lord Bentinck was appealed to, but declined to interfere. Civil war broke out, which was only settled by Lord Bentinck's successor. In Scindia's territories the situation was the same. Scindia's widow, after adopting a son, studiously neglected everything which would tend to fit him for his duties, saying that 'no one ever wished to qualify another for the exercise of that power which he himself wished to retain.' Lord Bentinck visited Gwalior, but refused to decide between the two parties. When civil war threatened, the British interfered, and the ambitious woman withdrew with her treasure into private life. In Jeypore the queen-mother quarrelled with the nobles respecting the appointment of a prime minister, and disorderly scenes were enacted. The life of the British Resident was attempted by one of the parties, and his assistant was slain in a riot. Here, too, the British had refused to interpose. Maun Sing, the Rāja of Jodhpore, presuming on the pacific inclinations of the British went to great lengths—refused to attend the Governor-general's *durbar*, pay his tribute, or give up criminals who took refuge in his territories. A force was assembled to compel him, but there was no need for it to march. The rāja submitted at once, when he saw that the English were in earnest. 'Why assemble an army,' asked his envoy, 'when a single constable bringing the Governor-general's orders would have been enough?'

In the two instances of Mysore and Coorg Lord Bentinck found himself compelled to depart from a neutral policy. The case of Mysore was peculiar. The country had been in Mohammedan hands forty years. On Tippu's death, the English might have annexed the country, and this course was strongly advocated by Sir Thomas Munro. Instead of this, the heir of the old Hindu dynasty, a mere child, was sought out and placed on the throne. But Lord Wellesley clearly intended the sovereignty to be nominal. The customary allusion to heirs and successors was omitted from the treaty. It is true that the phrase occurs, ' as long as the sun and moon shall endure '; but this is a diplomatic formula inserted in every Oriental treaty. Power was also reserved to resume the management of the kingdom, if the support of the British force or the welfare of the people should require it. This contingency arose about 1830. On attaining his majority in 1811 the rāja dismissed Purnia, his able and faithful minister, and ran the usual course of Indian princes—favouritism, corruption, waste. The country went to ruin. The people rose against oppression, and the rebellion could not be put down. The rāja was warned of the consequences in 1825 by Sir Thomas Munro, but the improvement was only temporary. In 1831 the country was taken from the rāja and placed under a British commissioner with four superintendents of divisions, the rāja receiving a pension of a lac of pagodas and a fifth of the net revenue. The country then flourished as it had never done before. Under General Cubbon's administration of twenty-five years, while taxes were reduced eleven lacs of rupees, the revenue increased from forty-four to eighty-two lacs. The rāja, of course, never ceased to agitate both in India and England for the restoration of the country, but his request was refused by Lord Hardinge, Lord Dalhousie, Lord Canning, Lord Elgin and Sir John Lawrence. The rāja, who had no natural heir, then requested permission to adopt a son with right of succession. This was refused. But the present Lord Salisbury, in 1867, when Secretary of State for India, granted the request, and the country is restored to native rule now that the young rāja has come of age. The decisions of one Governor-general after another are thus reversed, and the fruits of British administration for fifty years imperilled. The Mysore is one of the chief fields of the Wesleyan Missionary Society.

A still stronger measure was the annexation in 1834 of the little mountain territory of Coorg, adjoining the Mysore. A former rāja had rendered valuable service to the English in the war with Tippu. But the rāja who succeeded in 1820 acted like a maniac. He prohibited all intercourse with the English, sheltered rebels against English authority, tried to form a hostile league with the Rāja of Mysore, and encouraged disaffection among the sepoys at Bangalore. To his own subjects he manifested the ferocity of a tiger. No one was safe from his fits of passion. Twelve possible rivals among his kinsmen he had taken into the jungle and beheaded. He would kill people with his own hand. One of his chief grievances was that the English would not surrender his sister and her husband, who had fled from his fury. He imprisoned a native envoy whom the English sent with remonstrances, and wrote insulting letters to the Governor of Madras and the Governor-general. Whatever the technical rights of the question, there can be no doubt that interference in some way was necessary, and that the course eventually followed was the best for the people. Four columns of British troops entered the country. One from the east, under Colonel Lindsay, took the capital on April 6th; and another from the west, under Colonel Foulis, reached the same point on the 7th. Two other columns, one from the north under Colonel Waugh, and another from the Wynaad under Captain Minchin, received a severe check, and had to retire. This showed the resistance which might have been made by a brave people in a country all rock and jungle. But the rāja, who was as cowardly as he was cruel, surrendered himself a prisoner on April 10th. The political agent, Colonel Fraser, called the heads of the people together, and, at their request, assumed the government of the country. Coorg has since become famous for coffee-plantations. The German missionaries have long been settled in the country.

In October, 1831, a meeting took place between Lord Bentinck and Runjeet Sing, the powerful ruler of the Punjab. The Punjab kingdom was now in the height of its glory. The army consisted of eighty thousand men,—with three hundred and seventy guns,—trained, and in great part officered, by French leaders like Generals Court and Avitabile. The annual revenue amounted to two and a half millions, and Runjeet's savings to ten millions more. The British were anxious to keep on good terms with the Punjab ruler because of the movements of Russia in the direction of Persia, which were supposed to constitute a danger for India. Now begins the panic about Russian designs which has wrought so much disaster in Indian history. To gratify Runjeet's passion for horses the English government in the previous year had sent a team of English dray-horses, which had been brought up the Indus by Lieutenant Alexander Burnes. Lieutenant Burnes had not failed to make observations of the river and neighbouring countries, especially Scinde, during his progress. At the same time Sir John Malcolm had sent an old state-carriage. The dray-horses, gorgeously caparisoned, formed part of the pageantry at the interview in October, 1831, which took place at Roopur. The visits, presents, military reviews, conferences took up a week. No such magnificence had been seen in India since the palmy days of the Mohammedan empire. Both powers learned to know and respect each other more. Lord Bentinck gained all he sought, but not so Runjeet. His principal object was to gain the tacit consent of the British to his designs of conquest in Scinde, the wealth of which, he said, had been accumulating for a century and lay open to the first invader. The riches of the great commercial city of Shikarpore especially excited his cupidity. But the British officials gave no answer to his representations. The fact was that at this very moment Lord Bentinck had sent Colonel Pottinger to conclude a commercial treaty with the Ameer of Hyderabad in Scinde. This treaty, after some difficulty, was concluded, and Runjeet Sing shrewdly remarked that these commercial treaties of the

English checkmated all his schemes of conquest. One clause of the treaty was to the effect that the contracting parties should never look 'with the eye of covetousness on the possessions of each other.' Within eleven years Scinde was a British province.

Lord Bentinck returned to England in March, 1835. He was the first Governor-general who won the affection of natives as well as Europeans. Natives joined in erecting in Calcutta the statue, for which Macaulay wrote the inscription :

'This statue is erected to William Cavendish Bentinck, who during seven years ruled India with eminent prudence, integrity and benevolence; who, placed at the head of a great empire, never laid aside the simplicity and moderation of a private citizen; who infused into Oriental despotism the spirit of British freedom; who never forgot that the end of government is the welfare of the governed; who abolished cruel rites; who effaced humiliating distinctions; who allowed liberty to the expression of public opinion; whose constant study it was to elevate the moral and intellectual character of the government committed to his charge;—this monument was erected by men who, differing from each other in race, in manners, in language, and in religion, cherish, with equal veneration and gratitude, the memory of his wise, upright, and paternal administration.'

Nobler or truer words were never spoken of a public man.

CHAPTER X.

LORD AUCKLAND—AFGHAN WAR. 1835-1842.

HE charter of 1833 abolished the last remnant of the trading character of the East India Company and vested in it the government of the country for a further term of twenty years. The assets of the Company realized not much less than twelve millions, their estimated value. Other principal changes were the conferring of legislative power on the Governor-general in council for the whole of India, the admission of natives to office, and permission to Europeans to hold land. The last provision swept away the old jealousy of interlopers.

During the interval which elapsed before the arrival of Lord Auckland in March, 1836, the Governor-generalship was held by Sir Charles Metcalfe, who thus achieved the ambition of thirty-four years of Indian service. His great official act was the abolition of all restrictions on the press. During Lord Bentinck's term those restrictions had been a dead letter, but they still stood on the statute-book. Sir Charles Metcalfe's liberal instincts erased them. With the exception of the temporary restrictions imposed in 1857 and those of 1878, which we trust will prove as temporary, the Indian press has retained its freedom, and, on the whole, has justified the anticipations of its early friends. But this measure cost its author the favour of his English masters and his position in the service. The Court of Directors had often smarted under the criticisms of the Calcutta press, and they could not forgive Sir C. Metcalfe for having struck off its shackles. At the earnest request of Lord Auckland and the home authorities he accepted the Lieutenant-governorship of Agra on retiring from Calcutta; but when the Madras chair became vacant he expected the appointment, but in vain. Lord Bentinck urged his claims

CABUL.

without success. His one offence outweighed his long services. Such ungenerous treatment compelled him to resign, and his great abilities and long experience were lost for ever to India. He entered the colonial service of the Crown. If he had been confirmed as Governor-general, we should most probably have been spared the painful story we have now to relate.

The history of Lord Auckland's administration of six years is the history of the Afghan War. One other circumstance must be mentioned—the abolition in 1840 of all connection between the British government and Hindu idolatry. Salutes were no longer fired in honour of Hindu gods and festivals. Temples, like that of Jagannath, were no longer managed by British officers. The tax on pilgrims ceased. While the people were assured of perfect liberty of worship, they were left to conduct their own affairs in matters of religion. This was a tardy concession to the long-continued protests of the conscience of a Christian country against a public scandal.

The Afghan War can never be a pleasant subject of reflection to Englishmen. But it is as impossible to pass it over as to erase it from the page of history. A war more unnecessary, more unjust, more disastrous it would be hard to find in the history of the world. Retribution in this instance followed swiftly on the heels of wrong. A fatality of misfortune seemed to attend the war from first to last. Every new step was a new blunder. But it must be remembered that the war was condemned from the first, on military, on political and on moral grounds, by much of the highest opinion both in India and England. But a nation, committed to an evil policy, finds it difficult to recede. The war in its beginning had not the sanction even of the Calcutta Council, but was decided on and carried out by Lord Auckland along with a few advisers at Simla. Nay, in reality, it was not even Lord Auckland's war, but that of one or two rash, strong-willed counsellors, who completely domineered the weaker mind of their master. Those were Mr. Macnaghten and Mr. John Colvin, chiefly the first. The official responsibility of the enterprise rests of course with the Governor-general, but the real responsibility rests with those who used him as a tool. Mr. Macnaghten was high-minded and honourable, but reckless and daring in his views. The policy of the Afghan War was his more than any one else's. Sir John Hobhouse, President of the Board of Control, assumed a share of the responsibility, denying that Lord Auckland was alone to blame. When questioned by a Commons' Committee, he said, 'Alone I did it'; implying that the directors were as little consulted by the supreme authorities at home as the Calcutta Council was by the Governor-general.

The motive of the war was fear of Russia, which was seeking to acquire influence in Afghanistan by way of Persia. The prevention of Russian supremacy in Afghanistan is a perfectly legitimate object of British policy, always providing that the means are wise and just. In the present case they were neither the one nor the other.

Russia had beaten Persia in the field, and wrested from her two of her best provinces, chiefly owing to the refusal of the English to fulfil those provisions of the treaty of 1810 which bound them to help the Persians against foreign enemies. The English said that the fault of the war rested on Persia. The Persians then sought to repay themselves by conquering western Afghanistan, the key to which was Herat. Pretexts for war were always ready in the raids made on Persia by Shah Kamran, the ruler of Herat. In November, 1837, the Shah of Persia appeared before the city with an army of fifty thousand men. The walls were extensive and dilapidated. The Persian artillery had been drilled by British officers, and was now directed by Russian engineers. The place must have inevitably fallen, but for the presence there by chance of a young British officer. Lieutenant Eldred Pottinger, a Bombay engineer, had been sent by his uncle, Colonel Pottinger, Resident in Cutch, to travel and observe in Central Asia. Just as the Persians arrived he reached Herat in native dress. He saw the peril at once, offered his services to the government, and from that moment became the ruling spirit of the siege. His energy and example repaired the walls, put heart into the garrison, and for ten months kept Persians and Russians at bay. On June 24th, 1838, the grand assault took place at five points. Beaten at four points, the besiegers made good a footing at the fifth. Yar Mohammed, the Afghan commander, sat down in despair. Pottinger went, and by main force dragged him to the breach, where he fell like a madman on his own troops, who roused themselves for a last'effort, and drove back the assailants. The siege was turned into a blockade, and the town suffered the extremities of famine. In November the appearance of a small British force in the Persian Gulf, and the representations of Colonel Stoddart, our envoy, had such an effect on the Shah that he broke up the siege and retired to Persia. The designs of the Russians, who hoped to rule Afghanistan through Persia, were thus completely baffled. The heroic defence of Herat by Lieutenant Pottinger is too little known in this country. Let it be observed that with the departure of the Persians from Herat all present danger of Russian designs in Afghanistan vanished. The rest was matter of negotiation at Cabul. How were the negotiations managed?

Captain Alexander Burnes arrived at Cabul as British envoy to Dost Mohammed in September, 1837. The presents which he brought—a pistol and telescope for the Dost, and a few pins and needles for his ladies—were in sorry contrast with what the Afghans remembered of Mountstuart Elphinstone's mission in 1809, and gave too faithful an indication of the nature of the terms proposed by the English. These terms, in brief, were that Dost Mohammed must break off all connection with Persians, Russians, and Central Asia, and in return receive —nothing. Dost Mohammed wished the good offices of the English to enable him to recover Peshawur and its dependent province from Runjeet Sing, who had conquered it so lately as 1835. The mere exertion of our influence would have satisfied him, and it is not unlikely that this would have sufficed, for the Sikh troops detested residence at Peshawur, and it was a common saying that the mere mention of the Khyber Pass gave them colic. Captain Burnes urged consent to the request; but Lord Auckland would promise nothing, and would hear of nothing but absolute submission to his demands. His reason for refusing to intercede with Runjeet Sing was that 'it is not the practice of the British government to interfere with the affairs of other independent states,'—a curious preface to the Afghan War. Dost Mohammed then came to terms with the Russian officer who was in his capital, and Captain Burnes finally left in April, 1838. When the latter arrived at Simla, he asked with wonder why we could not form an alliance with Dost Mohammed. 'He is,' he said, 'a man of undoubted ability, and has at heart a high opinion of the British nation; and if half you would do for others were done for him, he would abandon Persia and Russia to-morrow.' But Lord Auckland and his advisers were possessed with an incurable distrust of Dost Mohammed. The plan they resolved upon was to send an army into Afghanistan, depose Dost Mohammed, an able and popular ruler, and set up Shah Soojah, who was so weak that he had been already driven out, and who was now a refugee in our territories. As to the question of right, there was no difference between Dost Mohammed the Barukzye and Shah Soojah the Dooranee. The former was the acknowledged ruler of the country, in peaceful possession of the throne. The British made a treaty with Runjeet Sing and Shah Soojah in accordance with their designs, but the whole burden fell on the British. Runjeet would not even allow our force to cross his kingdom, and Shah Soojah had everything to gain and nothing to lose. It is worth while to quote some contemporary opinions. Mr. Elphinstone said that 'if twenty-seven thousand men were sent up the Bolan Pass to Candahar, and we could feed them, there was no doubt that we might take Cabul, and set up Shah Soojah; but it was hopeless to maintain him in a poor, cold, strong and remote country, among a turbulent people like the Afghans.' Lord Bentinck characterized the whole scheme as one of incredible folly. Lord Wellesley called it infatuation. The Duke of Wellington said that our difficulties would begin as soon as we had succeeded. India had often been invaded from Afghanistan with good reason, for it was worth invading. This was the first time that Afghanistan, a land of rocks and snow, where every man is a born fighter, had been invaded from India.

Beyond the difficulties of the route, the invading force had no others to encounter. Cabul was occupied with as little resistance on the part of the enemy as has been met with in the recent expedition. The British force numbered twenty-one thousand men, with thirty thousand camels and thirty-eight thousand camp-followers. Sir John Keane was commander, Mr. Macnaghten minister at the court of Shah Soojah. As the Punjab was closed, this vast body had to go one thousand miles down the Indus into Scinde, and march through the Bolan Pass. It set out from Ferozepore in December, 1838. We need not linger by the way: at the Bolan Pass, Quettah, the still more terrible Kojuk Pass where guns had to be lowered down precipices by ropes. The soldiers were worn out with hunger and fatigue; twenty thousand camels perished. Candahar was reached in April, 1839. Here Shah Soojah was proclaimed Ameer with great state. Two hundred and thirty miles north-east of Candahar, ninety south of Cabul, lay the strong fort of Ghuzni, once the splendid capital of the conqueror Mahmud. Sir John Keane was told that the place was one of no strength, and left behind his battering-train which had been brought at such pains over mountains and passes. The wall rose to a height of sixty feet, and the ditch was filled with water. But from a nephew of Dost Mohammed, who sold the information for money, the British learnt that all the five gates were built up save one. This it was resolved to blow open. The daring suggestion was made by Captain Thomson, the engineer, who carried it out. On a dark, stormy night nine hundred pounds of powder were laid and fired, and over the ruins Colonel Dennie rushed with the 13th Light Infantry. The defenders fought bravely, but at last were overpowered, and the British flag floated on the great fort of Ghuzni. An incident which occurred at Ghuzni showed the Afghan in Shah Soojah. A number of Mohammedan fanatics attempted his life, but they were beaten off by Captain Outram, and fifty taken prisoners. When the latter were brought before the Shah they gloried in their deed, and one of them stabbed an attendant of the Shah, upon which, by the Shah's orders, they were taken outside the tent and all butchered in cold blood.

Dost Mohammed fled from Cabul to the Hindu Koosh mountains. He was pursued six days and nights by Captain Outram and a few officers at the head of a small force, and would have been overtaken but for the treachery of the officer of Shah Soojah who accompanied the force, and who always took care to keep a march or two behind. On August 2nd, 1839, Cabul was occupied, and on the 7th Shah Soojah was formally installed amid, not the blessings, but the outspoken curses of a people who, in their fierce love of independence, refused to acknowledge a ruler forced upon them by foreign bayonets. So far the expedition was an easy success. Honours were showered upon all engaged in it, with the exception of Captain Thomson, the real captor of Ghuzni, who retired from the service.

At this point our troops should have been withdrawn, and Shah Soojah left face to face with his own people. But the conviction forced itself upon the Governor-general that to do this would be to throw away all the cost of the expedition, and the force remained. Then came the first fatal blunder. It was essential that the British should take up the strongest position possible among a people plainly hostile to our presence. The citadel of Cabul, the Bala Hissar, furnished such a position. It would hold five thousand troops, and commanded the whole city. Captain Havelock and Lieutenant Durand both urged its occupation. The former said: 'All depends, in a military point of view, on a firm hold of the Bala Hissar. It is the key of Cabul.' But our creature, the Shah, wanted the fort for his seraglio, consisting of one hundred and sixty females, and objected to the presence of British troops in it. To his whim the whole army was sacrificed. The cantonments were planted on an open plain, in a position which so far from having any natural protection was actually commanded by surrounding heights. Such an act of course shows that the British leaders never dreamt of any opposition. And yet the whole country was full of smouldering disaffection, which manifested itself in frequent outbreaks. Nor must it be concealed that the unpopularity of the occupation was aggravated by the licentions conduct of some of the British officers, who disgraced their name and country. Such was the security felt by the British that the envoy sent for Lady Macnaghten from India, and other officers followed his example.

Dost Mohammed, who had taken refuge with the Ameer of Bokhara grew tired of exile, and resolved to strike another blow for his throne. At the close of 1840 he descended from the Hindu Koosh at the head of a few thousands of Oosbeg Tartars, expecting that the people would rally round him. His force was easily dispersed by Brigadier Dennie with a handful of troops, and after this he was pursued incessantly by Sir Robert Sale, and wandered about with a few ragged Afghan followers. A slight advantage which he gained over some native cavalry, when the latter abandoned their officers and fled, enabled him as he thought to surrender with honour. The next day, as Sir W. Macnaghten was riding in the vicinity of Cabul, a horseman galloped up, saying, 'The Ameer is at hand!' 'What ameer?' asked the envoy. 'Dost Mohammed Khan,' was the answer; and immediately Dost Mohammed appeared, dismounted, and presented his sword to the envoy. Sir William returned the sword, and the two rode together to the cantonments, the ameer telling of his wanderings and sufferings during the last fifteen months, and inquiring after his family, who were already in British hands. He was treated honourably and sent to Calcutta, where he received a pension of two lacs a year and played chess with the Governor-general's family.

The capture of Dost Mohammed afforded another opportunity for withdrawing from the country. Again the Governor-general decided against the course, but adopted the fatal policy of withdrawing a part of the force, and, at the same time, reducing the payments to the chiefs, by means of which alone the British retained any hold upon the country. The Ghilzye chiefs who commanded the eastern districts, through which lay our road to India, were told that their subsidies were to be reduced, and Sir Robert Sale was despatched with a portion of the troops towards Jellalabad. The Ghilzyes seemed to assent, but at once began to plunder and slay British detachments. The movement grew rapidly into a national rising.

Nothing awakens more indignation in an English heart in

the review of these events than the fact that the British force at Cabul contained a whole host of heroic spirits, any one of whom, placed in command, would have averted the impending disaster. To say nothing of Sale, Havelock, Broadfoot and Dennie, who had left for Jellalabad, there were Pottinger, Colin Mackenzie, Durand, Eyre, Griffiths, George Lawrence. But the commander at this time was General Elphinstone, a good and amiable man, but old and incapable, both physically and mentally, of coping with an emergency. He was feeble and vacillating to the last degree. Brigadier Shelton, the second in command, was brave as a lion, but as self-willed and cross-grained as he was brave. With them the whole military responsibility of the failure rests. Sir William Macnaghten, who had been a cavalry officer, had the instincts of a soldier, and never ceased to urge the commanders to the path of honour; but in vain. English commanders, with a host of strong hearts and keen swords at their disposal, preferred to trust their own lives and their country's honour to Afghan treachery. At Candahar the British force was surrounded by no less difficulties; but General Nott and the political officer, Major—now in an honoured old age Sir Henry—Rawlinson, held their ground without flinching.

The British leaders had been warned of the seething disaffection; but so confident were they, that at the beginning of November, 1841, Sir William Macnaghten was about to leave for the governorship of Bombay, to which he had been appointed. On November 2nd the house of Sir A. Burnes in the city was attacked by a mob, he and his brother were treacherously butchered, and the British treasury was plundered. The commanders had ample notice of the rising, and could have prevented the murders and plunder with the greatest ease, but their conduct was imbecile in the extreme. One reverse came after another. The provisions, on which the very existence of the force depended, were stored in a small, ill-manned fort four hundred yards away from the cantonments. When the fort was attacked General Elphinstone refused to send relief, and the soldiers sat down, helplessly watching the Afghans as they carried off the stores. Sometimes the hesitation of one commander, sometimes the obstinacy of the other, ruined every movement. They would neither retreat into the Bala Hissar, as Shah Soojah begged, nor take the field against the insurgents, as the envoy urged and entreated. On November 23rd Brigadier Shelton, under much pressure, led a force against the hills from which the enemy were cannonading the cantonments; but the arrangements were so unwise, and the troops so demoralized by hunger, cold and defeat, that the spectacle was seen of English soldiers pursued by Afghans. General Elphinstone refused to send out any supports. This was the last effort made by the commanders.

The envoy was forced to request an interview with the Afghan chiefs, who insolently boasted of their victory and demanded unconditional surrender. Soon afterwards Akbar Khan, a younger son of Dost Mohammed, arrived in Cabul, and took the direction of the rising. He was able, but cunning as a serpent, relentless as a tiger, faithless as an Afghan. He saw that starvation would do his work more effectually and cheaply than fighting, and he forbade the people on pain of death to supply provisions to the British. On December 11th only one day's supply remained, and as the commanders would not fight, the envoy was forced to accept Akbar's terms: the evacuation of the country, Shah Soojah to receive a pension or to leave with the British, four officers to be given as hostages, the army to be supplied with carriage and provisions. It was a shameful treaty, but the envoy had no choice. 'Environed and hemmed in by difficulties and dangers, overwhelmed with responsibility which there was none to share—the lives of fifteen thousand men resting on his decision—the honour of his country at stake—with a perfidious enemy before him, a decrepit general at his side, and a paralyzed army at his back, he was driven to negotiate by the imbecility of his companions.'

The Afghans had no sooner signed the treaty than they began to break it. Assured of the fulfilment of the British conditions, they never intended to perform the conditions on their own side. Instead of supplying provisions they shamelessly stole what remained, and the British allowed them to do so. Akbar Khan swore an oath that of the British only one should reach Jellalabad, to tell the tale of destruction. The British still lingered in expectation of the promised supplies, instead of marching in the best fashion they could. On December 18th snow began to fall, and interposed another difficulty. And now came the envoy's great error. He had made it known that if other Afghan tribes would help the British, he would break with the Barukzyes. In return, the crafty Akbar proposed that he, the Ghilzyes and the British should fall on Ameenoolla, the chief insurgent, and that Shah Soojah should remain king, with Akbar Khan as vizier, as though Afghan would help the English against Afghan. The envoy was earnestly dissuaded, but he fell into the transparent snare, and proceeded on December 23rd with Captains Trevor, Mackenzie and Lawrence, and a small guard, to an interview with Akbar on an open hillside. When the officers saw Ameenoolla's brother and the large number of armed men with Akbar, they suspected treachery. After a haughty greeting, Akbar gave a signal, and each officer was seized from behind, placed on a horse with an Afghan, and carried off to the city. Captain Trevor fell off the horse, and was instantly cut to pieces. Akbar Khan himself seized the envoy, who resisted, whereupon Akbar drew a pistol, the gift of the envoy the day before, and shot him dead. His body was mutilated by the knives of fanatics and paraded in the streets of Cabul. Akbar afterwards asserted that he had not intended to take the envoy's life, but only to hold him as a hostage for his own father. The deed was probably committed under the impulse of sudden passion. It was thoroughly characteristic of the Afghan nature.

Neither the murder of the envoy nor the entreaties of Major Pottinger, who now stepped into Sir William's place, could rouse the army to effort. The only cry was, 'Negotiate, negotiate.'— with foes whose treachery was so patent! On December 26th news arrived of promised help from India, and General Elphinstone was almost ready to make a bold stand, but Brigadier Shelton vehemently opposed. By a new treaty on January 4th, guns, wagons, small arms, and ammunition and four officers were given up, besides a bond for fourteen lacs of rupees. The latter fortunately was made contingent on the safe arrival of the troops at Peshawur.

On January 6th, 1842, the army, still four thousand five hundred strong, with eleven thousand camp-followers, marched out of the cantonments, less prepared for the journey than they were a month before, and with the snow ankle-deep on the road. The cantonments were instantly fired by the Afghans. Next day the army was a mere rabble, and lost baggage and men at every step under the attacks of the wild Ghilzyes. Instead of pressing with the utmost speed, the commanders halted again and again. The suffering reached its height in the Khoord Cabul Pass. The pass was five miles long, deep, narrow, dark, the road crossed and re-crossed twenty-eight times by a rushing torrent, and snow was on the ground. From every height the Ghilzyes poured in a deadly fire on the struggling mass of men, women and children. Human misery never rose to a higher point than in those horrible defiles. At every halt Akbar Khan appeared, demanded new hostages, who were surrendered, made new promises of provision and safety, and then protested his inability to restrain the bloodthirsty savages who were really obeying his orders. On January 8th, Captain Lawrence, Captain Mackenzie and Major Pottinger were surrendered; on January 9th, Ladies Macnaghten and Sale, nine other ladies, fifteen children and eight officers; on January 10th, General Elphinstone, Brigadier Shelton and Captain Johnson. Akbar, who had gained all he wanted, withdrew to Cabul, and left the rest to the Ghilzyes. The poor sepoys and camp-followers were slaughtered in masses. Four hundred and fifty famished Europeans still struggled on, but they fell one by one. At the Jugdulluk Pass twelve brave officers met their fate. Twenty officers and forty-five European privates reached Gundamuk, but these also gradually sank under the Ghilzyes' matchlocks and knives. On January 13th, a solitary horseman was seen from the walls of Jellalabad approaching slowly, wounded and faint. It was Dr. Brydon—save the one hundred and twenty prisoners, the only one left alive of fifteen thousand men. The eighty miles between Cabul and Jellalabad were strewn thick with the relics of a great army, not killed in fair fight, but butchered like sheep, with dastardly treachery. Akbar Khan had kept his vow.

The news of the catastrophe, the worst that ever befell British arms, reached Calcutta on January 30th, 1842. The Governor-general, after recording a brave minute, did nothing worthy of the occasion. The wreck of his one great enterprise seems to have plunged him into despair. His only thought was, not of retrieving British honour and recovering British prisoners, but of withdrawing the forces at Jellalabad and Candahar in safety. He left India in February, and the work of retribution fell into other hands.

KHYBER PASS.

CHAPTER XI.

LORD ELLENBOROUGH—AFGHAN WAR—CONQUEST OF SCINDE—
AFFAIRS OF GWALIOR. 1842–1844.

THE first relieving force was entrusted to an incapable officer, and got no farther than the mouth of the Khyber Pass, where it allowed itself to be driven back by the mountain tribes. The next commander was General Pollock, an old campaigner of Lord Lake's days, who had also seen service in Nepaul and Burmah. Arriving at Peshawur in February, 1842, instead of risking another failure, although importuned to advance by General Sale at Jellalabad, he wisely devoted two months to improving the order and tone of his troops. In April everything was ready. As the Afreedis demanded an exorbitant sum for a free passage, it was necessary to force the pass. Before daylight on April 5th the troops marched in silence upon the heights on either side, and when the sun rose the Afreedis saw their flanks turned and the barricades attacked in front and rear. By evening Ali Musjid, five miles within the pass, was reached, and on April 15th Jellalabad.

Here General Sale had held his ground since November 13th. When he arrived, the walls were in such a state of dilapidation that roads ran over them. Buildings of all sorts came close up to them on the outside, affording excellent shelter for assailants. These were cleared away, and the place soon made secure against native foes by the energy of Captain Broadfoot and the army, who all worked with a will. The people of the town and neighbourhood showed themselves as hostile as the Ghilzyes. Five thousand armed ruffians at once assembled, shouting curses and threats at the infidels; but the day after the occupation Colonel Monteith sallied forth with eleven hundred men of all arms, and taught them a lesson which did not need to be repeated.

Demands came from Cabul for the evacuation of the town in pursuance of the treaty with Akbar Khan. There were long and stormy councils. General Sale and the majority inclined to compliance upon certain conditions. Captains Havelock and Broadfoot always opposed this, and in the end their views carried the day. On February 18th an earthquake destroyed the labour of months; but the enemy were prevented by the same cause from taking advantage of the occasion, and the damage was repaired so quickly that the natives declared that there had been no earthquake at Jellalabad. Fortunately, Akbar Khan and his army were kept at Cabul by internal dissensions, and when they arrived everything was ready for their reception. At first they kept a respectful distance, and when they advanced to attack the town were put to ignominious flight. They next attempted the tactics of Cabul—blockade and starvation, but here also found that they had different leaders to deal with. On April 1st a sortie was made, and a flock of five hundred sheep and goats brought in. But as the besiegers were drawing their lines closer, more effectual relief became necessary. Captain Havelock proposed an attack in force. The general opposed for a time, but at last yielded, and allowed the captain to draw up the plan for the following day, April 7th. The force was to be formed into three successive columns, disregard the flanking forts, and strike boldly at the enemy's camp. General Sale, who commanded the second column, was so annoyed by the fire of a small fort that he detached Colonel Dennie to take it. During the delay the first column of three hundred and sixty men, under Captain Havelock, was left to contend with the whole strength of the enemy, who launched against it fifteen hundred fine cavalry. However, they repelled two charges, and when, in answer to urgent messages, the other columns came up, the victory was complete, the enemy's baggage and guns being taken and his camp burnt. The needless attack on the fort cost the valuable life of Colonel Dennie. Mr. Marshman may well say, 'One such day at Cabul would have saved the army.' The Jellalabad garrison was a mere brigade, the Cabul one was an army. On April 15th the garrison, rightly denominated 'illustrious' by Lord Ellenborough, marched out with drums beating and colours flying to meet General Pollock's delivering force.

Lord Ellenborough was a man of immense vigour and ability, but singularly capricious. Nothing could be more magnanimous than his minute of March 15th, in which he said: 'Whatever course we may hereafter take must rest solely on military considerations and regard to the safety of the detached bodies of our troops, to the security of those now in the field from all unnecessary risk, and finally to the establishment of our military reputation by the infliction of some signal and decisive blow upon the Afghans, which may make it appear to them, and to our own subjects, and to our allies, that we have the power of inflicting punishment upon those who commit atrocities and violate their faith, and that we withdraw ultimately from Afghanistan, not from any deficiency of means to maintain our position, but because we are satisfied that the king we have set up has not, as we were erroneously led to imagine, the support of the nation over whom he has been placed.' But in April came a change. The Governor-general forgot all about the necessity of inflicting a 'signal and decisive blow,' forgot even the English captives in Afghan forts, and determined to withdraw the forces from Jellalabad and Candahar. The cause of this sudden change seems to have been, partly a check sustained by an incapable commander who was conducting relief to General Nott, partly the influence of a vivid imagination in magnifying distant, unseen dangers. Both General Nott and General Pollock were aghast at the thought of retiring without marching upon Cabul. They prepared to obey, but prolonged the preparations to such an extent as to give time for another change to take place. Happily, the ignoble course proposed was rendered impossible by the thrill of indignation (one advantage of a free press) which ran through India when the orders leaked out. In July Lord Ellenborough sent the generals fresh instructions, most curiously worded. General Pollock was still to retire, but if he could do so, with absolute safety, he might retire by way of Cabul; which was like saying that an army might retire from Manchester to Edinburgh by way of Birmingham. General Nott received similar instructions, which was like permitting a general to withdraw from Manchester to Edinburgh by way of Hull, supposing Hull to be three times the distance to the east that it is. In other words, Lord Ellenborough, instead of assuming the responsibility, threw it upon the two generals, who accepted it with delight.

General Pollock could not leave Jellalabad till assured of General Nott's cooperation, and then it became a struggle which should reach Cabul first. The latter left Candahar on August 7th, and had the longest march. The former left Jellalabad on August 20th, and had battles to fight by the way. Akbar Khan had offered to restore the captives if the force would withdraw without marching on Cabul, but the offer was rejected with scorn. Pollock's force numbered eight thousand men in splendid condition. They were wrought up to the highest tension, not only by the mission that lay before them, but by the sight of the remains of their murdered comrades of eight months before. At Jugdulluk Pass the Ghilzyes mustered all their strength to bar the way, but were chased and scattered in every direction. In the valley of Tezeen, one of the chief scenes of massacre, Akbar made his last stand. The fight was spread, not only over the plain, but over the surrounding heights. First, the cavalry routed the Afghan horse, then the artillery inflicted great slaughter, and finally the infantry cleared the hills. Akbar fled to the northern highlands of Afghanistan. On September 15th the British flag again waved over the Bala Hissar.

The Candahar force arrived the following day. As the Candahar occupation exerted no decisive influence on the result we have not thought it necessary to follow its history in detail. But it must not be forgotten how General Nott's determination and Major Rawlinson's political tact held the place for months and even years amid treachery, insurrection and attacks on all sides. They so effectually checked disorder and license among their own troops as to secure the respect of the populace. The very Doorânees, Shah Soojah's own tribe, joined the hordes of the insurgents. Safder Jung, Shah Soojah's son, and Mirza Ahmed, a chief in Major Rawlinson's confidence, did the same. Once, when General Nott had marched out to beat up the enemy's quarters, Mirza Ahmed with bands of fanatics doubled back upon Candahar, and reached the Herat gate at sunset. Brushwood, soaked in oil, was piled up against the gate and fired. For six hours the enemy, reckless of their own lives, tried to force an entrance, but Major Lane and Major Rawlinson repelled every attack. On the force leaving for Jellalabad the renowned fortifications of Ghuzni were blown up.

One of the first things which General Pollock did after reaching Cabul was to despatch two columns under Sir Richmond Shakespeare and Sir Robert Sale to recover the prisoners, who on the English advance had been sent by forced marches day and night by Akbar over the heights of the Hindu Koosh to Bameean. They had not been treated with any exceptional harshness during the interval. Their first keeper was the blind old chief, Zemaun Shah, the same whose reported intention to invade India had spread consternation so far back as Tippu's days. Singularly enough, he remained faithful to the British cause, 'faithful among the faithless.' The English called him 'the good nabob.' Afterwards they came into Akbar's possession, and were taken from place to place. At Tezeen, one of their places of detention, General Elphinstone died, worn out with age and trouble. His body was taken by a servant to Jellalabad for burial. At Bameean Saleh Mohammed, the officer of Akbar who had charge of the party, showed the officers two letters, one from Akbar commanding him to take the prisoners farther on and give them up to the Oosbegs, which meant perpetual captivity or death, and another from Mohun Lall, a former moonshee of Sir W. Macnaghten at Cabul, offering him in General Pollock's name a present of twenty thousand rupees and an annuity of twelve thousand to set them at liberty. 'I know nothing,' he said, 'of General Pollock; but if you three gentlemen will swear by your Saviour to make good to me this offer, I will deliver you over to your own people.' The agreement was made, and Major Pottinger assumed command. On September 15th a horseman brought news of the victory at Tezeen. On the 16th the party set out for Cabul, and at night a note came from Sir Richmond Shakespeare to say that he was approaching. On the afternoon of the

17th the two parties met, and all danger was over. On the 20th General Sale came up at the head of the second brigade, and met his wife and daughter after months of suspense. On the 20th the whole party reached Cabul, where the British troops were wild with delight at the recovery of the captives, for whose fate all India and England were anxious.

Ameenoolla, the inveterate foe of the British, endeavoured to revive the struggle, and collected large forces at Istaliff, a mountain fastness in the north. But an expedition was sent against him, and by Captain Havelock's admirable dispositions the place was taken and the enemy's force broken up.

On October 12th the British set their faces towards India. Before doing so, as a mark of retribution, they destroyed the Great Bazaar, in which the envoy's body had been exposed to public insult. The building was so large and so solidly constructed that its destruction took two days. There is something more painful to record. Surrounded by memorials of British dishonour and suffering and Afghan perfidy and cruelty, the army broke through all the restraints of discipline, and, in spite of every exertion of commanders and officers, for three days plundered and ravaged the city at will. Cabul suffered the fate of a captured city. This is the only blot on the doings of 'the avenging army.'

At Ferozepore, on the banks of the Sutledge, whence four years before the ill-starred expedition had set out with such high hopes, Lord Ellenborough met the returning army, and indulged to the full the love of display and vaunting which was his greatest weakness. Two hundred elephants were made to kneel to the victorious legions. Remembering those who were left behind in Afghan graves, such scenes might have been spared. In the same strain was the Governor-general's order to bring back from Ghuzni the sandal-wood gates which Mahmud had carried away from the temple of Somnath eight centuries before. The original gates had no doubt perished in the course of time, and those brought back were copies. The temple of Somnath had also perished, and the gates lay, and perhaps still lie, as useless lumber at Agra. For the fifteen millions spent and the army lost in Afghanistan a pair of fictitious gates was all we had to show.

N

SIR CHARLES NAPIER.

We may mention the fate of our puppet, Shah Soojah. He was compelled by the insurgents to place himself at the head of the force marching to the attack of Jellalabad, but was murdered on the road, his body being stripped of its jewels and thrown into a ditch. The result of much strife was that Akbar Khan remained master of the situation until his father's return from India. Dost Mohammed took leave of Lord Ellenborough privately. On being asked his opinion of all he had seen he replied: 'I have been struck with the magnitude of your power and your resources, with your ships, your arsenals and your armies; but what I cannot understand is, why the rulers of so vast and flourishing an empire should have gone across the Indus to deprive me of my poor and barren country.' The reason of course was, not ambition to possess Afghanistan, but fear of Russia.

The conquest of Scinde was, if possible, even more shamefully unjust than the attack upon Afghanistan, but unlike the latter was successful. It has always been regarded, and justly, as the darkest stain on British fame in India; but it would be unjust to quote it as an illustration of the way in which India has been acquired. The country was governed by a crowd of poor chiefs, called ameers, who were grouped round three centres: Khyrpore in the north, Meerpore in the middle, and Hyderabad in the south. Of the first group Meer Roostum, a venerable man of eighty-five years, was the principal; of the second, Shere Mohammed. These chiefs again were in the hands of swarms of tributaries. During the Afghan troubles, a few of the ameers had shown a hostile spirit, and for their alleged fault the whole country was held responsible. In September, 1842, Sir Charles Napier was sent, with full power to investigate and act. Sir Charles was a most brilliant and daring soldier, but arbitrary, impulsive and from the first prejudiced against the ameers. On his first coming he wrote: 'We only want a pretext to coerce the ameers; they have given a pretext, they have broken treaties. The more powerful government will at no distant period swallow up the weaker, and it would be better to come to the result at once, if it can be done with honesty.' And again: 'We have no right to seize Scinde, yet we shall do so; and a very advantageous, useful and humane piece of rascality it will be.' Major Outram, the Resident, was the soul of honour, the Bayard of India; but he was placed under Sir Charles, and could not go beyond his instructions.

The gist of the dispute turned upon certain treasonable letters ascribed to some of the ameers. Their genuineness was strenuously denied; and, considering that the forging of seals was a regular business in Scinde, the denial may be accepted. But without hearing the ameers in defence, Sir Charles decided on his sole authority that the letters were genuine, and that the old treaty between the British and the ameers was abrogated. A new treaty was to be imposed, in which, beside other concessions, the ameers were to cede land to the value of eight lacs in lieu of the subsidy for the support of the British contingent. This was double the amount which Major Outram had suggested as sufficient for the purpose. He pointed out the mistake, which was not acknowledged until the issue had been decided by force.

On the other side, it must be stated that Sir Charles Napier was the victim, if that is an excuse, of the wiles of a crafty intriguer, Ali Morad, brother of Meer Roostum. By national usage Ali Morad was heir to the office of *rais*, or suzerain, held by Roostum. The latter was anxious to secure the office for his own son. So far Ali Morad had right on his side, but not so in the means he used. These means consisted in embroiling Meer Roostum with the British, and then obtaining the coveted dignity at the hands of the latter. He poisoned Sir Charles's mind against the old ameer, induced the former to send haughty messages and refuse a request for a personal interview, got his brother into his power, and forced him to sign an abdication. When Sir Charles Napier proposed in a personal interview to ascertain whether the abdication was genuine or not, Ali Morad persuaded his brother that the intention was to seize him, and induced him to flee. The flight was construed as proof of guilt, and on Meer Roostum sending a full statement of the facts, the answer was a charge of deceit and double-dealing.

Another act of Sir Charles's well illustrates his high-handed policy. In an inaccessible corner of Scinde stood the fort of Emamgur, which enjoyed the fame of never having been captured. The chief to whom it belonged had done nothing to offend the British. But Sir Charles thought that the capture of the place would impress the people with a sense of British prowess. He mounted three hundred and fifty European soldiers on camels, and with these and fifty horse and two twenty-four pounders crossed a desert in a march of four days, found the fort abandoned, and blew it up with the powder in its stores. The Duke of Wellington called this 'one of the most curious military feats he had ever known.' The moralist, as well as the soldier, is compelled to regard it as 'curious.'

A great conference was held at Hyderabad in February, 1843. The ameers protested their innocence, but on February 12th, conscious of their weakness, signed the treaty, hard as it was. Their only request was that Meer Roostum might be restored to the office of which he had been unjustly deprived. This concession, they said, might appease their followers, who threatened an outbreak. Major Outram said that he had no power to grant the request. On leaving the conference, Major Outram and his officers would undoubtedly have been murdered by a turbulent mob of citizens and soldiers but for the protection of a special guard commanded by the principal chiefs. Next day a deputation waited upon him with the same request, and at the same time urged him to remove from the residency to a place of greater safety. He could not grant the request, and he would not run away from danger. On February 15th the residency was attacked by masses of cavalry and infantry. Major Outram fortunately had with him a company of the 22nd Foot, and after a brave defence for three hours and a loss of seventeen men withdrew to an armed steamer in the river five hundred yards distant. After this of course nothing remained but war.

On February 17th was fought the hardly contested battle of Meanee, about six miles from Hyderabad. Sir Charles Napier had barely three thousand troops; the Beloochees amounted to twenty thousand, and were strongly posted. For three hours the latter stood their ground without flinching. After firing their matchlocks, they would rush sword in hand upon the British bayonets. The issue was decided by a cavalry charge on their right, while another body fell on their camp in the rear. They then retired, fighting at every step. Their camp and stores were all taken. No quarter was asked or given. The Beloochee loss was five thousand against the British two hundred and fifty-seven. The day after the battle ten thousand fresh Beloochee troops arrived, and Shere Mohammed had as many more in the neighbourhood.

On March 22nd a second battle was fought at Dubba, near Hyderabad, of a similar character and with similar results. Sir Charles had received reinforcements, and led six thousand troops to the attack on twenty thousand Beloochees, who were posted behind a river-bed. Across this the 22nd Foot charged in the teeth of a withering fire, while cavalry made an attack on the enemy's left flank. The Beloochees fought with their usual valour, but discipline and skilful generalship prevailed.

It is not too much to say that but for the Afghan and Scinde episodes the British history in India would present a comparatively fair record. Sir John Hobhouse believed that if Lord Ellenborough had known all the facts, Scinde would not have been annexed, but facts and documents were kept back from him. It is a poor province, and has never paid its way. Great quantities of prize-money fell to the conquerors, the Commander-in-chief's share being seven lacs. Major Outram's share was three lacs (£30,000); but he refused to accept the spoils of an unjust war, and devoted the amount to charitable institutions in India. Sir Charles Napier made a pun of his conquest. In reply to the charges of injustice he said, '*Peccavi*, I have sinned (Scinde).' To the rebellious ameers fell the hard lot of exile.

In the same year (1843) Lord Ellenborough was compelled to interfere by force of arms in the Gwalior state, which was in great confusion. The adopted son of Dowlut Rao Scindia's widow died February 7th, 1843, without heir or recognized successor. His second wife, Tara Bai, whom he married in 1838, and who at his death was not thirteen years old, immediately adopted a boy eight years of age. A dispute then arose between the palace and the British as to who should be regent. The rānee wanted Dada Khasji, the hereditary chamberlain and steward; Lord Ellenborough preferred Mama Sahib, uncle of the late rāja. The latter was installed February 23rd. But the rānee and her party thwarted him in every way, and at last expelled him from the country. The English Resident was then instructed to withdraw to Dholpore, a frontier town, and demand the surrender of the dada, who was set against the English, and ready to risk a conflict with them. The demand was refused. The chief reason why the Governor-general was anxious to have a regent favourable to the English was for the purpose of carrying out a reduction in the Gwalior army, which had outgrown the necessities of the country. It numbered thirty thousand infantry and ten thousand horse, with two hundred guns, and absorbed two-thirds of the revenue. It had also received a European training. As the country was under British protection, such a force was utterly unnecessary, and was a standing menace to the British power. But the army knew its strength, refused to allow any reduction to be made, and domineered over the whole country. At this time there was every prospect of speedy trouble with the splendid Sikh army across the Sutledge, and a simultaneous attack by such an army as that of Gwalior in the south would have placed the British power in the greatest peril. On November 1st the Governor-general issued an able and temperate paper stating these circumstances, and showing the justice and necessity of the British demands. In this paper he formally claimed for the British the position of the sovereign power throughout India, assuming the control and responsibility belonging to this position, and concluded, 'If the Governor-general, who is now on his way to Agra, should not find the dada there on his arrival, God alone knows what orders may be issued.'

He reached Agra December 11th, and the next day wrote to the rānee to say that as his demands had not been complied with the armies would advance forthwith. Both the ranee and the dada were now thoroughly alarmed. The dada arrived at Dholpore with a letter requesting that the march of the troops might be arrested. On December 18th the Governor-general replied, and presented his demand for the reduction of the army within reasonable limits. But, with a touch of weakness, he based it, not on present exigencies, but on the old treaty of 1804 which Lord Wellesley had forced on Scindia, and which had really been superseded by Lord Hastings's treaty in 1817. The ranee then sent three of the chief nobles to urge the request in more earnest terms and, if possible, prevent a collision. But the Governor-general was immovable. The Gwalior army cut the knot by advancing to meet the English, boasting of their ability to give a good account of the invaders. On the night of December 28th they took up a strong position at the village of Mahārajpore, where next day the British general was surprised at finding them. The first intimation of their presence was the balls whistling among the elephants which carried the Governor-general and the ladies of the chief English officers. It is surprising that the English had formed a low estimate of the troops they had to deal with. An English general who fell in the battle talked of his only needing a horsewhip. As we have seen, Scindia's troops had fought with the utmost stubbornness at battles like Assaye and Laswaree.

The battle of Mahārajpore was eminently a soldiers' battle on both sides. The British general, Sir Hugh Gough, had pushed on without his guns, having expected to meet the enemy farther on. To overcome powerful batteries he could only trust to living valour. Of his twelve thousand troops one thousand were killed or wounded. Generalship was as conspicuously absent here as it was present in the Scinde campaign. The Gwalior troops had no general at all: each regiment took up its position by instinct and fought for its own hand. The gunners were cut down to a man before the guns were taken. Even then the infantry fought on till they could fight no longer. On the same day another portion of their force was defeated at Punniar by General Grey, who advanced on Gwalior from the south.

On December 31st the rānee and rāja, together with their chief officers, proceeded to the British camp to learn their fate. The girl-rānee sat in a closed litter, and the Governor-general sat beside it. The conversation was held through Colonel Sleeman, the Resident, and two Mahratta ministers. The rānee pleaded her youth and inexperience and blamed the army. Lord Ellenborough simply replied that an orderly government must be established, holding out hopes that she might be recognized in it. But in the arrangement made she simply received a pension of three lacs, and the regency was entrusted to a council of six nobles, who were required to be submissive to the Resident. Instead of being annexed, like Scinde, the country was thoroughly mediatized. The army was cut down to ten thousand men, with thirty-two guns; and so broken was it in spirit by the recent defeats that it submitted quietly to the reduction. Many of the troops joined the British contingent, which became renowned for its efficiency, and signalized itself in the mutiny of 1857 by butchering its officers and marching off to work vast mischief in Bengal. So ended Scindia's dream of Indian empire.

Of Lord Ellenborough's three wars, two certainly were not of his seeking, but the directors thought, and his proceedings indicated, that he had become intoxicated by military success. A passion for military fame had taken hold of him—a dangerous passion for a ruler to whom war comes without seeking. The directors lost all confidence in him. They felt uncertain what he might do next. The dictatorial tone of his letters also offended them, and in June, 1844, he was recalled. Sir Henry Lawrence said that after his recall the natives of India ceased, on waking in the morning, to feel their necks to make sure that their heads were still on their shoulders. The internal reforms of his administration, such as the abolition of state-lotteries and the reorganization of the police, do not call for special notice.

CHAPTER XII.

LORDS HARDINGE AND DALHOUSIE—FIRST AND SECOND SIKH WARS.
1844-1848.

SIR Henry Hardinge arrived in Calcutta in July, 1844. He had highly distinguished himself under the Duke of Wellington in the Peninsula and at Waterloo, and was now in his sixtieth year.

The contest with the Sikhs, which had been long foreseen, and for which some preparations were made, now broke out. The battles which followed were battles of giants on both sides, and tried the qualities of the British troops to the utmost. In them the British encountered a foe such as they had never met in India before. The fiery valour of the Sikh nature had been trained to the utmost perfection by European officers like Avitabile, Court, Allard, Ventura. The artillery especially could not be surpassed. In discipline the Sikhs were fully equal to the British sepoys, and in physical strength and endurance far their superiors. The sepoys alone would have stood no chance against them. It was the combination of English with sepoy troops that decided the day. It is said that some of the English officers disparaged the Sikhs. If so, they were soon undeceived.

Runjeet Sing, 'the Lion of the Punjab,' died June 27th, 1839, at the age of fifty-seven, prematurely worn out by the excesses usual with Oriental princes. A characteristic story is told of his later days. He had sent a son of one of his nobles to Loodiana to learn English. The youth brought back a map of India, which Runjeet examined with great interest. He wished to be shown the Sikh dominions. After inspecting these, he asked, ' What mean these red lines everywhere ? ' 'Those,' it

BRITISH TROOPS ENTERING MOOLTAN.

was replied, 'are the British territories.' He kicked the map aside with the exclamation, 'All will become red.' His death was followed by six years of anarchy, intrigue and bloodshed. It may be worth while to epitomize the events. Runjeet's imbecile son, Khurruk Sing, died in November, 1840, of excess. The real power had belonged to Khurruk's able son, Nao Nihal, who was not unlike his grandfather, and to his minister, Dhyan Sing, brother of Golab Sing, the Rājpoot chief of Jummoo. But Nao Nihal was killed by the fall of a gateway at Khurruk's funeral. Khurruk's widow now became regent for the expected offspring of Nao Nihal's widow, with Dhyan Sing and Shere Sing, a reputed son of Runjeet, as ministers. But Shere Sing aspired to the sovereignty, and by bribing and flattering the army gained his ends. Dhyan Sing, who saw himself set aside, then induced Shere Sing to recall to court from banishment a powerful chief called Ajeet Sing, and, persuading the latter that his death was intended, induced him to shoot Shere Sing at a parade. Shere Sing's youthful son, Pertab Sing, was killed at the same time. Ajeet Sing next assassinated his employer Dhyan Sing, but was then himself assassinated by order of Heera Sing, son of Dhyan Sing. Heera Sing now became minister, and proclaimed Dhuleep Sing, son of Runjeet Sing and a favourite wife called Jhindun, a child now five years old, Mahārāja. Heera Sing was an able man, and saw that it was necessary to curb the overgrown power of the army. He wished to disperse the army over the country, but it refused to leave the capital. He had also offended the rānee, Jhindun, and her profligate brother Juwāhir Sing, and perished with his tutor, the pundit Julla. At his funeral twenty-five of his wives and female slaves burnt themselves on the pile. The rānee now ruled through her brother and a favourite called Lal Sing, a Brahmin of the lowest character, who had nothing to recommend him but a handsome person. The rānee's profligacy was such that the Governor-general called her the Messalina of the north. Next, Juwāhir Sing fell under the resentment of the army for the murder of Peshora Sing, a popular son of Runjeet, and was beheaded on the plain of Mean Meer, now the British parade-ground at Lahore. Thus, in

November, 1845, the ranee was regent, with Lal Sing as prime minister and Tej Sing as commander-in-chief.

Amid these scenes of confusion, the army had become the paramount power in the country. It made and unmade governments. Instead of being the servant, it had become the master of the state. It obeyed, not the orders of the state, but those of the *punches*, or army-committees, which met and settled all questions affecting the army. From the chiefs of Jummoo and Mooltan it exacted eighty-four lacs of rupees. The Sikh army was one in race and faith. Its enthusiasm was fed by national and religious traditions. Its one thought was for the glory of the Sikh Khalsa, or commonwealth. In religion the Sikhs are neither Mohammedan nor Hindu, but a combination of both. Their faith is an eclectic one, culled from both alike. All historians of the Sikh war assert that the Lahore rulers—the ranee, Lal Sing and Tej Sing—deliberately encouraged the army to attack the English; and the assertion is no doubt true. The army had broken loose from all control. It burned to try conclusions with the conquerors of India, and its desire was gratified with a view to bring about its destruction. It is also asserted that the army was betrayed and sold by its leaders. Whether this was the case or not, no troops could fight better than the Sikhs did. The British never won victories with greater difficulty or at greater cost. Often they were on the brink of defeat and destruction. It is true that some of the loss must be assigned to the tactics of the Commander-in-chief, Sir Hugh Gough, who hurled masses of troops on strong entrenchments, well constructed and fiercely defended, instead of clearing the way by artillery. But it is hard to believe that the troops were betrayed without their knowing it, or that knowing it such a people as the Sikhs allowed the traitors to escape. These points have never been satisfactorily cleared up.

There is comfort in the reflection that the great Sikh war was not brought on by the British. Nothing on their part could have prevented it. The Sikhs invaded British territory in full strength and with the avowed purpose of conquest. Captain Cunningham in his *History of the Sikhs* gives it as his opinion that the substantial responsibility lies with the English, but the grounds which he alleges are trifling in the extreme. The opinion is contradicted by the fact, admitted by Captain Cunningham, that the army was hurled at the British territories by the Sikh rulers as a measure of self-defence, and also by the fact that when the Punjab lay absolutely at the Governor-general's disposal, instead of annexing it, he did his best to re-establish the authority of the government. There were no such interferences of the British previously as might be adduced with respect to almost every other state. The Sikh pride and jealousy prevented anything of this kind. The only measure that wore even the semblance of provocation was the amassing of troops on the frontier in readiness to repel any invasion, and it would have been criminal in the British government to neglect preparation. Lord Ellenborough had increased the force to seventeen thousand six hundred men, with sixty-six guns. Sir Henry Hardinge increased it still farther to forty thousand, with ninety-four guns. He also wisely brought up from Scinde fifty-six large boats for the purpose of forming a pontoon.

The opening of the campaign reminds us of the prelude to Waterloo. Preparations were being made on December 11th, 1845, at Umballa for a state ball, when news came that the Sikhs' were across the Sutledge in force. The Governor-general and Commander at once hurried to the front with the Umballa and Loodiana divisions, eleven thousand strong. In six days they marched one hundred and fifty miles across a sandy country. But haste was essential, as Sir John Littler was exposed at the frontier town of Ferozepore, with ten thousand men and thirty-two guns, to the whole Sikh army of sixty thousand regular troops, forty thousand armed followers, and one hundred and fifty heavy guns. Four days had sufficed for the passage of this host. 'Every Sikh considered the cause as his own, and he would work as a labourer as well as carry a musket; he would drag guns, drive bullocks, lead camels, and load and unload boats with cheerful alacrity.' Wonder has been expressed that the passage was not opposed, but General Littler probably felt that to attempt opposition would be to expose his small force to destruction and give the enemy the first triumph. It is less intelligible why the Sikhs did not at once fall on General Littler. One reason alleged is the treason of the Sikh leaders, who had no wish either to anger the English or elate their own troops by the destruction of isolated detachments.

Lal Sing, with twenty thousand men and twenty-two guns, intercepted the advancing army before its junction with General Littler, and the battle of Moodkee was fought December 18th. The British troops had just ended a march of twenty-one miles, and had not tasted food since the previous night. It was four o'clock in the afternoon, and not much daylight remained, when the enemy opened a heavy, rapid fire and tried to outflank our force with cavalry. More than one sepoy regiment turned and fled, and was brought back with the greatest difficulty. Even European battalions shook under the fire. Lal Sing and his cavalry were the first to leave the field, and the infantry followed. Darkness effectually stopped pursuit. The loss of the British was heavier and the victory far less decisive than they had been accustomed to in India. The killed and wounded numbered eight hundred and seventy-two. After this experience of the enemy, the Governor-general set an example of devotion by serving as second in command under the Commander-in-chief.

At noon on December 21st General Littler, leaving a force sufficient to guard Ferozepore and eluding Tej Sing, who was watching him, joined the army with five thousand five hundred men and twenty-two guns. With the united force it was determined at once to attack the enemy's chief position at Ferozeshoor, to the west of Loodiana. The Sikh entrenchment was in the form of a parallelogram a mile long and half a mile broad, the longer sides facing Ferozepore and the east, the shorter the Sutledge and Moodkee. It was defended by thirty-five thousand men under Lal Sing, with one hundred heavy guns and two hundred camel-guns. The attacking force did not number more than sixteen thousand. The day was the shortest in the year, yet the attack was not begun till four in the afternoon. The Sikh artillery battered the light British guns to pieces, and the assail-

ants had to trust to the bayonet. Sir Hugh Gough led the right division, Sir Henry Hardinge the centre, and General Littler the left. Between the guns the Sikhs placed musketeers, and in the teeth of this double fire the columns advanced, but presently recoiled. On the western side, where General Littler was, the heaviest guns were massed. Here the 62nd regiment left seventy-six of its rank and file and seven officers within fifty paces of the entrenchments. Sir Harry Smith, who was with the centre division, penetrated the camp, and held the village of Ferozeshoor till two o'clock in the morning, when he was compelled to retire by the fire concentrated upon him. 'Guns were dismounted, and their ammunition was blown into the air; squadrons were checked in mid career; battalion after battalion was hurled back with shattered ranks, and it was not until after sunset that portions of the enemy's position were finally carried. Darkness and the obstinacy of the contest threw the English into confusion; men of all regiments and arms were mixed together; generals were doubtful of the fact or of the extent of their own success, and colonels knew not what had become of the regiments they commanded, or of the army of which they formed a part.'*
A wild, useless feat was performed by the 3rd Dragoons. 'Without orders from the Commander-in-chief they charged across the ditch while the battery in front mowed them down, till the yawning trench was choked up with their numbers, and those who followed crossed on a bridge of their own dead and dying comrades. This gallant band, after having silenced the battery in its front, faced the Khalsa army within the entrenchments, swept through the camp, with loud huzzas, over tents, ropes, pegs, guns, fires and magazines, and never paused till it emerged on the opposite side and rejoined their companions.' †

The army lay on the edge of the enemy's position, waiting for the morning. No permanent impression had been made. Living, dying and dead were all huddled together. The heavy guns still dealt out their thunder. One great gun was specially annoying, and just after midnight the Governor-general 'called

---

* Cunningham, *History of the Sikhs*, p. 308. † Marshman.

up the 80th Foot and the 1st Europeans lying around him on the frozen ground, and placing himself at their head, charged the gun and spiked it.' The night was called 'the night of horrors.' Some spoke of retreat to Ferozepore, but this would have been fatal, and neither Governor-general nor Commander-in-chief would entertain the thought. The next day, as light dawned, the scattered troops of General Gilbert's division, repulsed the night before, renewed the attack and met with little resistance. There had been quarrels and bitter recriminations among the Sikhs, Lal Sing's treasure-chest had been plundered, and either from treachery or cowardice he retreated. The British line halted on the northern side, and as the two commanders rode up they were received with a ringing cheer. Just at that moment Tej Sing came in sight with twenty-five thousand fresh troops and seventy guns. The British in their exhausted state must have been overwhelmed, if he had attacked vigorously; but he chose to join his companion in flight. The British loss in killed and wounded was two thousand four hundred and fifteen, fully one-seventh of the entire force, and among the killed were Major Broadfoot, a most able officer, and Major d'Arcy Todd, formerly minister at Herat. Seventy pieces of artillery were taken. Sir Henry Hardinge said that another such battle would shake the empire to its foundation. He had five aides-de-camp killed and wounded.

The Sikhs retired across the Sutledge, and the British were obliged to wait for heavy ordnance and supplies from Delhi. The wily Golab Sing was brought down from Jummoo to Lahore to try his skill in negotiation. He was told that the English would acknowledge a Sikh government, but must insist on the reduction of the army. This Golab Sing could not promise. The army would submit to nothing but force. It is said that the Sikh leaders again promised to desert it. Such consummate treachery is hard of belief, but certainly the whole conduct of the leaders is not inconsistent with the supposition.

The Sikhs took advantage of the British weakness to recross the Sutledge, under a leader called Runjoor Sing, to the number of ten thousand. Their object was to attack Loodiana and the approaching convoy. Sir Harry Smith was sent with four infantry and three cavalry regiments to foil them. At Buddowal, where the enemy stood across his path in such a way that he could not pass without engaging them, he suffered some loss, chiefly in baggage. The Sikhs were able to exhibit some European prisoners and artillery wagons at Lahore. But the object of the English was secured. Runjoor Sing now retired to Aliwal, on the banks of the Sutledge, and Sir Harry Smith, having received reinforcements which brought up his force to eleven thousand men, attacked him on January 28th, 1846. The key of the position was the village of Aliwal, which was held by some hill-battalions, who did not wait for the charge, but broke at once and fled with Runjoor Sing himself. This laid open the whole of the enemy's left to a cavalry charge, which was perfectly successful. The enemy's right was composed of regular troops, who stood firm and even gained ground. Against them a regiment of European lancers and one of native cavalry were launched. The Sikhs knelt to receive them, but at the critical moment their nerve failed them. Instead of retaining their kneeling position, they rose to deliver their fire at close quarters. Even then they were ridden through and through three times before they gave way. The Sikhs were driven across the Sutledge and fifty guns were taken. Aliwal recompensed General Smith for the discomfiture at Buddowal.

A more terrible conflict was impending. At the Kurreekee ford the Sikhs had gradually recrossed the Sutledge, fortified a bridge-head, and, under the eyes of the British, who were too weak to prevent, constructed a vast entrenchment with the river for a base, two and a half miles of outer crescent-shaped works, and a deep ditch. The British convoy of guns and ammunition arrived on February 8th, and it was resolved to attack on the 10th. From a neighbouring village the battle has acquired the name of Sobraon. The enemy had thirty-five thousand men and sixty-seven heavy guns. The English had fifteen thousand men. Tej Sing commanded in the entrenchments, and Lal Sing commanded the cavalry outside, who were held in check by Brigadier Cureton's horse. The fire from the

Sikh entrenchment on the other side of the river also assisted in the defence. On the English side 'the evening and the early hours of darkness of the 9th of February were occupied with busy preparations: the hitherto silent camp poured all its numbers abroad; soldiers stood in groups, talking of the task to be achieved by their valour; officers rode hastily along to receive or deliver orders; and on that night what Englishman passed battalion after battalion to seek a short repose or a moment's solitary communion, and listened as he went to the hammering of shells and the piling of iron shot, or beheld the sentinel pacing silently along by the gleam of renewed fires, without recalling to his mind his heroic king and the eve of Agincourt, rendered doubly immortal by the genius of Shakespeare?'* At daylight the batteries opened and continued on both sides for three hours. The Sikhs had the advantage in weight and number of guns, and the British ammunition began to fail. The bayonet had to decide. The English knew, it is said through Lal Sing's treachery, that the western end of the entrenchments was the weakest, as the sandy soil prevented the works being executed on the same scale. Here the chief attack was to be made under Sir Robert Dick. The centre under General Gilbert and the right under Sir Harry Smith were to serve as diversions. The main body of the left attack was driven back, but the extreme wing effected an entrance into the outworks, and this so encouraged the repulsed battalions on the right that they made another rush, charged with a shout across the ditch and up the ramparts, and made good their footing in the first trench. General Dick fell mortally wounded.

The Sikhs saw that here was the real attack, and brought every man and gun to bear against the assailants. The British centre and then the right division were therefore compelled to attack far more formidable defences. In each case the first columns were hurled back on the second with terrible slaughter, and it was only when the first and second columns joined and made a joint rush that they succeeded in mastering the batteries immediately

---

* Cunningham.

opposed to them. Tej Sing fled at the first assault, and by accident or design broke the bridge of boats across the river. But there were nobler spirits among the vanquished. The common soldiers disdained to ask for quarter, but either rushed on death in the British ranks or moved sullenly away to find it in the river. The old chief, Shâm Sing, clothed himself in white, rallied his shattered lines, again and again charged on the British, and at last found the death he coveted. 'Others might be seen standing on the ramparts amid showers of balls, waving defiance with their swords, or telling the gunners where the fair-haired English pressed thickest together. Along the stronger half of the battlements, and for the period of half an hour, the conflict raged sublime in all its terrors. The parapets were sprinkled with blood from end to end; the trenches were filled with the dead and dying. Amid the deafening roar of cannon, and the multitudinous fire of musketry, the shouts of triumph or of scorn were yet heard, and the flashing of innumerable swords was yet visible; or, from time to time, exploding magazines of powder threw bursting shells and beams of wood and banks of earth high above the agitated sea of smoke and flame which enveloped the host of combatants, and for a moment arrested the attention amid all the din and tumult of the tremendous conflict.'* By eleven o'clock the issue was decided. The horse artillery played on the Sikhs as they attempted to cross the river and completed their destruction. They are supposed to have lost eight thousand men, the British loss being not less than two thousand three hundred and eighty. Such was the great victory of Sobraon. The Governor-general, though severely injured by a fall from his horse, rode off at once twenty-six miles to Ferozepore, and the same night despatched six regiments across the bridge of boats which had been formed there.

On February 17th, Dhuleep Sing and Golab Sing appeared in the camp. On the 20th the whole British army encamped

---

* Cunningham.—It is to be regretted that this able history was not continued to the second Sikh war. The author lost his appointment under government on account of his inconvenient revelations.

on the plain of Meean Meer at Lahore. The fort was occupied, but the British soldiers were forbidden to set foot within the city. The terms imposed, by the treaty of March 9th, were the cession of the cis-Sutledge districts and of the Jullunder Dooab between the Sutledge and Beeas, which gave us a better road to Lahore, an indemnity of a million and a half, the reduction of the army to twenty thousand infantry and twelve thousand cavalry, and the surrender of the thirty-two guns still remaining which had been used in action against the English. As the Sikhs could not pay the money, Cashmere was taken instead, and at once handed over to Golab Sing, no doubt in accordance with a previous understanding. Golab Sing paid a million. As no cordiality existed between the Rájpoot Golab and the Sikhs, Sir Henry Hardinge thought that the former would serve as a bridle on the latter. From the bearing of the Sikh troops, it was evident that their pride was far from being humbled. The Lahore government was afraid of being left alone with them, and at its earnest request a British force remained till the end of the year, with Major Henry Lawrence as Resident. The Sikh authorities in Cashmere refused to surrender the country to Golab Sing. Major Lawrence had to march at the head of Sikh troops to enforce submission, and as it was found that Lal Sing had instigated the resistance, he was deposed on a pension of two thousand rupees a month, to the great grief of the ránee. At the close of the year the Sikh government earnestly desired the continuance of the British protection, and by a new treaty, dated December 16th, 1846, the British Resident was made supreme, a council of eight nobles was appointed to advise with him, and twenty-two lacs of rupees a year were assigned for the support of the British force. This was to last for eight years, till Dhuleep Sing came of age. Thus, to all intents and purposes, the Punjab came under British rule.

In order that the victories over the Sikhs might make their due impression on the Indian mind, the captured guns, to the number of two hundred and fifty, were taken in grand procession from Lahore to Calcutta, a distance of one thousand two hundred miles. At every station they were received with imposing ceremonies, which culminated in a state celebration at Calcutta.

Lord Hardinge is remembered with honour for more peaceful achievements. His predecessors had devoted considerable attention to the restoration of the splendid irrigation canals formed by the Mogul emperors in the north-west. The half million spent on these works had been repaid in increased revenue. In 1836, Colonel Colvin had also formed a plan for the construction of a new canal, to bring the waters of the Ganges to the Dooab, lying between that river and the Jumna. The scheme had so far lain in abeyance, but it was now pushed forward. The result is the magnificent Ganges canal.

Lord Hardinge also abolished Sunday labour in all the government establishments, exerted his influence against sutteeism, female infanticide and slavery in the independent native states; and by the promise of government employment to successful students in government and other colleges gave an immense stimulus to the cause of education. He left India in March, 1848, with the conviction that no war need be feared for at least seven years. How mistaken this expectation was, his successor soon discovered.

Lord Dalhousie, a second Wellesley, may be considered as closing the list of Governors-general which began with Clive, inasmuch as his successor passed into the service of the Crown. And as he was the last, so he ranks with the greatest of the company's rulers. His administration of eight years saw the British dominion extended to the Suleimans and Khyber Pass, at which point it remained till quite recently. His genius for government, force of character and strength of will were truly imperial, and these high powers were supported by the most indefatigable industry. He was the youngest Governor-general India has seen, being only in his thirty-sixth year.

The second Sikh war grew out of very small beginnings. In 1844, Moolrāj had succeeded his father as Governor of Mooltan in the south of the Punjab, where he was practically independent. There had been much dispute between him and the Lahore durbar about a succession-fine, in consequence of which, and of the new measures to be introduced under British influence, he offered to resign. It can scarcely be supposed that he really meant to part with power, but the offer was accepted, and a new governor appointed. With the latter went Mr. Agnew and Lieutenant Anderson to superintend the transfer. They had a guard of three hundred and fifty Sikhs and a few guns. The party arrived at Mooltan, April 18th, 1848. The next day Mr. Agnew conferred with Moolráj, and insisted on his submitting the accounts of the last six years. Moolráj wished to submit only one year's accounts. To do anything more, he said, would dishonour him before the people. Mr. Agnew, however, insisted, and he yielded reluctantly. Undoubtedly it was unwise in the circumstances to deal harshly. On the 20th the two officers went with Moolráj to inspect the different establishments. At the gate of the fort they foolishly consented, at Moolráj's request, to dismiss part of their guard, Moolráj, on some pretext, retaining his. As they were leaving the fort and crossing the drawbridge, Mr. Agnew received a spear-thrust from behind, was thrown from his horse and received three sabre cuts. Lieutenant Anderson was also felled to the ground. Moolráj at once galloped off. The officers were borne to the fortified mosque where they were staying, and Mr. Agnew wrote to Moolráj, appealing to his compassion. He replied that he was in the hands of the soldiers, who would not allow him to help. It was proved that he was in the plot. The English officers could have held their ground till the arrival of help, if the Sikh escort had remained faithful; but these went over bodily to the enemy, leaving the Englishmen at the mercy of the mob. A furious savage, called Goojur Sing, fell on Mr. Agnew, and, after violent abuse, struck off his head at the third stroke. Lieutenant Anderson was hacked to pieces. Their bodies were dragged out amid brutal yells, the heads sent to Moolráj and then tossed to the mob, who blew them to pieces with gunpowder. Moolráj now threw off the mask, and issued a proclamation, calling on the country to rise against the English.

Had Sir Henry Lawrence been still at Lahore, the rising

SIR HERBERT EDWARDES.

would have been dealt with firmly. However great Henry Lawrence's sympathy for the natives, it was not greater than his decision of conduct in emergencies like this. But he had gone to England in ill-health, and his place was filled by Sir F. Currie, a civilian pure and simple. At the first news of the attack the latter ordered out a military force for immediate action; but on hearing of the assassination he recalled the order, and threw the responsibility of action on the Commander-in-chief and the new Governor-general, who both agreed that nothing should be done till the cool season at the end of the year. The insurgents were thus allowed time to prepare, and a local rising grew into a national rebellion.

A revenue officer showed what might have been done by energy and determination. Lieutenant Herbert Edwardes was stationed at Bunnoo across the Indus. Acting on his own responsibility, he crossed the river with one thousand two hundred foot, three hundred and fifty horse, and two guns, and took up a position at Leia. Moolrāj marched at once to engage him. Edwardes discovered that his Sikh soldiers had agreed to sell his head for twelve thousand rupees, and had to recross the Indus. Colonel Cortland, one of the durbar's officers, had some Mohammedan troops who could be trusted to fight the Sikhs, and the two officers strained every nerve to increase their number. Their troops were wild fellows, who cared as little for other people's lives as their own. He also obtained troops from our faithful ally the Nabob of Bhawulpore, to the south-east. When Moolrāj attacked Colonel Cortland, Edwardes marched to his help, fifty miles in twenty-four hours. On June 18th, Colonel Cortland was able to repay the service. Edwardes fought a sharp action with Moolrāj at Kineyree, and the colonel came up in time to turn the scale against the enemy. On July 1st, Lieutenant Edwardes inflicted another severe defeat on Moolrāj at Sudoosain, compelling him to fly from the field and take refuge in his capital. In this engagement the decisive cavalry charge was led by an office clerk called Quin.

These events roused the Resident on his own responsibility to send General Whish with seven thousand men and thirty-four guns to Mooltan; but he accompanied the measure by another which completely neutralized its advantage. He sent Shere Sing, a leading Sikh noble, with a body of Sikhs at the same time. Neither leader nor men could be trusted, and General Whish had enough to do to guard against the treachery of his ally. The battering-train did not arrive till early in September. The place was summoned, not in the name of Dhuleep Sing, but of the Queen of England, the suspicions of the Sikhs being thus confirmed. The fort was exceedingly strong, having walls of solid brick forty feet high, thirty towers, and a ditch twenty feet wide. Moolrāj had in the fort two thousand men, in the town ten thousand, and fifty-two guns. The outworks of the town were taken at considerable loss, and the batteries established, when the siege was brought to an end on September 14th by the defection of Shere Sing and his troops. General Whish retired to a secure position near the town, where for three months he waited for the arrival of reinforcements from Bombay. Shere Sing joined Moolrāj, and issued a proclamation requiring all true Sikhs to join in the extirpation of the Feringees.

The rāja and durbar at Lahore stood aloof from the insurrection, but they were in the power of the English. The whole country beside sympathized with it. Guns buried after Sobraon were dug up and brought into action. The old Khalsa soldiers sharpened their swords for a second struggle. The chiefs all went with the people. Whatever treachery there may have been in the first war, there was none in the second. But the Sikhs of course fought with diminished resources. Their best soldiers had perished. They had been unable to repair their former losses. The present outburst was sudden. It was found that the rānee, Jhindun, whom it had been necessary to remove from Lahore, was engaged in far-reaching intrigues against the English. She had tried to corrupt the troops at Lahore, and written to Cabul, Cashmere, Rājpootana. She was now sent to Benares and placed under surveillance. A paper was received by the English, which alleged as the grounds for the rising, the honour conferred on Golab Sing, a Rājpoot, the banishment of the rānee, the promotion of Mohammedans, and above all the slaughter of the cow which, with Sikhs as with Hindus, is a sacred animal.

The British officers scattered over the Punjab, in the midst of hostile troops and peasantry, had a difficult part to play, and needed all their resources and courage. Such were George Lawrence at Peshawur, Captain Nicholson at Attock, Captain Abbott at Nara, Lieutenants Lumsden, Lake, Taylor, Herbert Edwardes, whose deeds added fresh lustre to the English name. Chutter Sing, father of Shere Sing, commanded in the neighbourhood of Peshawur, and did his utmost to seduce from their allegiance the eight thousand Sikh troops under Major Lawrence. Nothing but the popularity and personal influence of the latter kept them true. What Chutter Sing could not do was done for him by Sultan Mohammed, brother of Dost Mohammed of Cabul, 'the impersonation of Afghan perfidy.'* Mohammed was under special obligation to Henry Lawrence, who had procured him the restoration of his estate at Peshawur, and he repaid the obligation by betraying Henry's brother. Under his instigation the troops attacked the residency on October 24th with shot, shrapnel and shell, and the officers left under an Afghan escort. As soon as Mohammed had them in his power, he sold them to Chutter Sing, who kept them prisoners, but otherwise treated them respectfully. Dost Mohammed also joined the Sikhs in their insurrection, and sent Afghan cavalry to their assistance.

On October 9th Shere Sing marched away from Mooltan to assume the general direction of the movement. His numbers increased at every step. He marched towards the Ravee, to the north-west of Lahore, where he was near the latter place and at the same time joined hands with his father, Chutter Sing. He talked of attacking Lahore, and if he had done so before the brigade arrived from Ferozepore under Colonel Cureton he might have succeeded; but he allowed the opportunity to slip. He then took up a strong position at Ramnuggur on the right bank of the Chenab.

° Marshman.

Lord Gough took the field in November at the head of a most effective army, consisting of four English and eleven native regiments of foot, three English and five native regiments of cavalry, with eight howitzers and ten eighteen-pounders. The irregular horse was commanded by Hearsey, who fought at Seetabaldi thirty-one years before. Lord Gough's wisest course would have been to keep Shere Sing employed till Mooltan was taken, and then fall upon him with all his force. But this did not suit the commander's temperament. His plans failed, and eventually he had to adopt the waiting policy. Then followed two slight actions, and the great battle of Chillianwalla, which, if they were not defeats, were not victories for the British.

Shere Sing lay with fifteen thousand men and twenty-eight guns on the right bank, but had pushed a few troops across the river. Lord Gough's heavy guns had not come up. On November 22nd he easily drove off the forces of the enemy on the left bank, but his light artillery then came under the heavy fire from the other side. In retiring, one gun and two wagons became imbedded in the sand. Instead of destroying them, the English troops wasted time in bringing them off, and gave time to the enemy to push a strong force and guns across the river. The troops were extricated, but with loss. The British infantry made a demonstration to the front and came within range of the cannonade. This was bad enough, but worse followed. Colonel William Havelock, of the 14th Dragoons, requested permission to charge, and it was given. He was supported by Colonel Cureton, at the head of the 5th native cavalry. Men and horses sank in the sand amid a plunging cannonade from the opposite bank. Both commanders were killed, and nothing was gained.

The next move was far more judicious. On December 2nd Sir Joseph Thackwell was sent with a strong brigade to cross the river at Wuzeerabad, twenty-four miles up the river, and march down on the flank of the Sikhs, while Lord Gough attacked in front. Lord Gough, however, was unable to cross for want of boats, and intended sending another division across, under General Godby, by a ford. But this intention was anticipated by the Sikhs. Shere Sing, on hearing of the passage of the river, marched out of his camp to attack General Thackwell's force. At two in the afternoon of the 3rd, the English troops were snatching a hasty meal after forty-eight hours of marching and fasting, when they were startled by a cannonade, to which they quickly replied. After two hours of firing the Sikhs gave up the contest. General Thackwell had full permission to attack, but the hour was late, he remembered Moodkee and Ferozeshoor, and wisely refrained. It would have been well if his commander had always been as prudent. At midnight the Sikhs withdrew from the Chenab altogether, 'leaving not a goat behind,' and fell back to the Jhelum.

On January 13th, 1849, Lord Gough advanced to Chillianwalla, and wisely postponed all action till he knew more of the enemy's position. The next day the army advanced again, and found that the enemy had abandoned their strong camp on the heights of Russool and taken up a position on the plain. Here was the very opportunity the British wanted. But the Sikh position was a strong one, and moreover was covered in front by a dense jungle, which like a curtain effectually concealed their movements. There was every need for caution and thorough reconnoitring. It is said that some stray Sikh shots fell near Lord Gough, and so irritated him that, in spite of all remonstrances, he ordered an immediate attack. But this report can scarcely be correct. Lord Gough's mistake was in advancing, without scouts, to a position in which he was compelled to fight at a disadvantage.

By the time the army was ready it was three o'clock. One would have thought it impossible for the commander at Moodkee and Ferozeshoor to commit the same blunder again. The infantry attacked in two divisions under General Campbell, afterwards Lord Clyde, on the left, and General Gilbert on the right. General Campbell's two brigade-leaders were Hoggan and Pennycuick. The former carried the positions in his front, but the latter was unfortunate. The 24th Foot in its eagerness outstripped the native regiments, arrived at the batteries spent and breathless, and was there torn to pieces by grape in front and musketry from the jungle on the flank. The native regiments, when they came up, were involved in the confusion. The Sikhs fell, sword in hand, upon the discomfited battalions and drove them back. Brigadier Pennycuick's brigade was sent in support, but missed its way in the forest. General Campbell saw the disaster, and, taking Brigadier Hoggan's troops, stopped the Sikh pursuit and captured the guns. Twenty-three officers and four hundred and fifty-nine others were killed or wounded, and among the former were Brigadier Pennycuick and Colonel Brookes of the 24th. The regiment also lost its colours. The left attack was thus eventually successful. General Gilbert's division also succeeded in its object after terrible conflicts. Generals Mountain and Godby led on this side. The 56th native infantry lost its colours, its commander, Major Bamfield, and his son being slain. The 2nd Europeans under Godby had driven the Sikhs before them, and were collecting the wounded, when they were taken in flank by a party of Sikhs, who had crept round unperceived in the jungle. Major Dawes came to their relief with his battery, and saved them from disaster. 'The struggle was terrific; and, to use the language of an eye-witness, it seemed as if the very air teemed with balls and bullets. The Sikhs fought like demons, but the Europeans succeeded in sweeping them from the ground and remained masters of the field.'

The cavalry had been placed in the front line on both wings, to prevent the longer line of the Sikhs outflanking the British. The cavalry division on the right was miserably handled and suffered grievous disaster. The commander, Brigadier Pope, was old and incapable. He advanced without scout or skirmisher into the jungle in front, where his line was broken up by clumps of trees and brushwood. In this state he was attacked by a body of Sikh horse, infuriated with drugs. The commander was wounded, the native regiments gave signs of wavering. Suddenly some one in the ranks of the dragoons called out, 'Threes about,' whereupon the whole body retired. The retreat became a rout. The Sikhs pursued and carried off four of the guns of the horse artillery in the rear. The cavalry on the left were under General Thackwell, and were managed better. A party of Sikh horse having crept round the flank, he sent against it three squadrons of the 5th native cavalry and a squadron of Greys under Captain Unett. The native squadrons broke under a heavy matchlock fire and fled, but the Greys rode through the enemy and then rode back, losing forty-eight in killed and wounded. Night put an end to the conflict.

Want of water and a night of rain compelled Lord Gough to withdraw at once to Chillianwalla, the field being thus abandoned to the enemy, who barbarously plundered the dead and murdered the wounded. They also recovered their guns with the exception of the twelve carried off by the British, besides retaining the four captured. The British loss in killed and wounded was two thousand three hundred and fifty-seven privates and eighty-nine officers. Both sides claimed the victory, and perhaps with equal reason. Certainly the Sikhs had cause for elation. The result of all the three actions was indecisive. There was a great outcry in India and England. The ministry and directors recalled Lord Gough, and sent Sir Charles Napier to replace him. Before he could arrive, Guzerat had restored to the general and his army their lost prestige.

Lord Gough had now to wait for the fall of Mooltan. The Bombay force did not reach Mooltan till Christmas, 1848. General Whish had now seventeen thousand men and sixty-four heavy guns. The siege reopened on December 27th, and was pushed on vigorously. The suburbs were again taken at considerable loss, and the batteries began to play with tremendous effect. For five days and nights an unbroken shower of fire streamed on the town. Two thousand Sikhs made a sally and were driven back by Lieutenant Edwardes and his levies, aided by Sir Henry Lawrence, who was on his way from England to Lahore. On the third day of the bombardment an appalling explosion took place in the town. Four hundred thousand pounds of powder, stored in a mosque, were ignited by a shell, and exploded with a roar like a volcano. Besiegers and besieged stood silent for a few moments and then resumed the contest. On January 2nd the town was stormed and carried. There was not a whole building of importance in it. The streets were littered with dead and dying. In spite of every effort the victorious army was guilty of excesses and plunder. Moolráj now withdrew to the fort, which he held with three thousand men. On the 5th he wished to negotiate, but was told that he must surrender unconditionally. He resolved to fight to the last. The fire, both direct and vertical, which then rained on the citadel for a fortnight, was such as had never before been seen in India. At length, the only whole roof left was one over a bomb-proof gateway. The garrison then insisted that he should lead them in an attempt to cut a path through the besiegers' lines, or surrender. On January 22nd he rode out and gave himself up, 'his soldiers and chiefs prostrating themselves before him in passionate devotion as he passed along.' Lieutenant Edwardes assumed the command at Mooltan, and the army marched to join Lord Gough.

The British and Sikh forces lay watching each other at Chillianwalla and Russool. But on February 6th, Lord Gough heard that the Sikhs had left their strong camp and marched past his right in the direction of Lahore. If Shere Sing had acted with energy, he might have fallen on General Whish's advancing columns and done considerable harm. But, as previously, he failed in decision, and gave the British time to secure all the fords of the Chenab and thus prevent his escape in that direction. He fixed his camp under the walls of Guzerat. The Mooltan force joined on February 20th, and Lord Gough at once moved towards the enemy. He had twenty thousand men and one hundred guns. Shere Sing had fifty thousand men and only sixty guns. The Sikh position was a strong one. On one side was the deep, dry bed of the Dwara; on the other a narrow, deep rivulet. Behind was the town; in front two villages, which were loopholed and strongly occupied.

In the battle of Guzerat, February 22nd, all the old mistakes were avoided. The attack began early in the morning, so that daylight was available for pursuit. The superiority of the English in artillery was thoroughly made use of. The position of the enemy was carefully reconnoitred under the direction of Brigadier Cheape, the artillery commander at Mooltan. It is curious that a suggestion about the use of artillery had come from the enemy. George Lawrence was a prisoner in the enemy's camp. To him the Sikh leaders often expressed their wonder at the British not employing their artillery and sending their infantry to the muzzle of the guns. Major Lawrence was released on parole, and mentioned the remark to his brother Henry at Lahore; Henry Lawrence repeated it to Lord Dalhousie, and Lord Dalhousie to Lord Gough. Guzerat has been called 'the battle of the guns.' The infantry were held in reserve, while the artillery beat down the fire of the Sikhs. After a cannonade of two and a half hours, the infantry advanced to the attack, supported by field-batteries. At the larger village, where General Penny led the attack, a terrible hand-to-hand struggle took place. The Sikhs seized the bayonet with the left hand, while using their sabres with the right. At length they were overpowered. The smaller village was also carried by Colonel Franks and the 10th. The Sikhs then gave way. At a later hour a fine body of Sikh horse and one thousand five hundred Afghan horse under Akram Khan, son of Dost Mohammed, bore down upon the cavalry under General Thackwell. The latter sent against them the 9th Lancers and a regiment of Scinde horse, raised by Sir Charles Napier and commanded by Captain Malcolm. They not only drove back the Afghan and Sikh horse, but converted the flight of the infantry, whom the latter were seeking to cover, into a hopeless rout. Their pursuit continued for fifteen miles. A more complete victory never rewarded British skill and valour. Camp, colours, fifty-three guns fell to the victors. The rest was hopeless flight and pursuit.

The day after the battle General Gilbert was despatched with twelve thousand men of all arms, and gave neither his own men nor the enemy any rest. On March 12th, Shere Sing and Chutter Sing gave their swords into his hands. Thirty-five minor chiefs laid their swords at his feet, and sixteen thousand Sikh soldiers with tears piled their arms. Forty-one guns were also surrendered. No Sikh army was left in the field. The veteran Gilbert, the first rider in India, now flew on the trail of the Afghans, whom he chased into their hills. The sepoys said, 'Those who rode down the hills like lions ran back into them like dogs.' When George Lawrence returned into the Sikh camp after the victory, the Sikhs received him with shouts of admiration at his good faith.

Lord Dalhousie had no orders respecting the disposal of the country, and he decided that a second war so soon after the first left him no choice but to annex. 'On the 29th March, 1849, the young mahārāja (Dhuleep Sing) took his seat for the last time on the throne of Runjeet Sing, and in the presence of Sir Henry Lawrence, the Resident, and Mr. Elliott, the foreign secretary, and the nobles of his court, heard Lord Dalhousie's proclamation read in English, Persian and Hindostanee, and then affixed the initials of his name in English characters to the document which transferred the kingdom of the five rivers to the company, and secured to him an annuity of five lacs of rupees a year. The British colours were then hoisted upon the ramparts, and a royal salute announced the fulfilment of Runjeet Sing's prediction that the Punjab also would " become red." The Koh-i-noor, which he had destined to the great idol of Orissa, was set apart for the crown of England.'* The rebel leaders were punished with confiscation. Moolrāj was tried for the murder of the two officers, and sentenced to death. The sentence was, however, commuted to imprisonment for life, 'in consideration of extenuating circumstances discovered in the course of the inquiry.' He died in a short time. The mahārāja became a sincere Christian, and has long lived in England. The usual honours were bestowed on the Governor-general, Commander-in-chief and others, although some, as usual, were overlooked.

Under the administration of the Lawrences and their coadjutors—men like Montgomery, Nicholson, Edwardes—the Punjab became the model province of India, the border tribes were pacified, Sikh warriors settled down into peaceful cultivators, infanticide, slavery, dacoity and thuggism were suppressed, two thousand two hundred miles of road constructed, and mag-

---

* Marshman.

BRITISH RULE IN THE PUNJAB.

nificent works of irrigation accomplished. The road from Lahore to Peshawur runs two hundred and seventy-five miles, and includes one hundred large bridges and four hundred and fifty smaller ones. Colonel Napier—now Lord Napier of Magdala—superintended these great works. While taxes were lowered and transit duties abolished, the revenue increased. Many of the old soldiers entered the police or took service under the British colours. Sikh soldiers fought as bravely for us in Burmah and China and during the mutiny as they fought against us from Moodkee to Guzerat.

LUCKNOW.

CHAPTER XIII.

LORD DALHOUSIE (CONTINUED) AND LORD CANNING—ANNEXATIONS —SECOND BURMESE WAR—INTERNAL IMPROVEMENTS—SEPOY MUTINY. 1848–1862.

LORD Dalhousie's annexation policy has been severely condemned. It is asserted by some that one of the causes of the mutiny was the distrust and alarm inspired by his annexations. At present the tide of feeling runs against further additions to British territory. But we hope it will never be laid down, as a principle, that under no circumstances will England add to its imperial responsibilities. The gain to the districts in India brought under British rule is immense. The question has excited great controversy among Indian politicians. A great party, comprising eminent names—like Henry Lawrence, Outram, Sleeman, Low, Clerk, Malcolm and many others as great, —has always advocated the cause of the native princes and the wisdom of conserving their position by all legitimate means. Another great party, looking chiefly at the interest of the millions, has advocated the extension of direct British rule, when this can be done without injustice. It is evident that no single principle can be laid down governing all cases. Each case must be judged by itself. It makes considerable difference whether the dynasty in question owes its origin to British power or not. Much also depends on the terms of existing treaties. A chief element in the question is that of the right of adoption. Hindu law recognizes the right of princes, in default of natural heirs, to adopt a successor. But it is also certain that in the case of dependent states the consent of the suzerain was necessary to render the adoption valid. Much turns on this point in the cases in dispute in India.

Lord Dalhousie was called on to decide the Sattara case soon after his arrival, the rāja dying in April, 1848. It will be

SIR JAMES OUTRAM.

remembered that, on the peshwa's overthrow in 1817, the British, instead of annexing all the territory, as they might have done, set up the representative of the name of Sivaji. The last rāja, who had no heir, had often asked permission to adopt, but was refused, for what reasons we know not. A few hours before his death he adopted a boy, whom he had not known before. The question was, whether in these circumstances the boy should be acknowledged as sovereign. As to the act of adoption carrying with it the right to personal property, there was no question. The matter was long and earnestly debated. The Governor-general collected opinions and information from all quarters, and at last decided against the recognition. His action was approved by the directors, who said : 'By the general law and custom of India, a dependent principality like that of Sattara cannot pass to an adopted heir without the consent of the paramount power; we are under no pledge, direct or constructive, to give such consent; and the general interests committed to our charge are best consulted by withholding it.' The Sattara State long ago sank into insignificance.

The case of Nagpore was still clearer. Appa Sāhib forfeited the throne twice over, in 1817 and 1818. Native rule was then continued by the favour of the British. The rāja, who died in December, 1853, a low debauchee, left no heir. Though often importuned to adopt, he always refused. His widow also declined to adopt. On every ground of right and expediency, therefore, Lord Dalhousie decided to annex. Colonel Low, one of his council, advocated an opposite course. Mr. Halliday, another member of council, said that on the question of right there could be no doubt, and added : 'Here is a territory actually without a claimant, a territory full of available resources of a kind important to the government of India, and still more so to the people of England ; a territory whose teeming population is avowedly hoping, praying, expecting to be taken under our government; and at such a juncture, we are to be deaf to their call, and leave the widows and relatives and principal men to settle this affair; or still more, to invite and solicit them to take some spoilt boy from a nursery, or some obscure and uneducated youth from a village, and place again in such hands the rod of iron with which the late rāja so scourged the nationality out of his unfortunate subjects, that they are now impatient for the rule of the stranger rather than suffer such another tyranny.'

Jhansi was on the same footing as Sattara in all respects. Even Colonel Low concurred in this annexation, saying: 'The native rulers of Jhansi were never sovereigns; they were only subjects of a sovereign, first of the peshwa, and latterly of the company. . . . I consider that the government of India has now a full right, if it chooses to exercise that right, to annex the lands of Jhansi to the British dominions.' In all these transactions Lord Dalhousie kept chiefly in view the welfare of the people, and he had the full concurrence of the directors.

The Governor-general had a difficult question to arrange with the Nizam of Hyderabad. The arrears of the military contingent, which the nizam was bound, not indeed by treaty but morally, to support, had reached a large sum. After years of remonstrance, Lord Dalhousie's patience was worn out, and in 1853 he proposed that the nizam should cede territory sufficient for the expenses of the force, but at the same time intimated that, as the chief use of the contingent was to watch the hordes of troops the nizam kept in pay, the right method of lessening the expense was to dismiss some of the latter. The proposal was of course equivalent to a command. The nizam was exceedingly unwilling to consent, saying that he never parted with territory or soldiers; but at last under private influence yielded. The lands ceded were those which the British had once given to the nizam, and, as the debt was reduced and the revenue from the ceded districts improved, they were restored with the exception of the rich cotton-lands of Berar.

The ex-peshwa, Baji Rao, died at Bithoor, near Cawnpore, in January, 1853, at the age of seventy-seven. Under the treaty conceded by Sir John Malcolm he had drawn as pension no less a sum than £2,500,000. Great efforts were made both in India and England to obtain the continuance of the pension, or a part of it, to his adopted son, Nāna Sāhib, but the claim was instantly rejected. It was distinctly stated and understood at the time of the treaty that the pension was for life only. On no other condition would Lord Hastings have consented to so large a grant. The refusal was the cause of Nāna Sāhib's enmity.

Some writers have implied that Lord Dalhousie delighted in war and annexation, but there can be no doubt that he did his utmost to avoid the Burmese war of 1852. There is nothing in the war worthy of detailed notice. It arose out of petty annoyances to British Residents at Ava, and oppression and outrage practised on British merchants at Rangoon. Commodore Lambert was despatched to Rangoon in the *Fox* to investigate and, if necessary, to require compensation. When the governor refused to hold communication with him, he despatched the letter entrusted to him for the purpose to the king at Ava. A new governor was sent down, who trod in the steps of the first. A mission which the commodore sent was kept waiting, exposed to the heat of the sun and the jeers of a mob, under the pretext that the governor was asleep, whereas the dignitary in question was seated at a window enjoying the sport. Commodore Lambert now demanded an apology in addition to compensation. When this was refused, he seized a ship belonging to the king, and returned to Calcutta. The governor sent after him his own version of the proceedings. The only answer was a repetition of the commodore's demands.

In January, 1852, the Governor-general hastened down from the north-west to take charge of the business. He wrote to the king, and gave him till April 1st to make reparation, meanwhile pushing forward preparations with the utmost energy. In two months all was ready. The experience of the war of 1826 was not forgotten. Wooden huts were prepared to house the troops at Rangoon. The immense development of steam-marine greatly facilitated operations, the Irrawaddy rendering even the capital open to our vessels. When a Bengal regiment objected, as before, to go by sea, Lord Dalhousie replaced it by a regiment of Sikhs. The united Bengal and Madras force, five thousand eight hundred strong, under General Godwin, who had served in the former war, appeared before Rangoon on April 11th. On the 14th the great pagoda was stormed, and carried after an obstinate defence. During the following months there was the usual scattered stockade-fighting, but nothing occurred of a serious nature. Our war-steamers commanded the river. The population of Rangoon did not desert the place as formerly, but lived on the most friendly terms with the British. The whole province of Pegu, of which Rangoon was the capital, was most anxious for incorporation with the British territories. Since its conquest by the Burmese three-quarters of a century before, it had suffered endless oppression. In 1826 the people of Pegu had wished for annexation, and, after the English left, had been frightfully punished for their wish.

When Lord Dalhousie arrived at Rangoon in September, he discouraged an advance upon Ava, as this would open up larger questions; but he insisted on the cession of Pegu. As the royal envoys would not agree, the province was annexed by proclamation without treaty. Pegu has flourished wonderfully under British rule. The population of Rangoon has grown from a few thousands in 1852 to sixty-six thousand. The town is now as healthy as formerly it was unhealthy. The people are among the most contented and industrious under the British sceptre. In 1857 the province was left without European troops, who were all sent to assist in quelling the mutiny. The exports of rice from British Burmah reach an enormous amount.

The most considerable of Lord Dalhousie's annexations, and the one which has made most noise, was that of Oude in 1855. The misgovernment of the king was a perennial subject of dispute between Calcutta and Lucknow. Every Governor-general in turn had remonstrated and threatened. In 1847 Lord Hardinge visited Lucknow, and gave the king two years of grace to carry out reforms. In 1851 Colonel Sleeman, the Resident, a constant friend of native princes, presented an exhaustive report on the condition of the country, which was as bad as it could be. The king was sunk in sloth, folly and indulgence. His chief singer was practically king. Rapacious revenue-farmers were desolating whole districts. An army of seventy thousand men did whatever it pleased. The country swarmed with petty chiefs, who from their forts tyrannized at will over the people.

Colonel Sleeman, after referring to his well-known sympathy with native princes, said, 'he did not think that with a due regard to its own character, as the paramount power in India, and to the particular obligations by which it was bound by solemn treaties to the suffering people of the distracted country, the government could any longer forbear to take over the administration.' General Outram, who was appointed Resident in 1854, and who belonged to the same school as Colonel Sleeman, endorsed everything that the latter said. Lord Dalhousie reviewed the whole question, and recommended that, retaining the king as nominal sovereign, the British should assume the entire management of the country. The four members of council, one of whom was General Low, all concurred; two of them going farther than the Governor-general, and proposing the abolition of the sovereignty and the annexation of the country. The latter was the course adopted by the home authorities. General Outram carried out the measure. No difficulty was experienced. The king, refusing to sign a treaty of cession, was set aside with a pension of fifteen lacs, and the country annexed by proclamation.

Lord Dalhousie's administrative reforms were designed on the largest scale and carried out with the greatest boldness. The Public Works Department was his creation. The average amount spent annually in the previous seventeen years on public works was seventeen lacs. During Lord Dalhousie's last year of office it reached three hundred lacs. India is now blessed with a system of roads unsurpassed in the world. The case of the Punjab, already mentioned, may be taken as a specimen of all the districts under direct British control. One of the most difficult works of this class was the road connecting Bengal with Pegu. We have already seen how in the first Burmese war British troops attempted in vain to penetrate by this route. A road was now cut from Dacca to Aracan at great cost of life and money. The further difficulties of the extension to Pegu were even greater—lofty mountains, dense jungles, scarcity of water, fever. Lieutenant Furlong, however, organized a band of Burmese labourers and carried out the work in two years. A similar work is the road to Simla and beyond to the Vale of Chini, in the very heart of the mighty Himālayas, and opposite the sacred peak of Kailāsa, which towers twenty-one thousand feet above the level of the sea. The Ganges canal was completed during Lord Dalhousie's reign, under Colonel Cautley's superintendence. 'In its class and character, it stands among the noblest efforts of civilized nations. It nearly equals the aggregate length of all the lines of the four greatest canals in France, and its length is five times greater than that of all the main lines in Lombardy.'

In these and other tasks the Governor-general found a zealous helper in Mr. Thomason, Lieutenant-governor of Agra, one of the most able and philanthropic of the many good rulers India has had.

The question of Indian railways had been long in debate. Happily, debate now ended and action began. The principle adopted was that of a state-guarantee and state-control. Indian railways are now advancing towards independence and self-support. The advantages to the country in providing means of communication and to the government in the transport of troops are obvious. Great praise is due to Sir Macdonald Stephenson and Sir James Hogg in connection with the railways. In Sir William O'Shaughnessy the Governor-general found a zealous and able agent in extending telegraphic communication throughout India. Lord Dalhousie also gave India a uniform postage of half-an-anna=three farthings, besides reducing the postage to Europe. He said, 'The Scotch recruit at Peshawur might write to his mother at John o' Groat's house for sixpence.' He was equally zealous in the service of education, English, vernacular, female. During his administration Sir Charles Wood's despatch of 1854, which has been called 'the intellectual charter of India,' sketched the lines on which the future educational policy of the country was to proceed. 'It embraced vernacular schools throughout the districts; government colleges of a higher character, a University at each Presidency, to which all educational establishments, supported by the state, by societies, or by individuals, might be affiliated; and above all, the great measure of grants-in-aid to all schools, without reference to caste or creed.' An Education Department was organized to work out this scheme.

No administration has left a deeper mark on India than Lord Dalhousie's. His industry was untiring. He traversed and re-traversed the several provinces, seeing everything for himself. At Penang he found a structure like a gibbet within the jail, and was told that this was the gallows. 'He ordered it immediately to be placed without, with the facetious remark that if its position came to be known in England, he should be liable to an impeachment for having permitted an infringement of the most ancient and indefeasible right of an Englishman—to be hung in public.'

Lord Dalhousie quitted Calcutta for England in March, 1856. The demonstration of the natives on his departure resembled that on Lord Wellesley's departure in 1805. Eight years of toil like his in a tropical climate had fatally undermined his constitution, and he died in less than five years after his retirement. He was still comparatively young.

Lord Canning was a son of the great Canning, once President of the Board of Control. One of his first acts was to direct the formation of a Penal Code applicable to Europeans and natives alike. It was completed in 1861. He was obliged in 1856 to declare war against Persia on account of the disrespect shown to the British representative at the capital and the seizure of Herat. The expedition was commanded by General Outram, and soon brought the Persians to terms. In 1857, a treaty of alliance was concluded through Sir John Lawrence with Dost Mohammed at Cabul, an old quarrel, in which we had first done and then suffered wrong, being thus healed.

But the great event which overshadowed all others, and which with its issues occupied the rest of Lord Canning's administration was the sepoy mutiny of 1857, the centenary of Plassey. It might seem incredible that the main division of the army, by whose aid the British empire in India had been built up, and whose heroism we have again and again recorded, should suddenly turn round, massacre its own officers and deliberately attempt to exterminate the English from the soil; but such was the fact. There has been endless speculation as to the causes and character of the revolt, but everything points to the conclusion that in its origin it was purely military, and remained such for the most part to the end. The people took no part in the struggle between the sepoys and their late masters. There was no disturbance where sepoys did not lead the way. No doubt the rising was fomented and employed by others, by the Mohammedan princes at Delhi, by Nāna Sāhib of Bithoor, by princes like those of Oude whom we had dispossessed, by chiefs with whose exactions we had interfered. The sepoys became tools in their hands. But in the beginning the mutiny was simply a military rising, which weakness and mismanagement allowed to assume the proportions it did. Let it be remembered that the mutiny was confined to the Bengal army. It might, and if the fall of Delhi had been postponed much longer probably would, have extended to the Bombay and Madras armies, but it did not. The other two armies remained staunch, while the Bengal army failed us almost without exception. The Bengal army had always been far more difficult to manage than the other two. There had been partial risings in the Burmese war, the Scinde war, and on other occasions. The Bengal sepoys objected to cross the 'black water' to Rangoon, maintaining that they were only enlisted for service in Hindostan. Lord Canning had issued an order to the effect that all future enlistments must be for service anywhere. A report got abroad that the grease for the new Enfield rifles was made up of pig and cow fat, and was intended as a means of breaking down the religion of the Mohammedan and Hindu sepoys. No explanations could persuade the sepoys to the contrary. The rumour was no doubt secretly encouraged by agents of outsiders for their own purposes. One rumour led to others. 'The wells had been defiled.' Pure water is essential to the preservation of caste. Caste people cannot use the same wells or vessels as casteless people. 'Bone dust had been mixed in the flour. Animal fat had been mixed with the *ghee*, or butter.' *Chuppatties*, thin cakes, were circulated all over India. To this day their meaning has never been discovered. That they were a sort of signal, like the fiery cross, is certain; but there our knowledge ends. From city to city, from regiment to regiment, they flew, no one knew whence or how. From Peshawur to Calcutta barracks were burnt, while the hands that kindled the fires were never discovered. Nightly meetings of sepoys took place. The simultaneousness of these symptoms indicated a common purpose. Among Hindus example and custom are all-powerful. Regiments mutinied wholesale for no more definite reason than that others did. It was fortunate for us that no leader of genius appeared to give unity and aim to the efforts of a great army drilled to the highest point of perfection and well supplied with arms and arsenals. On the other hand, no crisis of English history ever produced a larger number of great men capable of dealing with the emergency. Henry Lawrence, John Lawrence, John Nicholson, Neville Chamberlain, Henry Havelock, James Outram, Neill, Colin Campbell, Hope Grant, Inglis, Franks, Hugh Rose, all surrounded by trusty subalterns, would have quelled half-a-dozen mutinies. We wonder at first how an army without leader or unity could do the mischief and make the resistance the sepoy army did. But we must remember that it was scattered over the breadth of half a continent, that each regiment mutinied where it stood, and that a body of disciplined soldiers holds a civil community at its mercy. Moreover, while the sepoys fought like lions behind entrenchments, they fled at once in the open.

Of all the absurd reasons alleged for the mutiny the most absurd is the supposed alarm caused by missionary operations. Every one who knows anything of the sepoys, of the Indian government and of missionaries, knows that the army was peculiarly secluded from missionary influence, that the Indian government had been studiously neutral on matters of religion and respectful to Hindu rites and that, as matter of fact, the amount of influence exerted by missionary operations on the army was infinitesimal. The vengeance of the sepoys was utterly indiscriminate. It was not particularly directed to Christian teachers and buildings. Its chief victims were the officers and their families. The blow was struck at the government. Far more real and potent circumstances, aggravating the mischief, can be indicated. The European army, in spite of Dalhousie's strong protest, had been reduced, under the stress of the Crimean war, below the point of safety. The proportion of European to sepoy, instead of being one to three, was one to six. Between Calcutta and Agra, a distance of eight hundred miles and among a population of fifty millions, there were only three white regiments. With only a hundred miles of railway open from Calcutta, it was months before reinforcements could arrive in strength sufficient to make any impression; and during those months the sepoys were masters of the field, and free to do whatever the most infamous treachery and cruelty could suggest. Again, the Bengal army was permeated by caste, which made it feel and act as a single unit. Two-thirds of its number, *i.e.*, forty thousand, came from the single province of Oude, the most recently annexed territory, and teeming, from long misrule, with dangerous elements. Again, there was most culpable indecision and weakness at critical points like Meerut and Dinapore, where old and incapable commanders, with ample European force at command, allowed mutinous regiments to march off and set the country in a blaze. It is also said that general discipline had become lax, and that, while the best officers were drafted off to staff appointments and civil employ, the officers with the colours were mostly young men, unacquainted with the native officers and men, and therefore having little influence over them.

The first great outbreak was at Meerut, one of the chief military centres of the north-west, on Sunday, May 10th. On the previous day some troopers of the 3rd Cavalry had been sentenced to imprisonment for refusing the new cartridges. While the English were at church at evening service the two sepoy foot regiments and the cavalry regiment rose in mutiny. Colonel Finnis and other officers, going to ascertain the meaning of the tumult, were shot down. Here, as everywhere, the first rush of the mutineers was to the prison, to release the prisoners and let loose the devilry of a district on the few Europeans. The horrors of that sultry May night are not to be described,—bungalows sacked and burnt, their inmates consumed in the flames, shot or stabbed, the exulting yells of triumphant ruffianism. All this time General Hewitt, with a splendid force on the spot of two thousand Europeans who were mad with rage, did nothing and would allow no one else to do anything. The mutineers, after plundering, destroying and slaying without let or hindrance, got off safely to Delhi forty miles away, to instigate and help in worse tragedies there. The General would not move a step till prevention and remedy were alike past.

The next morning some of the 3rd Cavalry brought the news of the night's triumph to Delhi. Here the only force was sepoy. The three native regiments at first made a show of loyalty, but soon revolted almost to a man. Before night not an Englishman was left in the city. The commissioner, Simon Fraser, the commandant of the palace, Captain Douglas, were slain in the palace, the chaplain and his daughter in the presence of the Mogul emperor. Every European within the walls was hunted to death. A small party of officers and others, who had gathered at the Flagstaff Tower in the cantonment, were at last obliged to hurry away in a flight, the sufferings and perils of which were worse than death,—men, women, and children—begirt by enemies, hungry, stripped by robbers. A few soon reached shelter at Meerut or elsewhere, others perished by the way, many lurked or wandered in hut or jungle, amid raging heats, days and weeks before reaching a place of safety. The incident of the Delhi arsenal should not be omitted. The first effort of the rebels was to secure this great magazine. Three English lieutenants and six ordnance conductors alone held it for a time. As the assailants swarmed up the walls, they were swept away by volleys of grape. But two of the little garrison were wounded, and the ammunition which they had hurriedly prepared was running low. Lieutenant Willoughby gave the word to fire a train previously laid, and a part, but only too small a part, of the magazine blew up. The defenders with one exception got safely away, though in one or two cases it was only to die of their injuries.

Would that a Gillespie, instead of a Hewitt, had commanded at Meerut! The imperial city of the north-west, with all its fortifications and military stores, fell into rebel hands, without a finger being lifted to prevent. From deference to the feelings of the Mogul sovereign a British force had not been stationed at Delhi, with the express understanding that a strong force should be kept at Meerut within striking distance. The force was there, but no hand to wield it. Delhi became at once the rendezvous for mutinous regiments from all quarters. After murdering every European within reach, they turned their faces towards the old Mogul capital.

There is good reason to think that the rising at Meerut was premature, and that it frustrated the main part of the conspirators' design, which was to effect a simultaneous and universal rising, perhaps on the centenary day of Plassey, June 23rd. If this plan could have been carried out, it is hard to see what could have prevented the extermination of the English throughout Hindostan.

Whatever failure there was elsewhere, the stern, strong man who ruled the Punjab, John Lawrence, rose to the full height of the occasion. When news of Meerut and Delhi reached Lahore on the 12th, he was at Rawul Pindi, but his trusty lieutenants, Montgomery and Macleod, acted promptly. A ball fixed for that night was held as if nothing were the matter, but a full parade was ordered for next morning on the plain of Mcean Meer. Brigadier Corbett so manœuvred the troops as to bring the four sepoy regiments face to face with four hundred European foot and two hundred artillerymen with loaded guns. They were then ordered to pile arms. Slowly, unwillingly, like men balked of their prey, they obeyed. The rising fixed for the 15th was thus anticipated and Lahore saved. There was like disarming at Peshawur, where Cotton, Chamberlain, Nicholson and Edwardes commanded. Many officers of the disarmed troops protested against the measure which saved their lives. All through the mutiny nothing is more wonderful than the blind confidence of officers in men. With mutiny on every hand, they never doubted the loyalty of their own men, and often paid the penalty with their lives. Of the Punjab sepoy regiments which broke out into open revolt not many succeeded in reaching Delhi. The 55th was pursued by Nicholson, many cut up, others brought

LORD LAWRENCE.

back as prisoners, and the rest perished, or were sold as slaves by the wild hillmen. The Sikhs were loyal almost without exception, and supplied regiments which rendered splendid service. All through those critical months Lawrence's one cry was, ' On to Delhi!' He kept not a single man who could be spared. Supplies were forwarded without stint. When the last reinforcement had been sent, he felt that he could do no more without incurring worse risk at home. It has been truly said : ' To John Lawrence, by the concurrent voice of Wilson's officers, of Wilson himself, of the Governor-general, of the Court of Directors, of every Englishman almost in Upper India, was assigned the place of honour as "Saviour of India," as the main author of Wilson's triumph, as the man to whom " more than to any other, more than to thousands of others, was owing the conquest of Delhi and the safety of the whole north-west." ' *

No time was lost in assembling a force at Umballa for the siege of Delhi, and toward the close of the month the army set out. On the death, from cholera, of the Commander-in-chief, General Anson, at Karnaul, on May 27th, Sir Henry Barnard assumed the command. On June 8th, after a sharply contested action with the rebels at Badlie Serai, British troops again occupied the cantonments on the Ridge from which less than a month before a few Europeans had fled for their lives. But four thousand British troops with no battering-train could effect nothing against a city seven miles round, defended by ramparts of our own construction, swarming with thousands of our own trained sepoys, and free to draw supplies from every side. For three months the little handful of British troops was more besieged than besieging. How during that time, under incessant attacks by day and night and the blinding heat and then floods of rain, it held its grip on that fateful Ridge is far more wonderful even than the heroic daring of the final capture. The Flagstaff Tower, Hindu Rao's house, Metcalfe's house, Ludlow Castle, the Subzie Mundie— scenes of many a fierce fight, where many brave Englishmen met their death—are henceforth sacred spots in British history.

---

* Capt. Trotter, *History of British India*, ii., p. 229.

The arrival of new sepoy regiments in the city, fresh from scenes of massacre, was announced by bands playing well known English tunes, and signalized by fresh assaults on the British position. Each new body came to the attack vaunting that it would succeed where its predecessors had failed, and returned to encounter the jeers of its comrades. The enemy could better afford to lose a score of soldiers than the British one, and yet every one of the numberless attacks told on the strength of the small force. Often, reinforcements went into action the moment they arrived in camp. Chamberlain, Hodson, Olpherts, Daly, Showers, Coke, Hope Grant, Tombs were to the front whenever fighting was going on. Many eager spirits in the camp were ardent for an attempt at surprise; but responsible leaders, who knew that repulse meant destruction, hesitated, and it never took place. On July 14th, the brave and gentle Barnard died. First Reid, then Chamberlain, finally Brigadier Wilson took his place. Nicholson arrived in camp on August 7th, with the last reinforcements from the Punjab, bringing up the force to eight thousand men, of whom about half were British.

At the beginning of September the siege-train was approaching from Ferozepore, and the enemy sent out seven thousand men with eighteen guns to intercept it. At the head of two thousand three hundred men with sixteen guns Nicholson started in pursuit. After a fatiguing march over swamps and cross-roads he overtook the rebels at Nujjafghur, and, charging across a swamp, where the water rose waist-high, routed them at every point, capturing guns and stores. In an attack in the dark on a village where a body of rebels stood at bay, without means of escape, Lieutenant Lumsden, a noble officer, was slain. After forty hours of marching and fighting, with little food or rest, Nicholson's force returned to camp.

On September 6th, the siege-train arrived, and next day the real siege began, under Colonel Baird Smith as chief engineer. Four batteries, containing fifty heavy guns and mortars, played day and night on the walls. On the 13th, two breaches were reported practicable, and the assault was fixed for next day. General Wilson could only reckon on six thousand men for the attack. Three thousand lay sick and wounded. To guard his camp from surprise he had but a few hundred horse, some scores of convalescents, and a troop or two of horse artillery. But nothing was to be gained by further delay. All India and England were listening for the fall of Delhi. The first column, one thousand strong, under General Nicholson, was to storm the main breach and the Cashmere Bastion ; the second, eight hundred and fifty strong, under Brigadier Jones, the Water Bastion ; the third, nine hundred and fifty strong, under Colonel Campbell, to enter by the Cashmere Gate, which had to be blown open ; a fourth, under Major Reid, to penetrate by the Lahore Gate ; a reserve of one thousand, under Brigadier Longfield, to lend support where necessary; while Hope Grant with his cavalry and horse-artillery checked any sorties and flank attacks by the enemy. At daylight Nicholson gave the word, and the two first columns sprang forward through a storm of fire, down the ditch, up the scaling-ladders, to breach and bastion. The blowing in of the Cashmere Gate was a brave deed. The little band of sappers rushed across a half-broken drawbridge amid a stream of fire. Sergeant Carmichael and a native corporal fell dead as they laid the bags of powder. Lieutenant Home was struck, though not disabled. Lieutenant Salkeld was struck twice while applying the match, and Corporal Burgess finished his work at the cost of his life. Seeing him fall, Sergeant Smith leaped forward, but at the moment there was a flash, a report, and he had just time to jump into the ditch when the gate fell in with a crash. Home's bugler sounded the advance, and Colonel Campbell's column rushed in over the ruins. The fourth attack failed from a variety of mishaps, and had to be withdrawn. On that day of trial Hope Grant's task was not the lightest. His force had to remain for hours quiescent under a heavy fire, guarding the flank and rear of the assailants. When the ramparts were gained, the real fighting began. On the first day only a fringe of the city was taken, and it took six days' conflict, street by street and building by building, before Delhi was in British possession. The loss on the first day in killed alone was eight officers and two hundred and eighty privates, and above all, the great Nicholson was mortally wounded. He was only thirty-four, the idol of English and native troops alike. He lived nine days, long enough to know that Delhi was taken.

The losses of the British were great. Some of the regiments—the 60th Rifles, Ghoorkas, Punjab Guides—lost half their strength. The engineers and artillery suffered heavily. The total of killed and wounded through the siege was three thousand eight hundred and thirty-seven. The victorious troops had all been gathered in the north-west. Not a soldier had arrived from Bengal. The greatness of the victory is to be measured, not simply by the material losses inflicted on the enemy, but by the moral impression made. The English in India breathed freely again. Native confidence was restored. The neck of the mutiny was broken. The victory came not a moment too soon. Had it been delayed much longer, the Bombay and Madras armies could hardly have been kept faithful, all India would have been dragged into the vortex, and this brief history would probably never have been written, as the writer was then resident in South India. Over the imprisonment and transportation to Rangoon of the king, an old man of eighty-four, and the shooting of two of his sons by Hodson, we need not linger.

We may here give a few specimens of the scenes which were enacted in those sad months of May and June over the broad spaces of Northern India. On Sunday, May 31st, at Bareilly, after the sepoys had killed several of the unsuspecting officers, Bahadoor Khan, a pensioner of the British, hung several of the English gentlemen who fell into his hands. On the same day at Shahjehanpore the 28th regiment surrounded the church in which the English were worshipping, and slaughtered all with the exception of a few, who perished in their flight at the hands of another regiment. At Jhansi in Central India, the rānee, widow of the late king, led the mutiny in revenge for the annexation of the territory. On June 5th the sepoys swore to protect their officers and then shot down several.' The rest of the officers took refuge in the fort, where seventy-three Europeans were assembled. After a siege of several days they were compelled by hunger, wounds, and despair of relief to surrender under a promise of safe conduct from rānee and sepoys. No sooner had they come forth" than they were tied together, the men in one row, women and children in another, and ruthlessly done to death by bullet, sword, and bayonet. At Allahabad, on June 6th, the 6th regiment was drawn up to hear read a letter of thanks from Lord Canning for their zeal in offering to march against Delhi. English and native officers shook hands. That same night as the officers were seated at mess a bugle was heard. Sallying out to learn the cause, they were nearly all shot or cut down by the same sepoys who, a few hours before, had cheered the Governor-general's letter. On June 4th a party of about one hundred and thirty men, women and children started from Futtehghur down the Ganges. Nearing Bithoor, they never dreamt of danger from the Nāna, the mild Mahratta who had always been on such friendly terms with the English. The wretch had them taken out of the boats and butchered to the last one. Here and there friendly chiefs and villagers were found who gave shelter to hunted fugitives, but many of the latter died of exposure and sunstroke or were cut off in their weary flight. We ought not to forget such fidelity as that of the three hundred native troops who remained with the English through the siege of Lucknow; the loyalty of the Mahārāja Scindia, who stood firm when his troops joined the mutiny; of the Rājas of Pattiāla and Jheend, and the help of Jung Bahadoor of Nepaul. These are bright rifts in the black expanse of perfidy.

There were noble examples of individual gallantry. On June 22nd at Mynpoorie, between Agra and Futtehghur, young Lieutenant de Kantzow, at the head of a few ill-armed police, prevented three hundred mutinous sepoys from plundering the treasury, and persuaded them to retire to Delhi without staining their hands with murder.

At Arrah, in Behar, a railway engineer, called Boyle, had fortified a dwelling-house in his grounds, and here for seven days, eighteen Europeans and fifty Sikhs held their ground against the attacks of four thousand rebels. A relieving force had been beaten back; but the gallant band, living on grain, and digging for water in the floor, stood fast till Colonel Vincent Eyre arrived with effectual relief.

But the most touching and tragical story of all is that of Cawnpore. Here in May were three infantry sepoy regiments and one cavalry. The only European force which their commander, Sir Hugh Wheeler, had at first, consisted of sixty artillerymen with six guns. Sir Henry Lawrence sent eighty men of the 32nd Foot, who could be ill spared from Lucknow, and from Calcutta came fifty men of the 84th Foot, and fifteen of the Madras Fusiliers,—who all came, not to victory, but death. The European community at such a central station as Cawnpore was a large one, including a large number of women and children. General Wheeler began to form and provision a hasty entrenchment. It was a poor affair,—standing on a broad plain, its only rampart a low breastwork, the only shelter two large hospitals and a few smaller buildings. One of the hospitals was straw-thatched. The whole was commanded by adjacent buildings. Probably this was the best preparation the time and place allowed. Here a thousand Europeans had to flee for shelter, when the sepoys rose on June 5th. After plundering the treasury and releasing the prisoners, the regiments set off for Delhi. Hitherto General Wheeler and the English had no suspicion of the Nāna at Bithoor, fifteen miles away. They believed implicitly his assurances of protection. Now he was to reveal his true character. He persuaded the sepoys to return to Cawnpore, and finish the Feringees before marching to Delhi; and on June 6th the whole host sat down before the weak entrenchments. Who can conceive the sufferings of the next three weeks, from the fire of the enemy, from a June sun on that bare plain, from hunger and thirst and exposure? Fourteen heavy guns kept up the bombardment. The English had but eight field-pieces, which stood in the open without a parapet for the gunners. Only by a miracle of coolness, skill, and endurance could such a position be held such a time against such odds. The fire told fearfully on the defenders. On June 13th the straw thatch of the hospital was fired, and, an attack being made at the same time, more than forty sick and wounded perished before help could be given. Captain Moore, of the 32nd, was the guiding spirit of the defence. With his arm in a sling he went about cheering the defenders. He and his brave marksmen would occupy an unfinished barrack outside the breastwork and deal out death to the assailants, on two occasions spiking the guns. Yet the cowardly sepoys never dared to approach the wall, which might have been cleared at a running leap. Once, on June 21st, they swore a great oath on the waters of the neighbouring Ganges, to destroy the English at a stroke, and came on from every side. Some rolled huge cotton bales before them as a shelter; but, when it came to the last rush, the cool, steady fire of the British put them to flight. Women took turns at night-watch with the men. The barracks were riddled and ready to fall; most of the guns rendered useless; rations reduced, medicines destroyed. Half of those who had entered the entrenchment three weeks before were dead. Then it was that the Nāna and his like-minded agent, Azimoollah Khan, swore by all that was sacred to furnish the garrison with boats and food for a passage to Allahabad. However excusable in the circumstances, the trust of the English, after their recent experience, was strange. The surrender on a Mahratta's * oath was General Wheeler's greatest mistake. On the 27th, four hundred and fifty men, women and children marched out to the boats; but they had no sooner embarked than a musketry fire was opened on them, the boats took fire, numbers were shot or drowned, the remaining men were dragged ashore and slain, and the women and children taken and shut up in a small building for another day.

One boat ran the gauntlet of the fire from both banks for two days, but then grounded on a sandbank near Futtehpore. A galling fire was rained upon it by sepoys on the bank. Lieutenant Delafosse and thirteen others plunged into the water and charged the pursuers, but in the eagerness of the chase were cut off from the boat by swarms of enemies. Thirteen of the number got safe into a small temple. Even there the enemy dared not assail

---

° The crafty Azimoollah Khan, as his name indicates, was a Mohammedan.

them, but was obliged to smoke them out. With a desperate rush, seven succeeded in reaching the water. Two of these were shot, a third came too near the shore and was slain; the other four— Lieutenants Delafosse and Mowbray Thompson, Private Murphy, and Gunner Sullivan—swam weary miles till a friendly Oude chief took them in, fed, clothed and ministered to them, and at last delivered them into the hands of Havelock's advancing force. They were the only survivors of the whole Cawnpore force.

The stranded boat was seized and taken back to Cawnpore, where it arrived four days after the fatal start. The men in it, including the aged Wheeler, who was mortally wounded, were allowed a moment's respite for prayer, and then shot in the miscreant Nāna's presence. One poor lady, who could not be torn from her husband's embrace, was shot with him. The other women and children were added to those already in captivity. Their doom was approaching swiftly. About forty-seven betrayed captives from Futtehghur had been added to the number. On July 15th Havelock had forced the bridge across the Pandu stream, in the neighbourhood of Cawnpore. That night the Nāna, determined that none of his victims should escape his vengeance, ordered all the prisoners to be butchered, and butchered they were. The men were first slain. The assassins then fired through the windows upon the heaps of women and children, and finally rushing in finished their hellish work with swords, bayonets, butt-ends, knives. The next morning the bodies were stripped, hacked and thrown into a well, over which a cross now stands. When Havelock's soldiers entered Cawnpore on the morning of the 17th the sight which met their eyes was the well with its awful contents and the slaughter-house littered with locks of hair, leaves of Bibles, children's frocks and shoes, combs, work-boxes, bonnets all swimming in blood. The victims numbered about a hundred and fifty. The world has no more touching story of suffering and heroism than that of Cawnpore. Heroism, we say, for the British were not conquered, but betrayed by the foulest treachery. The surrender led to a worse fate than resistance could have done. The whole history of the mutiny confirmed the wisdom of Henry Lawrence's dying charge to Colonel Inglis, 'Never surrender!'

SIR HENRY HAVELOCK.

LUCKNOW.

We must now turn to another great focus of insurrection —Lucknow. In March, 1857, Sir Henry Lawrence was sent as commissioner to Oude. If any one could have staved off the rising, the greatest Englishman in India would have done it; but he came too late. The dangerous classes in Oude were all to a man against us—the chiefs whose plundering we had stopped, the hangers-on of a corrupt court whom we had turned adrift, the relatives of the Oude sepoys who formed so large a proportion of the Bengal army. The annexation, instead of being made to press as lightly as possible, had been carried out with unnecessary harshness by the former commissioner, Mr. Coverley Jackson. All that Sir Henry could do was to secure the safety of the English garrison and community, and this he did. But for his timely forethought there is the strongest probability that Lucknow, at a still greater distance from relief and beset by a more numerous and hostile population, would have been another Cawnpore. Every European station in Oude was a scene of treachery and massacre. Seetapore, Sultanpore, Fyzabad, Azimghur, Shahjehanpore have all their pitiful tales to tell. Captains Fletcher Hayes, Samuel Fisher, Longueville Clarke, Major Gall—choice officers—were cut down by traitors among their own men, who had just sworn fidelity. We have no space for details of the sufferings of more helpless ones.

On July 1st, after details of the Cawnpore catastrophe had come to hand, the English were finally shut up in the residency, which had been made fairly defensible and provisioned for several months. On the 2nd Sir Henry was struck by a shell, and two days afterwards that chivalrous soul passed away. The defence fell on the shoulders of men like Colonel Inglis, Major Banks and the engineer Captain Fulton, who proved themselves worthy of the occasion. If the capture of Delhi was a marvel of daring, the defence of Lucknow was equally a marvel of endurance. Civilians vied with soldiers, women with men, in displaying the best qualities of English character. The few square yards of land held by the few hundred English and their few hundred native allies were all that the English owned in Oude. The rest was given over to hate and murder. Every foot of the position was searched by the fire at close quarters of twenty-five heavy guns and of skilled marksmen planted on neighbouring buildings, which Sir Henry's consideration for the natives had unfortunately left standing. Yet for three months the garrison, in the heart of a vast hostile city, defied every attempt of the swarms who thirsted for their blood. The chief reliance of the besiegers was on mines. On July 20th, August 10th, and August 18th mines were sprung and desperate attacks made. The second one levelled twenty feet of the wall and left the way open to the heart of the position, but the resolution of the stormers failed. The garrison not only baffled every attempt to overwhelm them by sheer weight of numbers, but made successful sallies and ran counter-mines. On September 5th, when the time of deliverance drew near, the enemy sprang three mines and attacked at every point simultaneously. A party even forced their way into the position, but were so decimated by musketry-fire that they withdrew. Several messengers had been sent out to ascertain the hopes of relief, but none returned till the spy Ungud on August 29th brought a promise of help in three weeks. The garrison was reduced to three hundred white soldiers and as many natives. It had one hundred and twenty sick and wounded and three hundred and fifty women and children to defend. The fidelity of the natives, so sorely tried, could not be depended on much longer. The sepoys consisted of the remnants of the 13th, 48th, and 71st regiments, the Europeans of the 32nd Foot.

Let us trace the march of the delivering force. Lord Canning summoned all available help from Rangoon, Madras and Bombay, and sent a message to Point de Galle in time to divert the Chinese expedition to Calcutta. The first regiment to land was the 1st Madras Fusiliers, commanded by Colonel James Neill. It seems incredible that with all the resources of an imperial government only twenty soldiers a day could be despatched at first, but such was the case. By the end of May only some eighty men of the 84th Foot reached Cawnpore, with what result we have seen. The first to start for the relief of Cawnpore and Lucknow was Neill. It showed the temper of the man that, when a station-master was for despatching a train without some of the troops, who were late, Neill had the official seized and kept prisoner till the men arrived. Reaching Benares on June 3rd with sixty Fusiliers, he speedily restored order where mutiny and weakness threatened disaster. On the 9th he left for Allahabad with forty of his men, and did the same there. On the last day of June General Havelock arrived to take the command. Reflections have been made on the supersession. But the issue proved the necessity of caution as well as valour, and while Neill overflowed with the latter quality he might have failed in the former. He had sent forward Major Renaud with a small force, but Havelock ordered that officer to halt until his own arrival. On July 7th he left Allahabad. His own force and Renaud's made a total of about one thousand three hundred Europeans, five hundred Sikhs and a few guns. The chief weakness was in cavalry. The only loss inflicted on the enemy was in actual fight, pursuit being impossible. The enemy therefore soon reappeared as strong as ever. The hot season was at its highest. Marching killed as many as hostile bullets. At Futtehpore on the 12th, at the Pandu bridge on the 15th, at Cawnpore on the 16th, Havelock fought and won four several battles. At the Pandu the brave Renaud fell mortally wounded. On the 17th the force reached Cawnpore, to wonder at the frail entrenchment held so long, and to sorrow over the remains of the recent massacre.

After a rest of two days the force marched out to Bithoor. The Nāna had fled, and all that could be done was to burn the palace and destroy the fort. Now followed a weary waiting of two months. Three times Havelock led his force across the Ganges with its face towards Lucknow, and as often was compelled, after routing the enemy in battle, to retrace his steps. He felt that to risk his small force, diminished by battle, by sunstroke and sickness, by the garrison left under Neill in Cawnpore, in a running fight of thirty-six miles, and then hurl it on a strong city, defended by thousands of desperate mutineers, would be to insure its destruction, and the destruction of the garrison he came to save. There was constant fighting around Cawnpore. On

August 16th, Havelock won a complete victory over the rebels, strongly entrenched at Bithoor. The position was carried at the bayonet-point.

By September 16th, Sir James Outram and his reinforcements were at Cawnpore. Outram, true to himself, declined to assume the command till Lucknow was taken, and served as a dashing cavalry leader. Neill commanded the first brigade of infantry. Sweeping aside opposition by the way, on the 23rd of September the force encamped at the Alumbagh Park near Lucknow. The 24th was a day of rest in preparation for the struggle of the morrow. On the 25th, a date to be ever remembered in British history, the British troops fought their way all day step by step, street by street, up to the gates of the residency. It was night before the goal was reached. Havelock and Outram ever led the advance. 'At length the last lane was threaded, and the leading column, with a long, loud hurrah heard above the thunder of the guns and the hurtling of bullets, rushed into a strange whirl of outstretched hands and joy-flashing eyes, and voices feebly emulating the shouts sent up to heaven by each fresh band of victors in its turn.' The loss in killed and wounded that day was four hundred and sixty-four. Sad to say, in the very moment of triumph, within a few yards of the residency gate, General Neill was shot dead by a concealed marksman. One of the bravest of the brave leaders whom those times brought to the front, he was only forty-seven years old when struck down.

Sir James Outram at once assumed the command, and on the morrow of the capture by some skilfully conceived attacks enlarged the area of the position. Even now the British force was too weak to convoy its charge down to Cawnpore, and had to submit to another siege till the arrival of Sir Colin Campbell in November. Another portion of the force, left to guard the stores in the Alumbagh, was besieged there. On November 12th, Campbell and Hope Grant were at the Alumbagh at the head of four thousand men with thirty guns. Instead of working his way through the streets of the city, Campbell advanced through a quarter studded with palaces and public buildings which had all been converted into so many formidable fortresses. These were the Dil-khooshah Park, or Heart's Delight, Sikunder Bagh, a mosque called the Shah Najif, the old Mess-house, and the superb Motie Mahal, or Pearl Palace. At the Sikunder Bagh fearful scenes took place. It was an enclosure, one hundred and twenty yards square, with massive, loopholed walls, held by two thousand picked troops and flanked by a fortified village and barracks. The outworks being captured, two eighteen-pounders began to play on the walls. At the end of an hour and a half a breach was made, through which the stormers poured. There was no outlet, and of the two thousand sepoys not one escaped alive. The advance through this chain of fortified posts took several days of hard fighting. On the 16th the generals met. General Campbell at once decided to withdraw from the residency, which for nearly five months had been the scene of such suffering and triumph. On the evening of the 18th the sick and wounded were removed to the new position at the Dil-khooshah, and the next two days the women and children were removed. The path was long and intricate, and crossed at several points by the enemy's fire, but no life was lost. Stores, treasure, supplies, prisoners were all safely carried off, some of the heaviest guns being burst. 'At length, on the night of the 22nd, silently and in perfect order, the last body of Outram's soldiers stepped forth from the lights and fires of the battered entrenchment into the darkness of the long, winding lane that still lay between them and comparative safety. Not a flaw seems to have marred the issue of a movement demanding the highest discipline on the part of the troops, the readiest cooperation among their leaders. Not a man was lost in that momentous night-march through the midst of forty or fifty thousand armed foes.' * Campbell was the last to leave. No, not the last. A luckless officer was forgotten, and left fast asleep. He awoke in time, and found himself to his horror alone in the entrenchment. Fortunately he took the right way, and came up breathless and bewildered, with the rearguard. So well was the secret kept, that the enemy fired for hours at the abandoned position. On November 25th

---

* Capt. Trotter.

Havelock, as good a Christian as he was a soldier, breathed his last, killed by fatigue, exposure and toil. General Campbell now retired with the bulk of the force to Cawnpore, leaving Outram in the Alumbagh to represent British authority and await happier days.

Campbell had not returned to Cawnpore too soon. The rebels were in great strength in the vicinity. The Gwalior Contingent had joined them in full force, and added greatly to their numbers and efficiency. On November 26th General Windham, instead of being content to hold Cawnpore, had moved out with his small force and routed a body of the enemy in advance; but on coming in presence of the whole army, after sustaining an attack of five hours from overwhelming numbers, decided to withdraw. The usual consequences followed. The next day he was attacked in force. The enemy threatened to surround him and cut him off from Cawnpore. The retreat became a flight, and baggage and stores were lost. The rebels of course were elated at the partial triumph, and hoped for still greater things. The town fell into their hands, and the British entrenchment was bombarded. The cannonade alarmed General Campbell as he was quietly marching along, and he hurried forward to Cawnpore, where he arrived on the evening of the 28th. After despatching the Lucknow women, children and invalids down the Ganges towards Calcutta, Campbell prepared to attack the enemy, who held the whole town from the river to the Great Trunk Road to Delhi with twenty-five thousand men and forty guns. By December 6th he was perfectly ready. He had to cross a canal in order to reach the enemy, and had only three bridges for the purpose. His plan was to strike heaviest at the enemy's right wing, while detaining the rest by slighter attacks. The result was a complete victory, with a loss of only thirteen killed and eighty-six wounded. The camp, seventeen guns, twenty-five ordnance wagons (all, of course, our property) were captured, and the pursuit was continued fourteen miles. On the 8th, Hope Grant led out a brigade in further pursuit, and the next morning beat up the enemy's encampment twenty-five miles away, at a ford of the Ganges, capturing fifteen guns and fifteen wagons with a loss of one horse killed!

LORD CLYDE.

General Campbell made a long pause before the final advance. When he appeared next at Lucknow in March, 1858, it was at the head of the finest British army both in numbers and efficiency that India had ever seen. It numbered twenty-five thousand men, most of them tried and seasoned in a hundred scattered fights during the past six months. The chiefs were such as Outram, Wilson of Delhi, Hope Grant, Hodson, Lugard, Franks, Norman, Mansfield, Robert Napier, each one competent to lead an army. Leaders and men alike might be trusted to dare and do all that is possible to man. The British had about ninety guns against one hundred. Jung Bahadoor himself supported the attack. The enemy too had improved their opportunity, learnt from past experience, and made every position as strong as possible. All their efforts, however, were rendered abortive by a clever device of Campbell, which his strong force enabled him to carry out. This was to attack all the rebel positions from two sides at the same time. In the course of two or three days Napier's engineers bridged the Goomty River with beer-casks, ropes and planks, and Outram passed over with a strong force to take the enemy in the rear and flank. Not till Outram had made a distinct impression, did Campbell address himself to the task of cutting his way through one line of entrenchment after another. The work occupied six days. Outram took the Chakkar Kotie, or Yellow House, the key of the position on that side, and advanced through the Padshah Bagh, or King's Garden, to the rear of the Martinière College. One of his officers climbed a height and waved on Campbell's stormers on the other side. At the Begum's Palace on the 11th the heaviest fighting took place. The pile of buildings had been converted into a perfect fortress, bastioned, loopholed, surrounded with a ditch, and filled with desperate men. After a bombardment of eight or nine hours, Adrian Hope (another Havelock, afterwards slain at the storming of a petty jungle fort) led on the storming party, consisting of the 93rd Highlanders, 4th Punjab Rifles and one thousand Ghoorkas. The palace was soon cleared, five hundred of the enemy being slain. Here the greatest British loss occurred. Major Hodson had accompanied the stormers as a volunteer. After the resistance had ceased he was looking over the rambling pile, when a sepoy started from a dark corner and shot him in the groin. He died the same night, bitterly mourned by his native followers, who almost looked on him as a demi-god. Outram from one side, Campbell from the other slowly closed in on the Kaiser Bagh, the royal palace, which at the last moment was feebly defended. The old positions—the Mess-house, Tara Kotie, Motie Mahal—were thus all taken one by one, and Lucknow again acknowledged British rule. The superb palaces, crowded with Oriental treasures, were very thoroughly plundered by the victorious army and their innumerable camp followers. On the present occasion two English ladies, Miss Jackson and Mrs. Orr, were rescued from the enemy's hands. The other prisoners, brought in from the country districts, had been murdered in November on Campbell's victorious retirement. The two ladies owed their safety to the fidelity of a native gentleman, who resisted all demands for their surrender. Sir James Outram became commissioner of Oude.

It is impossible for us to follow out the history of the numerous expeditions and engagements by means of which the last fires of rebellion were stamped out in Oude. The last rebel force was not dispersed or driven over the frontier into Nepaul before the early months of 1859.

We have omitted much in this account, but it is impossible to omit all reference to the splendid campaign by which Sir Hugh Rose (Lord Strathnairn) cleared Central India of rebellion in the summer of 1858. Starting from Bombay early in the year, capturing strong places like Rutghur, Garrakotah and Chandāri by the way, at the end of March he encamped before Jhansi, where the brave, bloodstained rānee stood at bay with ten thousand mutineers. The fort was exceedingly strong, both by nature and art. On one side a perpendicular precipice made it inaccessible, on the other sides massive granite walls and outworks frowned upon the town, which again was defended by wall, mound and ditch. It was on the fortified mound that the British brought two batteries to bear with such effect that the fire of the town was subdued and a practicable breach made.

But before the delivery of the attack, Sir Hugh was obliged to turn aside to encounter Tantie Topee, who had marched down, with twenty thousand men, from Calpee to the relief of Jhansi. On April 1st he encountered the enemy at the river Betwah. After a long and desperate fight the enemy fled, many perishing in the river, and others taking refuge in a jungle. In their despair they fired the jungle in the hope of checking pursuit. But dragoons and artillery charged through smoke and flame, and inflicted dreadful punishment on the beaten foe. Eighteen guns were taken, and one thousand five hundred of the enemy slain.

On the 3rd and 4th the town was stormed and cleared of the enemy, Brigadier Stuart leading the way. At least half the rānee's force, *i.e.*, five thousand, was destroyed. The English general had placed his cavalry all round the city, so as to intercept the fugitives. The siege of the citadel would have been a far more difficult task; but the English were spared this by the flight of the rānee, who in the night managed to creep through the encircling lines with a few hundred followers, and got clear away in spite of pursuers. The hot season was exceptionally severe, and the British troops lost more from this cause than from the enemy. Scudamore's cavalry did not undress for seventeen days. General Rose himself had five sun-strokes in a few days. One weak wing of a regiment lost twelve men in this way.

After a month's sorely needed rest Sir Hugh advanced to the attack of Calpee. With a view to cover this town Tantie Topee took up a strong position among gardens and woods near the town of Kooneh. The Jhansi rānee was with him, at the head of her horsemen. General Rose reached the point on May 7th, and, although one of his brigades had marched fourteen miles, prepared to attack at once. Pouring a heavy fire on the strong works on the enemy's left, he sent against the other wing dragoons and horse-artillery supported by infantry. The right wing was carried, and the strong works on the left, being turned, had to be abandoned. Tantie Topee was among the first to seek safety in flight. His troops at first showed their British training by observing order even in retreat; but, pressed unceasingly by alternate artillery volleys and cavalry charges, they soon broke into disorderly flight. The pursuit lasted eight miles, till the pursuers were dead beaten by the heat of a fierce Indian afternoon, and could keep up no longer. The thermometer registered 130° in the shade. The remnant of one mutinous regiment, the 52nd, was almost annihilated.

On May 16th the British reached Golowly on the Jumna, five miles from Calpee. Tantie Topee had received some reinforcements and took heart for a fresh stand. Calpee was in every respect as strong as Jhansi. But British forces were advancing from the north, and the enemy determined to attack General Rose before they could arrive. On the 20th an attempt was made on the British flank, and failed. On the 22nd a more desperate struggle took place. The sepoys had maddened themselves with *bang*, and fought with the utmost fury. But the Rifle Brigade and the 88th Foot bore them back, and Lightfoot's guns and Major Gall's dragoons completed the rout. At daybreak the next morning, without giving the enemy time to recover from the defeat, Sir Hugh attacked the town, and by two o'clock Calpee was ours, with all its vast munitions of war, arsenal, and cannon foundries.

Here the campaign should have ended, but an unexpected task emerged. Tantie Topee's troops, instead of making for Oude, marched on Gwalior, and raised Scindia's remaining forces in mutiny. The rāja fled to Agra, a new ruler was set up, and the city with all its treasures fell into the hands of seventeen or eighteen thousand armed rebels. After nine days' marching Sir Hugh Rose reached the Morar cantonments near the city, and by a swift attack drove the rebels posted there in headlong flight upon the city. The far-famed town of Gwalior, with its forts and defences, was much stronger than either Jhansi or Calpee. In a conflict on June 18th the rānee of Jhansi, fighting in a man's garb, was slain as she fled from pursuit by British hussars. On the 19th an attack in force was made on the Lashkar Fort, covering the city on the south. Soon the fort and city were in British hands, all save the renowned citadel on its rocky perch of three hundred feet. Next day, this fortress, in which only a score of soldiers remained, surrendered to a handful of sepoys. Robert Napier, who was sent with a small pursuing force to scatter the last remnant of the retreating foe, perfectly succeeded in his task, driving the enemy into pell-mell flight and taking twenty-five out of thirty guns. This was the last serious battle, both in the Gwalior campaign and in the mutiny. General Rose's career had been one unbroken series of rapid, brilliant victories. In five months he had marched more than a thousand miles through a difficult country, taken strong fortresses and defeated armies far outnumbering his own. The blows were as swift as they were heavy. If Delhi was a marvel of daring, and Lucknow of endurance, General Rose's campaign was equally a marvel of resistless energy.

We may note the fate of the chief rebel leaders. Tantie Topee, the ablest of the native chiefs, was tried by court-martial for his share in the Cawnpore massacre, and hanged on April 18th, 1859, at Seepric. Bahadoor Khan, of Bareilly, was shot on the scene of his crimes. On May 3rd, 1860, Jowāla Parsād, another of the Nāna's officers, was hanged on the spot where he had directed the firing upon the boats at Cawnpore. The two worst criminals, the Nāna and his tool or instigator, Azimoollah Khan, died in 1859 in Nepaul, where also another bitter enemy of the British, the Begum of Oude, spent the rest of her days.

The greatest among the results of the mutiny was the complete transference of the government of India from the famous company to the Crown. One advantage at least of this measure is that Indian affairs are discussed in Parliament in presence of the whole nation. There can be no doubt that since the mutiny the English people have taken a far livelier interest in their great dependency. India is better known, and the two peoples have been drawn together in closer bonds of mutual respect and sympathy. Lord Canning punished Oude for its rebellion by confiscating all the soil, a measure which was modified, at Sir James Outram's intercession, in favour of those who helped in the restoration of order. The company's European troops murmured against being transferred to the Crown without their consent being asked or acknowledged. The government undoubtedly showed a want of consideration for brave men, who had deserved well of their country. Most of the troops concerned elected to take their discharge, whereas they might have been kept by a little timely generosity.

In March, 1862, Lord Canning left India, and died in London in June of the next year, a victim to unprecedented anxieties and toils. Very different opinions have been expressed as to his character. There was probably a want of grasp and decision at the outbreak of the rebellion, and occasional indecision throughout. A man of the Dalhousie type would have crushed the danger sooner. But it would be unjust to complain that Lord Canning was not a Dalhousie or Lawrence. On one ground he deserves all honour, and that the ground of his chief condemnation; namely, the immoveable firmness with which he resisted the cry for an indiscriminate vengeance unworthy of a Christian nation. At one time he was the most unpopular man in India. His name became a by-word for effeminacy. But results have justified the course which he took. Punishment severe enough was meted out to the guilty. We should be glad to be able to believe that the innocent were never involved in it.

MOSQUE IN CAWNPORE.

VIEW OF CALCUTTA.

CHAPTER XIV.

HISTORY OF PROTESTANT MISSIONS IN INDIA.

AS the methods and results of missionary labour largely depend upon the general character and circumstances of the people, a few remarks on this subject may not here be out of place.*
With respect to the vernacular languages of India, it is to be observed that most of them are altogether independent of Sanscrit in their origin and structure. Sanscrit is strictly the language of the Brahmins, was introduced and has been exclusively cultivated by them. Whether it was ever spoken in India is unknown. The Brahmins are fond of representing Sanscrit as the parent, not only of all Indian languages, but of all the languages of the world, and support their position by words resembling each other in sound, but connected in no other way. In point of fact, the Indian vernaculars are purely indigenous. As might be expected, those spoken in the north, where the Brahmins, entering by the north-west, first settled, have the largest infusion of Sanscrit; but even in these the substance and structure differ fundamentally from Sanscrit, and in the south the Sanscrit element is much less. Here the influence of Sanscrit is far less than that of Latin on English. There are even translations of the great Sanscrit epics in the purest vernacular. In the villages a Sanscritized vernacular would be unintelligible. Dr. Caldwell in his *Comparative Dravidian Grammar* shows that the vernaculars belong, not to the Aryan, but to

---

* One of the best compends on the subject of Hindu life in general is *The Land of the Vēda*, by the Rev. P. Percival (London, G. Bell, 1854), now unfortunately out of print, but sometimes to be met with. On Hindu philosophy and literature, Williams's *Indian Wisdom* is full and trustworthy.

the Turanian family. Some of the distinctive features of this family, present in the Indian vernaculars, are the following: all nouns denoting inanimate objects and irrational beings are neuter; postpositions are used instead of prepositions; the governing word in the sentence invariably follows the governed; continuative particles are preferred to conjunctions; the verb has a negative as well as an affirmative form; there are no relative pronouns, their place being supplied by relative participles. It is remarkable that there should be a closer affinity between Sanscrit and English than between the former and the tongues now spoken by the Brahmins themselves in daily life. A few examples may be interesting. The English *father, mother, daughter* come directly from the Sanscrit *pitru, mātru, duhitru;* whereas the Canarese (one of the five Dravidian tongues) is *tande, tūye, magalu.* The connection between numerals like *two, three, seven,* and the Sanscrit *dwiti, triti, sapta* is obvious to the eye, whereas the Canarese has *yeradu, mūru, yēlu.*

Sanscrit literature is remarkable for its extent, richness and antiquity. It covers the entire field of mental activity. The most ancient portion consists of the four sacred Vēdas, which are generally placed somewhere between 2,000 and 1,000 B.C. These books are objects of extraordinary veneration to the Hindus. But it would be a mistake to suppose that they exert any practical influence, save in the most remote way, on Hindu life. Beyond their names little is known of them in India. It must be remembered that an intelligent acquaintance even with what may be called modern classical Sanscrit is by no means a common acquirement among Brahmins; and the Sanscrit of the Vēdas differs far more from classical Sanscrit than the English of Chaucer does from that of Addison and Pope. Again, the teaching of the Vēdas represents a phase of opinion and faith which India left behind many long ages ago. The Vēdic religion is nature-worship. It knows nothing whatever of the multifarious deities and incarnations of modern Hinduism. The Vēdāntists, who profess a desire to return to the simplicity of the Vēdic faith, represent the latter as a system of philosophical theism; but to do this is simply to read their own ideas into the Vēdic writings. Philosophical theism, or rather pantheism, is the doctrine of the Vēdāntist philosophy, which is a much later development of Vēdic teaching. In India at present 'the Vēda' is little more than a name to conjure by.

In reality, the authoritative religious books which sway the religious life of the masses are neither the Vēdas nor the Purānas—mythological works far more recent,—but the great epic poems, the Mahā Bhārata and Rāmāyana, as these are read in whole or part, known through translations, or rendered into popular song, story and drama. These wonderful creations of poetical genius—perfect forests of legend and myth, in which Eastern imagination has run riot—have for ages shaped popular religious faith in India. The Rāmāyana especially, the story of Vishnu's incarnation in the form of the hero Rāma, has taken a deep hold on the popular imagination, has been reproduced in numberless forms, and may be regarded as the gospel of the Hindus. The higher religious thought of the nation finds perfect expression in the Bhagavad-geeta, an extract from the Mahā Bhārata, which teaches the purest pantheism in the smoothest verse. Of the mere literary works, this is not the place to speak. It may be mentioned, however, that the drama of Shakuntala is beautiful, even in a foreign dress, and in its original form is perfect in grace and delicacy.

The philosophical systems of India remind us of the speculations of ancient Greece, only that they are elaborated and commented on with far greater fulness and precision. They are three in number, known as the Nyāya by Gotama, the Sānkhya by Kapila, and the Meemamsa by Jaimini. Each of these has been further developed into a supplement, the Vaishēshika of Kanāda, the Yoga of Patanjali and the Vēdānta of Vyāsa. In the case of the first and third, the supplement is the most perfect expression of the system. The Nyāya is analytic, the Sānkhya synthetic, the Vēdānta pantheistic. The seven Categories of the Vaishēshika, under which all existences are included, remind us of the Aristotelian Categories. The same system teaches the atomic theory familiar to us in connection with the names of Democritus and Lucretius. Certain ideas, such as the eternity of soul and matter, the inherent evil of separate individual existence, and the necessity of absolute emancipation by absorption into the great All, are common to all the systems. A full exposition would require too much space.

The most prominent feature of Hindu society is caste, which, according to Brahminical ideas, is the distinctive mark of Hindu blood. No one outside the sacred lines is acknowledged as a Hindu proper. The second and third castes, those of the Kshatriyas and Vaishyas, being now virtually extinct, Brahmins and Shūdras divide between them all Hindu society. The ideal of the Brahmin order is that of an aristocracy of culture and holiness, independent of the accidents of wealth and social position. How little the facts correspond with the ideal, experience shows. It is useless to deny that the Brahmins are superior in many respects to the other classes. This is simply the result of the exclusive possession for ages of all social and intellectual privileges. A Brahmin regards himself as the perfect flower of human life. 'All the universe is subject to the gods, the gods are influenced by incantations, incantations are in the keeping of the Brahmins, the Brahmins therefore are our gods,' is the common Hindu's creed. Roman Catholic missionaries and others represent caste as an innocent social distinction. Such is not the Hindu view. The proof is found in the fact that all transition from one caste to another is impossible, the orders being separated by impassable barriers. There is no rising from a lower caste to a higher, no falling from a higher to a lower. By eating and drinking with persons outside his own caste a Hindu simply loses caste altogether. The general effects of a system which restricts social intercourse, marriage and business occupations within the narrow limits of hereditary lines need not here be described. The way in which caste has acted as the most formidable obstacle to the spread of Christianity is by the intense unity and cohesion given to the Hindu nation and the terrible social penalties inflicted on all who withdraw from its authority. The converts hitherto made from the ranks of caste are comparatively few. The majority of the native Christians are drawn from classes whom the Brahmin regards with ineffable contempt and scorn. But under the pressure of British and Christian influences of all kinds, the power of caste is fast passing away, its bonds are in course of dissolution, and society is being placed on new foundations and taking new shapes. The greatest hindrance to the success of Christianity in India is thus being removed.

To Denmark belongs the honour of having founded modern Protestant Missions in India.* The first missionaries were Ziegenbalg and Plutschau, who landed at Tranquebar in 1705, and who worthily head the roll of Indian missionaries. They were gifted, bold, full of sustained enthusiasm. The king and royal family of Denmark manifested the deepest interest in the prosperity of the mission, but their sympathy was not shared by the local authorities, who did all in their power to annoy and thwart the newly-arrived missionaries. By 1711, Ziegenbalg had translated the whole of the New Testament into Tamil, and at the time of his death, in 1719, the Old Testament as far as Ruth. In the course of a visit to Europe he succeeded in interesting George I. of England and many of the chief persons in Church and State in his mission. The Propagation Society and Christian Knowledge Society gave him substantial help. Ziegenbalg's work was continued by men of like spirit and gifts, such as Grundler and Schultze, the latter of whom completed the translation of the Scriptures in 1725. The same missionaries broke ground in Madras in 1726, and ten years afterwards the converts there numbered four hundred and fifteen. Branch societies were also formed in Negapatam, Sadras, Fort St. David, Cuddalore and Pulicat.

In 1750, the greatest of all the Danish missionaries, and perhaps of all Indian missionaries, arrived in India—Schwartz, who from this time laboured forty-eight years without a break, acquiring an influence and witnessing results which have rarely been equalled and never exceeded in the history of Christian Missions. English and natives, even implacable enemies of the

---

° For the material of the following account, the writer is indebted to Sherring's *History of Protestant Missions in India*, Trübner, 1875.

English like Hyder Ali, reposed in him the most absolute confidence. Without mixing himself up in political affairs, he was able to render the greatest services to government and people alike. The Rāja of Tanjore looked on him as a father. No more perfect example of unselfish devotion to the good of others can be named. Xavier is often quoted as a peerless example of Christian zeal. But Schwartz equalled Xavier in his best qualities, and had other gifts which the great Roman missionary lacked. To the zeal and enthusiasm of an apostle he united a wisdom and sagacity which any statesman might have envied. He deserved, if any man does, the title of 'Apostle of India.'

The Danish Mission was successful in a numerical point of view far beyond the average of Indian missions. As the result of fifty years' labour, no fewer than fifty thousand converts were made. Yet, strange to say, this prosperity has not been enduring. Scarcely anything remains of these early missions. The decline seems owing chiefly to two causes, the neglect to train and organize a native ministry, and the toleration of caste within the Church. The last cause alone is enough to explain the decline. The early missionaries, few in number, without advice from others, perhaps shrank from declaring open war against a system so ancient and universal as caste; but in the end nothing was gained by treating it as a friend. The only result was to bequeath a legacy of evil to their successors, who had to do battle with the evil in an aggravated form and at greater disadvantage. Eventually the remnants of the Danish Mission passed into the hands of the Propagation Society. In modern days the Leipsig Lutheran Mission, which in 1841 established itself in the same district, is the only one that has adopted the same fatal policy with respect to caste. By this means, and by its open proselytizing, it has isolated itself from the sympathy of all other missionary bodies.

Missions in North India also were commenced by a Dane, Kiernander, who, on being driven from Cuddalore in 1758 by the French capture of the place, went to Calcutta, and laboured there many years with much devotion and success. But missionaries in North India, and indeed in India generally, will always look back to Carey as their leader, as having begun work on a large scale and with permanent results. He reached Calcutta in 1793, and played there much the same part as Schwartz in the south. His career was nearly as long, his character as high and spotless, his personal influence—one of the most essential factors in Indian missionary work—as commanding, while the breadth of his plans, his learning, and the enduring results of his work were far greater. If not by Danish hands, it was on Danish soil, that the first permanent mission-work was done. Forbidden a home on English territory, Carey and his two noble helpers, Marshman and Ward, settled at Serampore under the Danish flag. But for this timely hospitality, the period of India's redemption must have been postponed still longer. The great honour of the Baptist missionaries is that they entered India before the door was legally opened, which was not till 1814. Over against the hostility of the government must be set the sympathy and effective help of private officials like Mr. Udny and Charles Grant, and chaplains like David Brown, Claudius Buchanan, Henry Martyn, Thomason and Corrie. The missionary zeal of Henry Martyn has sometimes been disparaged because of his official position and salary; but surely all the greater merit is due to him for labours which were outside the line of strict duty. The most essential qualification of an Indian missionary is self-forgetting, burning zeal, like Martyn's.

The London Mission Society and the Church Missionary Society commenced work in Calcutta in 1816. Both societies, here as elsewhere, are distinguished for the prominence they wisely give to educational work. The Baptists everywhere pay less attention to education, and give themselves almost wholly to the work of direct evangelization. No absolute rule can be laid down as to the methods to be pursued. Much depends on local peculiarities, and still more on the skill, patience and energy of the labourers. Every kind of agency is in operation in the Indian mission-field, and every kind is successful somewhere. The capital city has naturally taken the lead in educational operations and in auxiliary philanthropic institutions of all kinds. 'The School-book Society' and 'Calcutta School Society' have done excellent service. Here also began the system of female education, which has since grown to such large dimensions, and is working the greatest changes in native society. English ladies, with the wives of Governors-general at their head, have always manifested the deepest interest in this movement. But the greatest change of all was that which made the English language the vehicle of higher education in India. The change was brought about mainly through the advocacy of Dr. Duff, who arrived in Calcutta in 1830, and who ranks in the length of his course and in missionary zeal and ability second only to Schwartz and Carey. The effects of the substitution throughout India of English for Sanscrit in collegiate and university education, and of the introduction in this way of the millions of Hindu youth to the broad fields of English literature, are simply incalculable. In this peculiar department of labour the Scotch Churches have led the way in all the three Presidency cities, where their institutions are the first in size and efficiency. Dr. Duff's institution in Calcutta began in 1830 with five pupils, and in nine years they numbered eight hundred. The eagerness of the Hindu youth belonging to the higher classes for a knowledge of English is extreme, and in this circumstance the Church sees a rare opportunity for communicating a knowledge of Christianity to classes who are reached with difficulty in any other way. Nothing destroys Hindu superstition more effectually than instruction in western literature and science. With all the educational activity of which Calcutta is the centre, the public preaching of the Gospel has not been overlooked. One of the best vernacular preachers India has ever seen was the Rev. A. Lacroix, of the London Society, who laboured in Calcutta through a long term of years. His eloquence and effective delivery always secured a good audience in the streets; but it would be a mistake to suppose that public preaching in India has been more fruitful in direct conversions among caste Hindus than schoolteaching.

The rest of Bengal is covered by the missionary agencies of various Churches. In Chittagong, Barisal and Dacca, to the east of Calcutta, the Baptists have had important missions since the beginning of the century. The Church Mission has found a peculiarly fruitful field in Burdwan to the west and Krishnagar to the north. Forty years ago, the latter mission experienced one of those spring-tides of religious influence to which Eastern peoples, usually so apathetic, seem liable. Hundreds came forward at once to receive baptism. A subsidence of feeling followed which lasted a long time, but of late there seems to have been a revival. The Krishnagar mission comprises four thousand eight hundred and seventy converts. In the district of Rajshye the English Presbyterians have a small but prosperous station under the Rev. Behari Lal Singh. Different societies are at work among the hill-tribes in the far north.

In Orissa, to the south of Bengal, the chief missions are Baptist, English and American. All the chief towns are central mission stations—Poree, near the great temple of Jagannath, Cuttack, Balasore, Midnapore, and Santipore. Among the Santals in the north of the province an industrial school and farm are in operation. Of the missionary in charge, the magistrate says: 'Mr. Phillips is quite a little chief in those parts. The people come to him on all occasions for advice and assistance; and his farming operations, assisted by the anicut he has constructed, and the canal leading from it, are gradually converting the wild forest country into a fertile agricultural tract.' The great province of Behar, to the west of Calcutta, is occupied by the Baptist, Church, Propagation and Gossner Missions. The following are some of the statistics for Bengal in 1871:

Protestant Native Christians	46,968
Increase in Ten Years	26,450
Native Communicants	13,502
Increase in Ten Years	8,783
Ordained Native Ministers	35
Unordained ,,	398
Pupils in 693 Colleges and Schools	27,950
Native Christian Teachers	548

Between Behar and Orissa live the Kōls and Santals, aboriginal hill tribes, on the same intellectual and moral level as the South Sea islanders. Among them Christianity has had to encounter the common vices of savage tribes, but not the artificial obstacles raised by Brahminical superstition and caste. The Gospel was first taken to the Kōls in 1846 by six missionaries of the Gossner Society of Berlin, four of whom soon fell victims to zeal untempered by prudence. In 1850, eleven converts were received, and year by year the number increased. Despite persecution by unbelievers and the severe sifting of the mutiny, the baptized Christians in 1863 numbered three thousand four hundred, and the communicants seven hundred and ninety. The religious services among these simple children of the hills are models of reverence and devotion. Bishop Cotton, after being present at one of them, was asked what he thought of it. After pausing a moment, he replied with quivering lip, 'Sublime! the only word to describe it.' Owing to disputes with the Berlin Committee, half of the missionaries joined the Propagation Society. Both missions are now prosperous, and the missionaries of both societies have joined in translating the Scriptures. The number of native Christians in 1871 was twenty thousand seven hundred and twenty-seven; communicants, six thousand two hundred and thirty-three; native ministers, one hundred and five; scholars, one thousand two hundred and ninety-seven.

Among the Santals four missions are at work. One of them, known as the Indian Home Mission, under the guidance of the Rev. Messrs. Skrefsrud and Boerresen, is conducted on a novel plan. Mr. Skrefsrud says: 'We have no native preachers, and do not believe in them. We have a preaching Church. All the Christians are preachers. They preach without pay, and without being told to preach. One single man has thus brought five villages to Christ. Last year eight Christian villages were formed by the native Christians, not by us. The most suitable convert in a village is made pastor. They support their own pastor. Their pastor is a ploughing pastor. Morning, noon and evening he prays with his people, and ploughs his land in the intervals. They pray for certain villages; then go to them and speak to the inhabitants; and then pray again. The Gospel is preached to a small circle, accompanied with much prayer on its behalf. The result is, that nearly all the persons within the circle become Christians. They have no endowments, but the pastor gets the piece of land which formerly heathen priests received.'

In the north-west provinces between Bengal and the Punjab stretch three chains of missions, those of the Church Socioty, American Presbyterian and American Methodist, in addition to some smaller missions. The Church Society alone has in these districts a staff of forty-five native preachers, seventy-one educational institutions, four thousand four hundred and seventy-seven pupils, and three thousand four hundred and eighty converts. St. John's College at Agra is a most complete and efficient establishment. The Presbyterian stations run in a continuous line from Allahabad to Rawul Pindi in the Punjao. Besides a theological college, the mission has five ladies who devote their time to zenâna visitation in Allahabad. In the charming valley of Dehra Doon it has established a boarding-school, in which the best education possible is given to Christian girls. The missions of the American Episcopal Methodists in Oude and Rohilkhund were established by Dr. Butler just before the mutiny. Like all the American missions in India, these are marked by great completeness, and pushed forward with the utmost energy. The Sunday-school has been established with signal success.

Benāres, the holy city of India, is an important and difficult field of labour. The Baptist missionary, William Smith, worked here forty years, acquiring universal confidence and respect. As in Ephesus of old, the population of Benāres is easily excited ; but Mr. Smith passed in safety where no magistrate would venture. Singularly enough, another William Smith, of the Church Mission, laboured in the same place contemporaneously a like term of years, and occupied a similar position in popular esteem. The Rev. C. B. Leupolt of the same mission is another fine example of the life-long consecration which Indian missions need. The Church Mission possesses here the Jay Narain College—which educates six hundred and fifty students—as well as girls' schools, orphanage, normal institution, Christian village and lace manufactory. The Revs. Messrs. Buyers and Shurman have given their lives to the service of the London Mission in the same city. At Mirzapore, Dr. R. C. Mather founded a London Mission station in 1838, and has lived to see schools, orphanage, press and Churches grow to maturity around him. In 1871 the numbers in these districts stood thus:

Native Christians	8,039
Increase in Ten Years	4,097
Communicants	3,031
Ordained Native Ministers	19
Unordained Native Ministers	185
Pupils in 344 Schools, etc.	17,265
Christian Teachers	328

In 1865, the London Missionary Society began a mission among the hill-tribes of Singrowlee, one hundred miles south of Mirzapore. The missionary, the Rev. W. Jones, lived an apostolic life, and thoroughly won the confidence of the people. 'Full of earnestness and love, he sacrificed health and comfort in his privations and toils, and died in the midst of his usefulness, and in the maturity of his powers, singing in his delirium the old Welsh hymns which his mother had taught him in his childhood.'

Imperial Delhi belongs politically, though not geographically, to the Punjab. Missionaries and missions, Baptist and Propagation, were alike blotted out by the mutiny, but they have been re-established in new vigour. The Propagation Society devotes seven ladies to zenâna visitation. These have eight hundred and forty pupils. One of the seven is a medical missionary among women. The Medical Mission has charge of nine thousand cases annually. Medical missions might be multiplied indefinitely, and would prove a most efficient agency. The Delhi *Female Medical Mission* was the first of the kind, and is excellent in idea.

In the Punjab proper eight societies have their home. As has been mentioned before, Dhuleep Sing, who but for British occupation would now be ruler of the Punjab, is a Christian.

In 1874, a prince of the state of Kupurthala received baptism at the hands of a native Presbyterian minister. The Church Divinity School at Lahore, under the direction of Rev. T. V. (now Bishop) French, deserves special notice. Mr. French trains his students on a principle new to us, but familiar enough in the East, that of close personal association between master and disciple. In taking this course he has the warrant of the highest example. At Peshawur, at the mouth of the Khyber, a strong mission is actively at work among the Afghans. The key to the Afghan heart is hospitality. 'A missionary to the Afghans should be careful to observe the apostolic rule, and be "given to hospitality."' In order to this, it has been the custom of the Peshawur missionaries to keep up guest-houses for the reception and entertainment of Afghan visitors.' The number of native Christians in the Punjab is one thousand eight hundred and seventy; native ministers, fourteen; scholars, ten thousand five hundred and forty-seven.

A vast field invites missionary enterprise in Central India, which until recently has been greatly neglected. In this territory, as extensive as Great Britain, France and Spain together, the missions are few and recent. The only mission in the ancient Hindu states of Rājpootana is that of the United Presbyterians, which began in 1860, and counts four hundred and ninety-four converts in towns bearing such famous names as Ajmir, Jeypore, Nasirabad. They also report sixty-seven schools, two thousand three hundred and twenty pupils, twenty-two native preachers and teachers. Medical work has been a strong point in the mission, one-half of the staff being medical missionaries. In Scindia's and Holkar's territories the only station is one belonging to the Church of England. The Scotch Free Church Mission at Nagpore, begun in 1844, is the oldest in the central provinces. Its founder, the Rev. T. Hislop, bade fair to equal his countrymen, Duff and Wilson, in extent of personal influence, interesting himself in all matters bearing on the elevation of the people, when he was drowned. Mr. Hislop came into conflict with the rāja over the baptism of a young casteman. The youth sought protection at the hands of the missionary.

His surrender was demanded by the rāja, and enforced by the Resident. He was imprisoned, and the Governor-general refused to interfere. But public indignation was roused to such an extent throughout India that he was released after three months' captivity. The Church Mission at Jubbulpore is of a very complete order. 'It has its native preachers ministering to the people in the streets of the city and surrounding villages. It has its orphanages for boys and girls. It has charge of as many as ten schools, in which about eight hundred children of both sexes are instructed.' The Free Church Mission at Jalna was begun in 1855, and then abandoned. Work was resumed under the oversight of the Rev. Narayan Sheshādri, and the progress since has been rapid. In 1871 there were three hundred and ninety-three Christians, one hundred and ninety-four of whom were communicants. The Christians are rendered independent by the possession of land granted for their use by Sir Salar Jung. Six hundred and fifty acres were granted rent-free for twenty-five years. Of this amount two hundred and fifty have been already brought under cultivation, and the village of Bethel is fully equipped with wells, church, manse, schools, roads, the houses being built on a uniform plan, with gardens before and behind. The number of Christians in Central India is two thousand five hundred and nine; native ministers, six; scholars, six thousand one hundred and thirty. It is truly said that the vast territories of Berar, the Gonds, Holkar and Scindia and the Nizam, are 'scarcely touched by Christianity.' In many respects the centre would be far more interesting soil than the coast, where missions are most thickly strewn. Hinduism and the people in the former case have been less modified in character by foreign contact, and it is not at all improbable that success would be more rapid.

The first mission established in Bombay was that of the American Board in 1813. The circumstances were singular. Two missionaries, Messrs. Nott and Hall, ordered by government to leave Calcutta, fled to Bombay. A similar order followed them there; but the governor, Sir Evan Nepean, a thoroughly Christian man, interceded for them, and obtained leave for them to remain. They were honoured to be the first to preach and translate the Gospel of peace in the tongue of the warlike Mahrattas. The same society has also a mission at Ahmednagar. The Church Society began work in Bombay in 1820. Here, at the old Mahratta capital of Poona and at Nasik, its missions are very complete. At the latter place the Christians, who number five hundred, manage an industrial establishment and have a separate village.

The mission of the Scotch Church in Bombay began in 1828. In the following year, Dr. John Wilson arrived, and by a long life, devoted to the highest objects and inspired by the purest love, made himself a name equal to that of Duff. Wilson was less absorbed than the latter in English work. His thorough mastery of native learning and thought, his high character and long course of labour, gave him an influence such as none else ever wielded in the western Presidency. Dr. Murray Mitchell, as an educationist, and Robert Nesbit as a popular missionary, rank high among their brethren. No missionaries have excelled, and few have equalled, those of the Scotch Free Church in commanding influence among the people. When Mr. Nesbit was cut off by cholera in 1855, natives of all classes wept like children at his funeral. At Bombay, as at the other capitals, the Christian press and the Bible Society are powerful missionary auxiliaries. The Parsees are numerous and influential in the west. The baptism of the first Parsee youths in 1839, by Dr. Wilson, gave rise to immense excitement. The Parsee community was wild with rage, tried the law and every means short of actual violence to recover the converts, but in vain. To the north-west of Bombay the Irish Presbyterians have five stations in Guzerat, and the Church Society two in Scinde. In the south of the Bombay Presidency six societies are at work on twelve stations. The following are the figures for the Bombay Presidency in 1871:

Native Christians	4,177
Increase in Ten Years	1,646
Native Ministers	20
Pupils in 132 Schools, etc.	7,184

The central portion of the western coast, including Canara and Malabar, is given up to the German missions of the Basle Society, which has also five stations in the south Mahratta country, and two in the hill country of Coorg. The languages used are the Canarese, Tulu, and Malayalim. The two chief stations on the Malabar coast are Mangalore and Calicut. The German missionaries are especially apt in the promotion of industrial training, in which they display the union of speculativeness with practical skill which characterizes their nation. At Mangalore a boarding school, the manufacture of sugar from cocoa-nut juice, coffee-planting, watch and clock-making, a smith's shop, have all been tried and abandoned. The manufacture of clocks and watches among a people who know nothing of artificial time-keepers was a singular enterprise. Printing and bookbinding, weaving, farming, silk-growing, are more suitable and successful. It was found essential to place the lay missionaries, who superintend these operations, on an equality with the ordained. The patience of the German missionaries in the face of many disappointments is altogether admirable. In the south Mahratta country the missionaries were imposed on by a sect called the Kâlagnânis, who professed to see in them teachers for whom they had long been waiting, and promised to become Christians in a body if land could be found for them. The land was found and buildings erected, when the Kâlagnânis, unable to compass their selfish ends, disappeared. The Basle Mission reports four thousand six hundred converts, of whom two thousand two hundred and seventy are communicants.

The Mysore country is occupied by the London and Wesleyan Missions, chiefly by the latter. The London Mission at Bellary dates from 1810. One of its missionaries, the Rev. J. Hands, began, and another, the Rev. W. Reeves, completed, a Canarese dictionary, which has been re-edited by a Wesleyan missionary, the Rev. D. Sanderson. The Wesleyan Mission has been in existence fifty years, and has worked to good effect through the press, schools and direct evangelization; but its continuity of influence has been greatly interrupted by sickness and death among its agents. It is now making an effort to cover with mission stations a country which, according to the principle of division of labour generally observed among Indian Missions, has been committed to it to evangelize. May it rise to its duty!

The chief numerical success of Indian Missions has been in the south. The Church Missions of north Travancore and Tinnevelly and the London Missions in south Travancore together contain one hundred and five thousand converts, fifteen thousand communicants, seventy native ministers, six hundred unordained preachers. The increase in converts in ten years has been twenty-five thousand. The great majority of the converts are from a particular class without caste, whom Hindus proper refuse to acknowledge; but under the combined influence of education and religion they will rise rapidly in the social scale. These large South Indian churches have a complete organization, and are advancing every day in intelligence and independent power. They have been wisely and ably led in the past. The London Mission has had agents like Messrs. Mault, Abbs, Russell, Whitehouse, Lewis, Baylis, Mateer, who have given their lives to its service. In the Church Mission, Caldwell, Fenn, Jœnicke, Sargent, Rhenius, Ragland, are names whose 'praise is in all the Churches.' The name of Rhenius is a proverb in South India for apostolic simplicity and devotion. No little romance is connected with the history of Mr. Ringletaube, of the London Travancore Mission. He came to South India in 1806, lived an ascetic life, travelled and preached everywhere, baptized great numbers, and suddenly in 1815, without saying a word to any one, left for Madras, where he disappeared, and was never heard of again. There was evidently a touch of eccentricity and genius in his nature. 'Scarcely an article of his dress was of European manufacture. He seldom had a coat to his back, except when furnished with one by a friend in his occasional visits to Palamcottah. Expending his stipend upon his poor people, his personal wants seem never to have entered into his thoughts. While at Madras, he had no coat, though about to undertake a voyage. The only covering for his head was something like a straw hat of native manufacture.'

T

In north Travancore is the singular phenomenon of an indigenous Christian Church, which has apparently come down from the earliest Christian antiquity,—a Syro-Greek Church, with prayers and worship in the Syriac language. The Churches on the coast were forcibly reduced to conformity with Rome by the Portuguese Inquisition at Goa, but the inland Churches have preserved their independence. The Rev. Claudius Buchanan visited and described them in 1806, since which time they have been objects of great interest to English Christians. At first the Church Society sought to reform the faith and worship of this ancient Church by friendly cooperation; but differences arose, and the Church Mission has since pursued an independent course and exercised a powerful influence for good upon the Syrian Churches. 'The demand for copies of the Holy Scriptures has increased wonderfully; meetings for prayer are held where such things were previously unknown; the *catharas*, or priests, are bestirring themselves for the instruction and reviving of their own people, and doing something, it is said, in some cases for the enlightenment of the heathen around them.'

The beautiful province of Madura, to the north of Tinnevelly, is occupied by the American Board and the Propagation Society. The latter missions are confined to Ramnad and its neighbourhood; the former occupy the heart of the province in full strength. The American Missions comprise eleven principal stations, and one hundred and thirty-eight separate congregations. The nine missionaries are assisted by eight ordained native ministers and above a hundred unordained preachers. In Madura there are seven thousand three hundred native Christians, of whom one thousand six hundred are communicants.

The interval between Madura and Madras is filled up by the Propagation, London, Wesleyan, and American Dutch Reformed Missions. The latter might fitly be called the Scudder Mission, having been founded and hitherto carried on by missionaries of the Scudder family. In 1861, seven of this name were at work, in 1871, five. The plan adopted has been vernacular preaching by means of 'concentrated itinerancy.' The number of Christians in this wide district is seventeen thousand, an increase in ten years of six thousand six hundred. The Scudder Mission has followed Schwartz's excellent method of instructing catechumens in the Lord's Prayer, the Ten Commandments, the Apostles' Creed, as well as in a simple Catechism.

As we have seen, mission work was begun in the city of Madras in 1726. The different Churches are employing the same methods as in the other capital cities. The name of John Anderson, who founded the Free Church Institution in 1837, is an honoured one in Madras. Like all other missionaries in similar circumstances, he had a hard battle to fight with caste. On his admitting two Pariah scholars the rest all withdrew and endeavoured to compel him to exclude the obnoxious students, but firmness for the right won the day. Again, on the baptism of three youths in 1841, the institution was left for a time nearly empty. Missionaries have had to take their trial in courts of justice on charges of kidnapping. Jealousy on the subject of caste has led to the establishment of purely native institutions for instruction in English.

Female education has advanced rapidly, and been a powerful auxiliary to missions in Madras. The Church School alone in 1871 contained four hundred and twenty-seven young women and girls, the Church of Scotland's four hundred and fifteen, the Scotch Free Church Schools eight hundred and eighteen. Of the latter sixteen, all native Christians, passed the government examination for female teachers' certificates.

Madras is also the head-quarters of the Christian Vernacular Education Society, which occupies itself in training teachers, publishing school-books, and supporting day-schools, and extends its operations all over India. It has issued in all four million tracts and books in fifteen languages, has three training institutions and twenty-seven depôts, and employs sixty colporteurs.

It should not be overlooked that the bishops of Madras have distinguished themselves for sympathy with evangelical missions. The Madras district contains five thousand native Christians, an increase in ten years of one thousand five hundred. There are two thousand two hundred communicants, eleven native ministers, forty-eight unordained native preachers, and eight thousand two hundred and fifty scholars, of whom two thousand eight hundred are females.

The Telugu country, to the north of Madras, has lately been the scene of a remarkable religious awakening. For many years the Missions of the Propagation and London Societies remained feeble, when suddenly, about the year 1850, there were baptisms on the same scale as in Travancore and Tinnevelly, and among similar classes of people. The London Mission at Cuddapah and Nundial sprang at a bound from one hundred to five thousand Christians, the Propagation Mission to three thousand, the Baptist Mission at Nellore to six thousand. Out of these Churches theological colleges and a native ministry are slowly growing. The Scotch Free Church has a large educational institution at Nellore. The total number of native Christians in the province in 1871 was thirteen thousand eight hundred, an increase in ten years of ten thousand four hundred and sixty; the number of communicants, two thousand eight hundred and twenty-eight; ordained native ministers, three; unordained, ninety-two; theological and training schools, nine.

The wide district of the Kistna and Godâvery rivers, stretching to the borders of Orissa, is occupied by various English and American societies. At the American Lutheran station of Palnâd a movement similar to the one in the Telugu country has been witnessed, the number of Christians having increased between 1861 and 1871 from three hundred and thirty-eight to two thousand one hundred and fifty, scattered throughout fifty-two villages, and forming thirty-two congregations. In the same time the converts of the Church missions, directed by fine missionaries like Noble, Fox and Sharkey, advanced from two hundred and fifty-nine to one thousand eight hundred and eighty-two. Among their sixty-one educational institutions are two colleges. The Godâvery Delta Mission has grown in the same proportion. The London Mission at Vizagapatam alone has not felt the movement.

We have thus completed the circle of Indian missions. The total statistics for India, Burmah, and Ceylon, as given in the government return of 1873, are as follows:—Twenty-five mission presses; eighty-five training colleges for preachers and teachers, with one thousand six hundred and eighteen students; twenty-eight training institutions for girls, with five hundred and sixty-seven students; one thousand three hundred zenâna classes, with one thousand nine hundred and ninety-seven scholars; one hundred and forty-two thousand nine hundred and fifty-two scholars; Christians, three hundred and eighteen thousand three hundred and sixty-three; communicants, seventy-eight thousand four hundred and ninety-four. Between 1862 and 1872 the students who matriculated from missionary institutions were one thousand six hundred and twenty-one; passed first examination in arts, five hundred and thirteen; B.A., one hundred and fifty-four; M.A., eighteen; B.L., six. The number of missionaries is six hundred, of stations five hundred and twenty. The Bible has been translated and published, in whole or part, in about thirty languages.

If there are many things in the history of British India to fill an Englishman with just pride, there are some things to suggest humility and moderation, especially in judging other nations. But no believer in a Divine government of the world can doubt that both the good and the evil will be overruled for the benefit of the millions thus strangely brought under British rule. It may be the case that the tendency of our rule is to abolish those divisions of caste, race, religion, and even of language, which alone have made our conquest possible, and to this extent to lessen the security of our power. But on the other hand our rule also tends to discourage warlike and promote peaceful habits, and what is gained on this side probably fully counterbalances what is lost on the other. The Mahratta, Pindâri, we might almost add Sikh, wars could not take place again. The hereditary troublers of the public peace are completely changed in character. Commerce, with its apparatus of roads, rail, telegraph, post, newspapers, is a powerful peacemaker and civilizer, and it is matter of sincere joy that commerce fills the place in India once filled by war. If we seek evidence of the blessings which British rule has brought to India, we only need to compare the condition of the country with that of other Asiatic states, China, Burmah, Persia, Turkey. In one case, progress, liberty, inducement to exertion, advancing knowledge and civilization; in the other, stagnation, barbarism and all the baleful effects of capricious despotism. The enjoyment by every one of the millions of a vast continent of a clear field for the exercise of his talents and of perfect security for his just gains, and this for the first time for centuries, is almost the greatest benefit which one nation can confer upon another.

There can be no doubt that the British government and Christian Missions in India have helped each other. Missionaries and all English Christians in India represent the best side of English character. The former come into contact with classes who have no personal knowledge of government officials. They study, as no other Englishmen do, the languages and literature of the people. In their schools, preaching, conversation, and discussion, they live on familiar terms with those who constitute the bulk of the population, and it is from them that the natives derive much of their knowledge of English thought and ways. That these relations tend to give favourable impressions of the spirit and purposes of our government is self-evident. On the other hand, the powerful action of the government in its own sphere tells indirectly in favour of Christianity, especially in undermining the artificial restrictions of caste. The direct influence both of government and Christianity has immensely increased since the mutiny. Education, means of internal communication, trade, missionary agencies have developed at a marvellous rate. Through a thousand channels a full tide of progressive influences has been pouring into the country without cessation. Under rulers like Lord Elgin, Lord Mayo, Sir John Lawrence and Lord Northbrook, the country has taken great strides forward, and nothing is wanting but the continuance of a peaceful policy for still greater improvement. In measuring the progress of Christianity in India, the difficulties already referred to must be taken into account. Some Anglo-Indians talk of the failure of Indian Missions; but these are persons who either have seen little or nothing of the inner working of missions, or are unable to appreciate the subtler changes taking place over a wide area in native thought and feeling. Large bodies move slowly. The heavy ironclad scarcely stirs where the tiny boat dances on the water. The Oriental mind is far less susceptible to change than the western. Not without reason do we speak of 'the changeless East.' But under the immense energy of British influence even India with its massive systems of philosophy and worship shows signs of change and movement. If not driving before the breeze, it is drifting with the current. Young India is breaking away from its ancient moorings and feeling its way to new anchorage ground. There the East and West, the youngest and old nations, have met together. Long may the union last to the advantage of both!

LAHORE.

www.ingramcontent.com/pod-product-compliance
Lightning Source LLC
Chambersburg PA
CBHW032104220426
43664CB00008B/1130